Western Primitivism:
African Ethnicity

Western Primitivism: African Ethnicity

A Study in Cultural Relations

Aidan Campbell

CASSELL

London and Washington

Cassell
Wellington House
125 Strand
London WC2R 0BB

PO Box 605
Herndon
Virginia 20172

First published 1997

British Library Cataloguing in Publication Data
A catalogue record for this book is available from the British Library.

Library of Congress Cataloging-in-Publication Data
Campbell, Aidan.
    Western Primitivism: African ethnicity: a study in cultural relations/
Aidan Campbell.
        p. cm.
    Includes bibliographical references and index.
        ISBN   0-304-70076-2 (hardcover).—ISBN 0-304-70077-0 (paperback)
        1. Ethnicity—Africa.   2. Africa—Public opinion.   3. Public opinion—
Civilization, Western.   4. Africa—Social conditions.   5. Africa—Ethnic
relations. I. Title.
GN645.C345 1997
305.8'00954—dc21

                                                                    97-607
                                                                    CIP

ISBN 0 304 70076 2 (hardback)
         0 304 70077 0 (paperback)

Typeset by Ben Cracknell Studios
Printed and bound in Great Britain by Biddles Limited, Guildford and King's Lynn

Contents

Acknowledgements

I wish to record a debt of gratitude to both Sybille Kuester and Miriam Marshall, who both – in their different ways – incited me to write this book (though I doubt if Sybille in particular will agree with any of it). Other people who have helped me on the way are Justine Brian, Paola Cerni, Ceri Dingle, Frank Furedi, Julie Heath, Cheryl Hudson, Mick Hume, Rachel Jordan, Michael Lester-Card, Suke Wolton and Jane Greenwood of Cassell. Special thanks to James Heartfield. I would also like to take this opportunity to thank Professor Terence Ranger of St. Antony's College, Oxford, for his kind invitation in February to present my reservations about the social construction of ethnicity at one of his regular 'Ethnicity and Nationalism' seminars. These remarks were briefly summarized in my 'Ethical ethnicity: a critique', *Journal of Modern African Studies*, vol. 35, no. 1, March 1997. Needless to say, responsibility for any errors and omissions is mine alone. Permission was obtained from Routledge to reproduce the maps of Nigeria on pages 170–1, which come from I. L. Griffiths, *An Atlas of African Affairs* (London, 1984).

Many years ago I was accosted on the streets of London by a racist South African who upbraided me for demonstrating against apartheid: 'How can you judge us when you've never even been to Africa?'. She did not convince me. I was still sure it was right to oppose apartheid. Unfortunately I still haven't been to Africa, so I suppose it is a trifle arrogant of me to have written a book about it. I can only explain myself along the lines of what I told that woman all those years ago as to why I backed the struggle against apartheid: nothing human is alien to me.

Introduction: An Ethnic World?

There is no doubt that ethnic consciousness still influences Africans, but it is worth asking why these cultural survivals are being so privileged today above all else.

In the West, African tribalism has traditionally been seen as the epitome of primitive savagery. The expression conjures up images of ghastly mobs baying for blood, with heads cut off and stuck on poles. Even today every newspaper and television commentator has a list of African atrocities – Rwanda, Somalia, Liberia – ready to hand whenever they wish to illustrate the barbarism.

The erroneous notion that ethnicity is intrinsic to human nature is as firmly entrenched as ever. For example, apart from African conflicts, the upsurge in petty national squabbles after the collapse of the Berlin Wall and the Soviet bloc in 1989 was widely portrayed as a revival of ancient ethnic rivalries. Yet times have changed. No longer are the old racist arguments that pit Western civilization against the barbarism of other societies accepted without question. For example, in a carefully written article by Andrew Marshall, the relevance of Joseph Conrad's *Heart of Darkness* (1899) to the modern predicament of Rwanda's Tutsis and Hutus is discussed. Marshall claims that, for Conrad, the 'Heart of Darkness' is located in Europe, not, as often thought, in the Congo, and consequently the novel is a polemic against imperialism. According to Marshall, however, the source of imperialism's 'darkness' lay in its 'ideas of progress, faith in science and rationality . . . the human destruction wreaked by industrialisation'.[1] Marshall concludes his piece with a flourish: 'A sense of doubt about Europe itself and its "civilised values" pervades the whole book. This, too, is bound to strike a chord with us'. For Marshall, progress leads directly to concentration camps and world war. The notion that the barbarism that the West unleashed upon Africa was the product of a heavily restricted conception of progress is entirely absent.

It is the argument of this book that these days illustrations of tribal barbarism from Africa tend to be employed by Western commentators with the intention of emphasizing humanity in general's potential for evil, rather than solely laying stress upon African atavism. For Professor Patrick Chabal, for example, the atrocities committed in Rwanda and Liberia are disturbing not just because we are concerned at the loss of African life, 'but also, and perhaps primarily, because it makes us wonder about the potential barbarity present in us all'.[2] Indeed, far from the Third World being seen as the quintessence of evil these days, the threat to the planet is now depicted as originating in the consuming ambitions of the modern world. For example, a prestigious American think-tank, the Worldwatch Institute based in Washington, DC, recently published a document, *Fighting for Survival*, which asserts that it is not good enough to blame ethnic conflict in Africa on 'ancient hatreds', because the underlying cause is more likely to involve 'environmental degradation':

> On the surface, many conflicts do seem to revolve around ethnic, religious, cultural or linguistic divisions, and these divisions will likely dominate the perceptions of the protagonists. Yet to gain a better understanding of the nature of these conflicts, we need to look beyond the easy excuse of 'ancient hatreds' and 'tribal bloodletting' to detect the underlying stress factors that help cause the fighting . . . disputes are often sharpened or even triggered by glaring social and economic inequities – explosive conditions that are exacerbated by the growing pressures of population control, resource depletion and environmental degradation.[3]

On the other hand, the report claims that 'multi-cultural society need not involve conflict. Tanzania, for example, is home to many different peoples – Zigula, Yao, Sukuma, Haya, Chagga, Asians and Arabs – with little evidence of tension among them'.[4]

Indeed primitive society is often presented as a source from which decadent modern nations can rejuvenate their humanity. Over the last decade and a half, the status of African tribalism has been undergoing a subtle change in the West. No longer is it automatically synonymous with barbaric events and terror. Indeed the rest of the world – especially the West – seems intent upon imitating African lifestyles. These seem to be closer to nature and more sustainable than our own high-octane, high-consumption ones. Once 'ethnic' was a term of abuse, especially in the USA. Now the whole world is made up of ethnicities apparently. Everyone can be a member of an ethnic minority, even if you're white. Lester Thurow, for example, contends that claiming rights as an ethnic minority has now become the easy way for Americans to improve their access to resources, 'Every American can now claim to belong to some minority group that deserves special treatment'.[5] According to popular television presenter and author of the *Naked Ape*, Desmond Morris, ethnicity is natural because 'Man is a tribal animal'.[6] While traditional values and institutions are greeted with cynicism and jaded mistrust, a wide-eyed naïvety appears to grip even hard-nosed critics of modern life when confronted by aspects of ethnic culture. All too often, the suspicious 'don't trust them' that is regularly applied to Western scientific achievements and political institutions is transformed into the gullible 'you never know' when it comes assessing the validity of obscure tribal customs.

The remarkable thing is that this elevation of ethnicity in the West is not confined to mavericks like the New Age anti-road protesters and crystal mystics. A positive image of ethnicity has made deep inroads among the ranks of the Great and the Good, and especially among the Western intelligentsia. In an article entitled 'The Return of the Primitive', American commentator Charles Krauthammer has pointedly remarked that, while we have had tarot reading, crystal therapy and homeopathy for decades now, 'What is new is that irrationalism is gaining official sanction', noting how Congress ordered the American National Institute of Health to set up an Office of Alternative Medicine in 1992.[7] Interestingly Krauthammer blames the modern world for this return to the primitive, 'An age in which we carry around boxes that can digitize information and rationalize thought at 133 MHz is an age even more susceptible to the call of the wild'. Out of the relatively narrow arena of anthropology studies, ethnicity has grown in an empire-building fashion to take the privileged position of being the answer to many otherwise confusing phenomena in modern society. According to University of Texas professor and author Edwin Wilmsen, in the decade since 1983 'the package of meanings wrapped in the word "ethnicity" has grown exponentially'[8]:

> A focus on ethnic processes enables us to investigate topics which are of crucial importance in social anthropology: the relationship between culture, identity and social organisation; the relationship between meaning and politics; the multivocality of symbols; social processes of classification; the relationships between action and structure, structure and process, and continuity and change.[9]

> Ethnicity is a descriptive concept that lends itself to a wide variety of theoretical interpretations. Evolutionary, sociobiological, and materialist analyses have been usefully applied to the explanation of ethnic phenomena. Likewise, psychological and hermeneutical approaches have been fruitful in understanding the relationship of individuals to their group affiliations.[10]

More and more academic fields are coming round to relying upon ethnicity and indigenism to provide their underlying explanation of human behaviour. According to a group of Dutch radical intellectuals,

> Ten years ago most of the academics working in the area of indigenous knowledge represented anthropology and geography . . . Today important contributions to our understanding of indigenous knowledge and decision-making are being made in the fields of ecology, soil science, veterinary medicine, forestry, animal science, aquatic resource management, botany, zoology, agronomy, agricultural economics, rural sociology, mathematics, management science, agricultural education and extension, fisheries, range management, information science, wildlife management, and water resource management.[11]

According to South African scholar Saul Dubow, the main reason why ethnicity has forced itself on to the mainstream agenda today is because 'the strength of materialist analysis, both as an analytical and a practical programme, has been severely fractured' due to the collapse of the Soviet bloc. Incredulity towards rationalism has encouraged academics to adopt ethnicity as a potent substitute for discredited Marxism:

Ethnicity, which, like nationalism, has often been dismissed by Marxists as a form of irrational false consciousness, cannot any longer be explained away or ignored in this way . . . Familiar categories of analysis based on notions of rationalism and progress are increasingly treated with scepticism or disdain. More and more we see an emphasis in the academic literature on the ambiguous, contingent and multiple nature of human identity.[12]

Ethnicity can now be used to explain almost anything that happens socially. This is attractive to Dubow's 'bewildered' intelligentsia since it means they can attach a multitude of different agendas to it. Hence, unlike Morris's thesis that links tribalism to base instinct, ethnic theories can now take on quite radical flavours. Of necessity, therefore, ethnicity has had to become a very fluid, highly mobile concept.

But there is an unfortunate drawback to this development. If ethnicity can explain everything, the implication is that ethnicity can explain nothing specifically. The consequence is a regrettable inability to comprehend the real basis of modern African ethnicity. The task for Africanists must be to cut through this confusion to reveal what is specific about modern ethnicity that demarcates it both from previous forms of African tribalism as well as from other current unrelated phenomena.

Currently, society is commonly assumed to be too complicated to be understood as an aggregate. Just as the market economy is viewed as the product of billions of individual decisions that are too intricate to be rationally comprehended as a whole, so society is pictured as billions of individuals with highly mobile identities who cannot be slotted into the 'totalitarian' compartments of race and class. Instead, these fluid identities are being grouped into either ethnic or gender categories.

In the modern conception, ethnicity appears as fluid because so many different agendas have been attached to it. It can therefore be portrayed as both fragmentary and dangerous, as well as a mystical or moral force that perhaps can cohere a disintegrating society. Through the creation of a new African élite and 'capacity-building' institutions, Western non-governmental organizations (NGOs) aim to offset the risks associated with unregulated ethnicity.

The term 'ethnicity' is much bandied about. But surely this promiscuous use of the term must raise a suspicion that it is more a mystification than an explanation of the phenomena we hope to examine. Though every concept is in general an abstraction which has to be qualified when dealing with specific cases, they are generally useful to us in that they help us to order and to clarify our random thoughts. Sometimes, however, concepts can form a barrier to clearer thinking when they block the development of a more profound analysis. In my opinion, this latter is the case with ethnicity.

The reader must not be distracted by the fact that either the word 'ethnicity' or the word 'tribalism' is mentioned on almost every page of this book. This is because in order to polemicize against the concept of ethnicity it is necessary to refer to the use others make of it. As a real and objective phenomenon innate to Africa, my proposition is that ethnicity does not exist. It is only 'real' because the persistence of the West's relationship with Africa makes it a reality. Like Saul Dubow, therefore, I also object to the notion that ethnicity is a 'false consciousness' that can simply be wished away.[13] Unlike Dubow, however, I do not believe that the failure of existing paradigms in and of itself makes ethnicity intrinsically more real. That is pure mysticism. As the ancient philosopher remarked, the word 'dog' cannot bite. So with the word 'ethnicity'. No matter how many times I use the word 'ethnicity' in my book, or others use the word in their texts, that does not make ethnicity really exist. From this perspective, I should also make clear here that, for purposes of brevity, when I use the expression 'ethnicity' in the text it is shorthand for 'the conception of ethnicity as an ideological framework for Africa constructed in the West'.

If we are clear then what is specific about the concept of ethnicity, a more realistic appreciation of it as a social phenomenon can be realized. That is the objective of this book.

Ethnicity takes different forms at different times, according to how confident the West feels about itself, that is, its sense of mission. In the aftermath of the collapse of the Soviet bloc in 1989, there was an explosion of interest in ethnicity as a source of conflict, as a threat to the West. This reflected the West's disorientation and loss of direction. It was deprived of an objective which could cohere its unity in every other sphere as well. Defeating communism was the mission by which the West justified its activities around the rest of the world. Ethnicity as 'threat' substituted as a motivating goal for the West that replaced the old bogey of communism.

The main problem with this substitution of the threat of ethnicity for the threat of communism was one of credibility. Despite occasional panics about the 'Fundamentalist bomb', the 'Islamic bomb', the 'bomb in a suitcase', etc., no ethnic threat could ever hope to replace a foe like the Soviet Union which had the *real* capacity to destroy the world several times over. As a consequence, the threat of ethnicity has proved to be almost entirely ineffective in helping to offset the fragmentation of the West and in particular its political and state structures. Rather than simply fade away, however, ethnicity is increasingly coming to be seen in the West as a source for celebration rather than fear.

Chapter 1 argues that the theory of a new and 'modern' version of ethnicity has emerged primarily as a response to profound despair towards the advancement of Western society. At the same time, anything old or traditional is also rejected in the West because it is irrevocably associated with the discredited institutions of the establishment. In this context, where both the past and the future are excluded, a cult of primitivism has blossomed in the West that is completely different to traditional notions of primitivism. This version of primitivism is often referred to by the oxymoron: 'modern primitivism'. It is primitive in so far as it defines humanity as being close to nature, rather than the ability to regulate nature. It worships high-technology but not because it enables the mass of ordinary people to exercise some control over society, but only in the more limited sense that it enhances the consumption – and therefore the comfort – of passive individuals. Though ostensibly liberating, this celebration of technology in fact helps reconcile people with a diminished ability to control their own lives, and therefore introduces a measure of stability into existing society.

To smudge over the numerous contradictions associated with this new version of primitivism, modern society is increasingly defined ethnically.[14] But, as we have seen above, it is an ethnicity that has been stripped of any of its former meanings. Instead ethnicity is being redefined 'morally', that is, in a way that presents the comfort of the diminished individual as the highest virtue that society should aspire to. In so far as they pose as champions of this new moral primitivism, the discredited state institutions of the West are able to rehabilitate themselves in the eyes of their constituencies.[15]

Because modern primitivism and moral ethnicity helps stabilize the *status quo*, the establishment in the West has altered its former hostility towards primitivism, and therefore ethnicity, with alacrity. This new conception of primitivism has therefore influenced the volunteers who staff the NGOs, the primary vehicles through which the West relates currently to Africa.

All the Western establishments have found that the most effective way to solve their domestic problems is to internationalize them. On the international stage, normally ineffectual figures like John Major and Bill Clinton can suddenly achieve the stature of Great Statesmen. As they strut about from one diplomatic conference to another with peace processes for Bosnia, Palestine or Rwanda, the only criticism to be heard is that they are not intervening enough. This view ignores the massive intervention being undertaken by the West's 'non-political' NGOs into Asia, Eastern Europe, the Middle East, Latin America and Africa.

The role of NGOs in propagating their carefully sanitized version of ethnicity in Africa – or 'ethical ethnicity' – is the subject of Chapter 2. Ethical ethnicity is favoured by NGOs because it enables them to reformulate the disrupted relationship between the West and Africa under the pretext that Africans are the principal victims of the globalized world market. At the same time, the chapter investigates the problems that arise for the NGOs when this alien, politically correct ethnicity is superimposed as a moral constraint upon the people of Africa. The resolution of these conflicts involves the construction – or the 'capacity-building' – of a new African élite committed to the moral form of ethnicity.

In Chapter 3, the implications of ethnic conflict for the creation of a morally ethnic agenda is studied. Ethnic conflict is either asserted to be the negation of authentic ethnicity, or ethnicity is denied. The West's emasculation of African nationalist leaders is briefly surveyed, and their lack of responsibility for ethnicity and ethnic conflicts established. The promotion of localism by the NGOs certainly helped subvert the only instrument that Africans had to control their own affairs, leaving the African nation-state little else but a hollow shell.

But Chapter 3 indicates that the privileging of localism is increasingly turning from rubbishing defunct African nationalism to trying to restore coherence to an increasingly atomized African society, allegedly the new source of ethnic conflict.

The first three chapters establish the themes that define modern ethnicity: modern primitivism, victimization and localism. Chapter 4, being primarily historical, is a marked departure from this approach. Generally, when the notion of progress flags in the West, the theme of ethnicity can be revived as a ready-made explanation to justify the *status quo*. In the heydays of the imperial mission to civilize Africa, Africans were generally denounced as tribal savages. When imperialism subsequently lost its momentum and nationalism arose as a threat to colonial rule, African tribalism underwent a transformation in the eyes of Western administrators who took to celebrating the virtues of indirect rule. During the 1950s and 1960s, in the heyday of the post-war boom and African independence, ethnicity was once again put on the back-burner. Each of these periods is examined in some depth in this chapter with the aim of distinguishing each of them from the present version of African ethnicity. This differs from all preceding definitions of ethnicity in that they assumed the political mobilization of Africans through a definite ethnic identity, whereas modern ethnicity celebrates the inertia of the individual African. It is only through traversing its past forms that the novelty of the present form of ethnicity can be properly demarcated.

As we have established both thematically and historically the foundation for modern ethnicity, it will then be appropriate to assess the theoretical frameworks that others have made to understand ethnicity. Chapter 5 scrutinizes the three main theories of ethnicity that are popular among academics today: primordial ethnicity, instrumental ethnicity and moral ethnicity. In particular, the chapter is concerned to debunk the fashionable dogma that ethnicity is created through the negotiation of personal identities.

Each of these theories of ethnicity possess certain insights as well as inconsistencies, but the chief problem that affects them all is that they approach the subject from the point of an appearance at any one time, which is then eternalized for all time. This is particularly true for social constructionist theory, despite its ostensible reliance upon contingency and fluidity. For social constructionists, ethnicity has become an eternal characteristic of humanity, though their theory will not permit them to recognize that, never mind justify it.

In the modern paradigm, the concept of 'ethnicity' is the link that ties the modern world to the primitive. Through a review of Marx's writings on primitive communist communities, Chapter 6 queries the popular notion that the conditions that governed those ancient societies are still valid today.

We have asserted that modern ethnicity is completely different from these past forms. But those who advocate that modern ethnicity is fluid readily admit to a change from past forms of ethnicity, and are even prepared to exaggerate this sense of change by imbuing it with an element of out-of-control turmoil and chaos. How does this fit in with the notion of an eternalized, or naturalized, ethnicity? We conclude the book by examining what has been the real change in the characterization of modern ethnicity.

The analysis contained in *Western Primitivism: African Ethnicity* does not pretend to be a general analysis of ethnicity. It is an assessment of only one particular form of ethnicity – modern moral ethnicity – which may or may not remain relevant in the future. In other words, the determinant factor for my analysis is not ethnicity as such, but the underlying social relationships that give rise to a particular form of ethnicity, chiefly the relationship between the West and Africa.

Notes

1. Andrew Marshall, 'Heart of Prejudice', p. 20.

2. Patrick Chabal, 'The African Crisis', p. 36.

3. Michael Renner, *Fighting for Survival*.

4. Ibid.

5. Lester Thurow, *The Future of Capitalism*, p. 240.

6. Desmond Morris and Peter Marsh, *Tribes*, p. 9.

7. *Time* magazine, 29 January 1996.

8. Edwin Wilmsen and Patrick McAllister (eds), *The Politics of Difference*, p. 4.

9. Thomas Eriksen, *Ethnicity and Nationalism*, p. 162.

10. David Levinson and Melvin Ember (eds), *Encyclopedia of Cultural Anthropology*, p. 395. Contribution on ethnicity by Walter P. Zenner.

11. Guss von Libewstein, L. Jan Slikkerveer and D. Michael Warren, 'CIRAN: Networking for Indigenous Knowledge', p. 441.

12. Saul Dubow, *Ethnic Euphemisms and Racial Echoes*, pp. 1–2.

13. The reasons for this are fully dealt with in Chapter 6.

14. To mention one major contradiction with modern primitivism: how can you produce high-technology for a society based upon the consumption of isolated individuals without at the same time maintaining a society that is geared to mass production, the rapid extension of scientific research, high energy consumption, etc.?

15. Given that the preferred objective of the establishment would have been to revive respect for its traditional institutions, in no way can the promotion of modern primitivism be ascribed to a 'conspiracy' or a 'plot' by the Western ruling élite. Rather, they are adapting to the conservative mood generated within society as a whole in order to buttress their own position.

CHAPTER 1

The Modern Primitive

The Western view of Africa has changed as Western self-perception has changed. When the West was confident of its own superiority it was happy to condemn the South. As Western self-confidence has ebbed, so African society has become a positive rather than a negative model.

The onset of the 1990s has seen all the ruling institutions of the Western establishment collapse in the aftermath of the fragmentation of the Soviet bloc. The world's major political traditions have seen faith in their most precious dogmas depreciate. The search is on for suitable replacements.

The modern Western condition can be summed up as anomy and alienation. The loss of faith in tradition and the lack of coherence in society has seen a retreat to the local as the only source of security in a world where little seems to make sense any more. Among Western conservatives, an increasing despair that capitalism can ever deliver the goods has provoked sympathy for ecological movements that present any technological change as a problem. Among radicals, a similar loss of faith in their socialist projects has resulted in their deprioritizing social change in favour of the small scale and local. With society at the international and national level seen as abstract and unrealistic, only the local is viewed as real and practical. When once every local phenomenon was examined from the point of view of its national or international ramifications, the reverse is more likely to be the case today. As Frank Furedi bluntly puts it: 'Paradoxically, the more the world becomes internationalised, with every region brought into an intimate relationship with world market forces, the more the singularity of the experience of the parish-pump is insisted upon.'[1]

Even trendy international globalization theories are posed as an opportunity for the local. Hence the current antagonism to all things national, and especially the nation-state, is far from expressing any progressive sense of internationalism. It should rather be located in a more general hostility to society at large as compared to the local and parochial.

In this atmosphere the establishment feels confident that, by adopting the programme of its former radical opponents, it can reinvigorate their system and give themselves a new sense of direction. Through associating with victims, they can portray state repression as justified moral retribution. Through extolling localism, they conceal their national and international operations as community awareness projects.

For those who accept the new agenda, the rewards are plentiful. For example, Britain's new National Lottery Charities Board (NLCB), a quango which describes itself in its literature as 'an independent body set up by Parliament', has been geared to fund those who adopt this new style of organizing. Its application form for NGOs applying for international grants demands that they 'encourage equality of opportunity in all aspects of your project, irrespective of age, race, religion, ethnic origin, marital status, colour, nationality, gender, disability or sexual orientation'.[2] Moreover, the project must be 'culturally sensitive, non-violent and respect social diversity'.[3] Through adopting the guise of a quango and by voicing the victim-friendly cliches of politically correct liberalism, organs of the state like the NLCB can distance themselves from despised state authority.

In this context of discredited establishment institutions, the popularity of primitivism has recently undergone an extraordinary transformation. In Western society, the concept of primitivism is notable since it contains two meanings that can often be opposed to each other – the savage and the simple. The former definition of the primitive was dominant so long as Western society identified itself with progress and civilization.

Nevertheless, the latter definition of primitivism has always attracted a significant minority of supporters who generally identified themselves with the myth of the 'noble savage'. Sentimental expressions in favour of the noble savage were made by those intellectuals who found the uncouth and the vulgar revolting. In particular, they objected to mass society. Instead, they indulged themselves in nostalgia for a primeval Eden peopled by graceful primitives. Oxford professor John Carey has debunked this romanticization beloved by sections of English intelligentsia in particular: '[The intellectuals merge] the masses back into a pastoral world of birds and wild roses, which redeems them but also eliminates them. For that pastoral world predated the revolt of the masses'.[4] However, as faith in progress and society diminishes across the board, this more exclusive cult of primitivism has accumulated broader appeal.

No longer is primitivism solely associated with atrocities and blood-letting. Whereas humanity used to be equated with civilization, that is, with independence from nature, the meaning of humanity has been transformed into proximity to nature. Indeed, many of the problems currently associated with society – wars, corruption, repression, pollution – are ascribed to the fact that humanity has lost contact with nature. In other words, it is the over-civilized who are now held responsible for the savagery of the world. Indeed, it is often claimed that primitive societies are the really civilized ones. This privileging of primitivism implies the degradation of humanity. The common assumption is that the closer to nature you are, the more human you can be.

Primitivism has acquired cult status in the rudderless West of the 1990s. Only the ethnic is held to be genuinely human nowadays. The argument is that if Western society is to recapture its lost humanity, it must immerse itself in the authentic values of primitive society and dispense with any expectations of modernization and progress. Extolling primitivism in this way prompts the formation of a milieu in which limits are spoken of with reverence.

When modern society adopts the primitive lifestyle as a yardstick, its deficiencies can be accepted as properly appropriate for sustaining a genuine humanity. Sympathy for primitivistic-influenced ecological ideas that present any technological change as a risk has increased enormously in the West over the last decade. Experimentation, whether in the sciences or the arts, is frowned upon as life threatening.[5] The prevailing mood that privileges a primitivist perspective helps offset any criticism directed against the system for failing to deliver the goods. Indeed Western society is often indicted for being obsessed with consumption. A sanitized image of the African primitive serves as a role-model to reinforce this message of limits preached at Western audiences.

The Primitive Individual

The charm of the ethnic today is confirmed by the fact that primitives epitomize the undeveloped individual for a West that has come to fear personal independent-mindedness. Standing in stark contrast to the uncooperative, self-assertive and demanding inhabitant of modern urban society, the ethnic is viewed as comparatively self-effacing and modest, almost childish in their dependence upon others.

This interpretation of the diminished individual as being more human than modern, urban-dwelling man was originally drawn out by those modern artists belonging to the Primitivist school.[6] Scientific racists despised savage peoples and grouped them together with children, women, the insane and the criminal, either as examples of the origins of humanity or as degenerate, undeveloped forms of it. Turning the tables on the racists, Primitivist artists like Paul Gauguin and Pablo Picasso elevated the tribal world into the fount of human creativity, thereby serving as a source out of which the rational but decadent West could revitalize itself. For art critic Colin Rhodes,

> [Primitive art] represents an attempt on the part of Western artists to retreat from 'reason' and thereby gain access to the very sources of creativity, which they believed was exemplified in its most authentic and liberated form in the minds of children, tribal peoples and the insane.[7]

Primitive art, and its immediate successor Abstract art, has always remained marginal to mass society. Its sermonizing on the moral rejuvenation of Western culture was chiefly aimed at the narrow constituencies of the intelligentsia and the establishment élite. The project of primitivizing the West is on a much grander mass scale today. It entails no less than the relativization of modern and tribal society.

According to Scandinavian anthropologist Thomas Eriksen, 'Virtually every human being belongs to an ethnic group, whether he or she lives in Europe, Melanesia or Central America'.[8] Or Africa, perhaps we may add. For sociologist Abner Cohen, there is little to choose between indigenous Africans and the business élite of the City of London: 'In the cases of both ethnicity and eliteness, different symbolic forms are combined to achieve the same organisational functions'.[9] Alluding to the masonic rituals practised by City stockbrokers, Cohen's concludes that, 'In many situations in modern society custom is as strange and as sovereign as it is in "primitive" society'.[10] Again, for Survival International campaign officers Barbara Gehrels and Aidan Rankin, 'Tribal societies are no more and no less "traditional" than others'.[11] The focus of these arguments is that tribal society is just like modern society. But the full implications of this relativist case is still only rarely drawn out – that the modern world is fundamentally primitive.

The thesis that equates modern and primitive worlds is derived from the influence of 'cultural relativism', and is almost 100 years old. The German–American anthropologist Franz Boas first posited the existence of many 'cultures', all equally valid, against the singular notion of Culture, meaning the state of civilization that every society can aspire to. Boas's theory reconciled his roots in the conservative particularist doctrines of German historians Dilthey, Ranke and Rickert with his experiences as an immigrant in America's 'melting pot'. Contrary to the scientific racists, Boas argued that humanity was not divided racially but culturally. His epigones, like Ruth Benedict, went on to maintain that society's culture moulded individuals from birth into traits that they kept for life. In many ways this determinist character of cultural relativism simply substituted cultural explanations of human diversity for racist biological ones.[12] Cultural relativism legitimates the universal application of techniques specifically developed for analysing primitive societies. Boas opened the way for anthropologists to apply their tribal perspectives to the workings of modern societies.[13] Exposing the primitive hidden within the modernist shell of society has since become an activity that everyone can engage in.

The Modern Primitive

The image of the primitive in Western society has gained in importance because it helps put a congenial gloss on frail individuals and their fragmented communities. Primitivism celebrates weakness and underdevelopment as being more humane than the rugged entrepreneur of the 1980s or the racist thug. Across a huge range of social activities, the primitive is now flavour of the month. Articulating the standpoint of the primitive has become a mark of social sophistication that encompasses everyone from members of the British royal family to anti-road protesters.

The celebration of African primitivist art in the West can be traced back to the influence of Paul Gauguin and Pablo Picasso, but has now spread beyond narrow Bohemian circles into the establishment. In the eyes of the Primitivist artistic school, primitivism was a radical challenge to the conventional classicism of the establishment, but nowadays this iconoclasm has almost completely dissipated. The London Royal Academy of Art exhibition *Africa: The Art of a Continent* (October 1995 to January 1996) featured numerous artefacts and was a great success.[14] The British Museum is to build a new African gallery so as to mount a more permanent display once the British Library vacates the Reading Room.[15] Literature also has its moments of celebrating the primitive in us: the 'Savage' in Aldous Huxley's *Brave New World* (1932), Sir William Golding's neanderthals in *The Inheritors* (1955) and Margaret Atwood's *Surfacing* (1972), to name but a few.

Body art has become high fashion because even if you are powerless to influence the world, you can still exercise a limited sense of power by experimenting on your own body.[16] Even the most elegant people sport pierced noses and tattoos these days. On the magazine racks, periodicals like *Skin Art* and *Piercing World* compete alongside *Cosmopolitan* and *Wired*. Pop musicians play alternative versions of their hits with 'unplugged' acoustic guitars. On the fashion catwalks wearing dowdy grunge outfits has given way to grungy-looking models. According to *Vogue* magazine's Lisa Armstrong, calling models like Kristen McMenamy and Jade Parfitt beautiful may be in 'breach of the Trade Descriptions Act'.[17] The 'wigga' phenomenon – 'white nigger' – where white males imitate black culture, is not just confined to the sink estates, but has also attracted youthful members of the middle classes.[18]

The influence of primitivism extends into higher reaches of the establishment as well. Scientists are increasingly seeking relief in religious explanations for sub-atomic and astronomical phenomena.[19]

New Age religions like paganism are reliant upon the growth of the notion of a secluded self. Their crystal-worshipping, tarot card reading followers are rapidly outstripping congregations in the official churches of the West.[20] The official churches are struggling to catch up. The young Anglican priest in the Sheffield parish, Chris Brain, sought to jazz up the traditional Mass along New Age lines, but was engulfed in a sex scandal.[21] Economists are transfixed by the need to keep growth within sustainable (that is, 'primitive') boundaries.

In the health sector, official approval for herbalism and primitive remedies like acupuncture is growing apace. In this context, even the London *Economist* has swung round to considering the merits of African spirit mediums and faith-healers. At the end of a survey on Sub-Saharan Africa, it noted how doctors in KwaZulu Natal believe that

> *there is also a role for the traditional medical practitioners in relieving pain and easing suffering. They include [herbalists, spirit mediums, faith-healers]. These traditional practitioners are available for consultation 24 hours a day, are often within easy reach of a patient's house, share a common language, and outnumber Western-trained doctors by ten to one even in South Africa.*[22]

About the only thing the *Economist* article did not say is what the average remuneration that a traditional African doctor receives is, but it is clear that they were thinking about it.

Even among cynics, sympathy for nature, ecology and sustainability is widespread. Man pollutes but a primitive man pollutes a lot less. In June 1996, Malidoma Some and his wife Sobonfu addressed a conference entitled 'Women and Men Working Together for Change' at the Royal Geographical Society (RGS) in London. Malidoma has a degree from the Sorbonne, as well as four BAs, three MAs and two PhDs from American universities. Based in Oakland, California, the couple travel the world speaking in favour of traditional initiation rites. They are both members of the Dagara ethnic group that straddles north-east Ghana and Burkina Faso. They attended the RGS conference to argue that the West is 'all mixed up' because it lacks its own version of the African initiation rites that bring boys to manhood. The Somes argued that the problem with relationships in the West is that 'Western males have remained boys', and that a traumatic initiation rite is necessary if they are to make the transition to manhood.[23]

But modern primitivism is not a simple reprise of traditional rites. Take Modern Primitivism, for example. According to Steven Mizrach (aka Seeker 1), the Modern Primitive movement

> *in essence is a combination of modernity and the premodern – a genre blurring of the abandoned and the untried. In a world where the old (tradition, superstition, folk beliefs, etc) is increasingly being abandoned, there can be nothing more new and avant-garde then [sic] to reintroduce it once more, thus the ironic state of postmodernity . . . Having at once embraced a mythical low-tech past and a mythical high-tech future, the modern primitives are the pre-eminent denizens of the post-modern, cyclical-time era.*[24]

Modern primitivism can be distinguished from the traditional Noble Savage myth because 'Mod Prims' reject traditional romantic anti-technology sentiments. They are fascinated by the high-technology instrumentation of the modern world. Modern primitives are also known as 'Zippies' – Zen-inspired professional pagans according to Fraser Clark, editor of the *Encyclopedia Psychedelica*, or 'hippies with zip'. For Clark, a Zippie is

> *someone who has balanced their hemispheres to achieve a fusion of the technological and the spiritual. The techno-person understands that rationality, organization, long-term planning, consistency and single-mindedness are necessary to achieve anything solid on the material level. The hippie understands that vision, individuality, spontaneity, flexibility and open-mindedness are crucial to realize anything on the spiritual scale.*[25]

Modern primitive sources of inspiration are the science fantasy genre, especially Michael Moorcock's novels. Moorcock was also lyricist for Hawkwind, who – together with the Shamen – were an important British musical influence on Modern Primitivism. Sci-fi films like *Bladerunner* (1982) and the novels of William Gibson (*Neuromancer*, 1983) and Neal Stephenson, focus on how technology can enhance the performance of the human body. In Stephenson's *Snow Crash* (1992), based in a futuristic Los Angeles, everybody is defined as a member of one ethnic group or another. The skateboarder couriers he features 'are an oppressed ethnic minority'.[26] But these skateboarders carry more high-technology on them than a present-day astronaut. Here Stephenson describes a single skateboard wheel:

> Each one consists of a hub with many stout spokes. Each spoke telescopes in five sections. On the end is a squat foot, rubber tread on the bottom, swiveling on a ball joint. As the wheels roll, the feet plant themselves one at a time, almost glooming into one continuous tire. If you surf over a bump, the spokes retract to pass over it. If you surf over a chuckhole, the robo-prongs plumb its asphalty depths. Either way, the shock is thereby absorbed, no thuds, smacks, vibrations, or clunks will make their way into the plank or Converse high-tops with which you tread it.[27]

The technology may be fantastic, but it's not fantastic enough to liberate people from oppression. No, in the modern primitive philosophy, technology only provides limited emancipation.

Mizrach claims that the limitations of the mind and body need not be obeyed but can be reworked via technology because it follows in the traditions established by tribal witch-doctors or shamen. For Mizrach, indeed, 'Shamanism is shown to have a basis in quantum mechanics':

> The technological modification of the body is seen as a reworking of the shamanic 'deconstruction' of a past era, where the shaman is torn apart by the gods of his tribe, and then his bones and flesh are replaced with quartz or fire or something else.[28]

Once the shaman has been reconstructed in this way by the gods, he returns to guide his tribe. Similarly, the mechanically reconstructed techno-shamen can offer us guidance today.

Through drugs like Ecstasy, Prozac or steroids, the body and the mind can be enhanced and the trances that primitive shamen experienced can be imitated: 'The use of mystical drugs like LSD really becomes a means to activate normally dormant "circuits" with the "biocomputer" known as the brain, thus making "metaprogramming" possible' (Mizrach). One example of metaprogramming being human–animal communication. So-called 'techno-shamen' like the late Timothy Leary, John Lilly and Terrence

McKenna are embraced as heroes. Whether the drugs used are organic or synthetic is besides the point. Modern primitivism also encompasses computer hackers and internet netheads as well as those ravers who pierce their ears with computer chips, juxtaposing magic and science as they seek to manipulate national and international computer systems with their 'gremlins' and 'bugs' and 'glitches'.

Ironically, alongside this growing popularity of primitivism, there is next to no nostalgia in our times for anything remotely associated with the past. Modern primitivism is sufficiently contemporary-looking to enable it to distance itself from that vast amalgam of obsolete institutions and establishment figures irrevocably linked with the passe and the antiquated. To be cool, you cannot get away with just being 'tribal'. Unless you also have a laptop computer on which to download your e-mail, tribal is just another word for 'muddy'.[29]

The popularity of television series like *The X Files* is typical of modern primitivism. For its two stars, FBI agents Scully and especially Mulder, modern problems are more susceptible to mystical explanation than rational analysis; memory – and especially buried memory – is more useful than history and forensic science.[30] Racists are considered intolerable because they imagine the US government is really run by aliens, either the United Nations or the ZOG (Zionist Occupation Government). But *The X Files* fans are cool because they think that Washington is run by aliens too, except that these ones come from outer space. The modern tribal shaman is more likely to present himself as a UFO abductee 'implanted' by aliens than to dress up in a grass skirt and live in a mud hut. In the summer of 1996 New York's prestigious American Primitive Gallery ran an exhibition devoted to works painted by people who claimed to have been abducted by aliens.

If the modern primitive idea that the human mind can become part of a 'global brain' through the cyberspace of the internet is a revolutionary notion, it is an indication of how degraded the concept 'revolution' has become. It is one step along from 'revolutionary' soap powder. The theme that modern primitivism pursues is to identify every single high-technology mechanism in modern society and imbue it with a primitive, irrational content. Unlike films such as *The Terminator* (1984), *The Lawnmower Man* (1992) and *Jurassic*

Park (1993), the techno-shamen of modern primitivism are prepared to celebrate technology so long as this reactionary context is accepted.

Ultimately the modern primitive individual reappears as just another train-spotting, anorak-wearing social casualty, isolated from everyone else and dependent upon his technological crutches just to get by. Given their inability to dynamize stagnating society on their own terms, both the establishment and the intelligentsia are fairly content to see primitivism developing into a 'mass' cult in this way. Of course it is a misnomer to talk about modern primitivists as a 'mass', and even less as a 'movement', because the whole point about it is that – by increasing access to video recorders and internet terminals, etc. – it makes the marginal lifestyle of the isolated individual seem attractive and even spiritual. Robert Pirsig's *Zen and the Art of Motorcycle Maintenance* was for a long time seen as the hippy's Bible. In fact it was a polemic against the hippy antagonism to technology: 'I just think that their flight from and hatred of technology is self-defeating.'[31] Pirsig's aim was to reconcile modern technology with ancient wisdoms such as Zen and the Buddha: 'The Buddha, the Godhead, resides quite as comfortably in the circuits of a digital computer or the gears of a cycle transmission as he does at the top of a mountain or in the petals of a flower.'[32] Pirsig made strenuous efforts to distance himself from the romantic 'noble savagery' of hippy culture, ruthlessly debunking the myth of a primeval paradise. In the mid-1970s, when he was writing, Pirsig even credited technology with the ability to solve ecological problems – which even the most hard-nosed scientists are reluctant to do today:

> *The primitive tribes permitted far less individual freedom than does modern society . . . A technology that produces debris can find, and is finding, ways of disposing of it without ecological upset. And the school-book pictures of primitive man sometimes omit some of the detractions of his primitive life – the pain, the disease, famine, the hard labor needed just to stay alive.*[33]

Pirsig remained overwhelmingly hostile to the deployment of technology for the benefit of mass society, however: 'God, I don't want to have any more enthusiasm for big programs full of social planning for big masses of people that leave individual Quality out.'[34]

For Pirsig, 'Quality' was a spiritual notion that an individual had to capture in order to avoid alienation from machinery, which for him was a dialectical transcendence of the natural and the human: 'technology is a fusion of nature and the human spirit into a new kind of creation that transcends both'.[35] Ultimately, for Pirsig, nobody should hate technology. By being applied to society rather than the individual, it was simply wrongly used: 'It's not connected in any real way with matters of the spirit and of the heart.'[36] There was occasional public recognition of this transcendence, during the first airplane flight, during the first moonwalk, but Pirsig wanted the individual to relate to technology spiritually as a matter of routine: 'This transcendence should also occur at the individual level, on a personal level, on a personal basis, in one's own life, in a less dramatic way.'[37] Pirsig was the first to see in modern technology a means by which the existence of the diminished individual could be a cause for celebration, that is, by presenting it as an opportunity to enter into spiritual communication with nature.

Before the primitive could become a cult in the West, an important facet of Western ideology had to be discredited: nationalism. In the early 1990s, the establishment and intellectual élites experienced a severe panic at the prospect of being engulfed by nationalist mobs emerging from the ruins of the Soviet bloc.

The Twilight of Nationalism
The fall of the Berlin Wall in 1989 witnessed a tremendous outburst of triumphalism and celebration in the West at its victory over communism. Yet the same events were also seen as creating a power vacuum which an angry populace could exploit. Both left- and right-wing strands of the political mainstream became obsessed with the prospect of uncontrollable mobs using ethnicity as a vehicle for mobilization. In the eyes of the radical left, this fear took the form of dire predictions of 'fascism' marching across Europe once again. In the eyes of the right, the same nightmare took the form of ancient ethnic hatreds or religious 'fundamentalism' being unleashed against comfortable Europe. As a result, the entire political mainstream took fright, not just against any movements committed to realizing ethnic goals, but against the whole notion of mass mobilization.

The establishment generally desires to achieve national harmony. In Britain, it is often ready to consider projects that promote a sense of national community – international sporting events, sentimental television dramas rehearsing past national glories, and rather tacky pageants like trooping the colour or changing the guard. This patriotic milieu helps consolidate all sections of 'the nation' behind the establishment. This consensus is particularly crucial at times like the present when there is great tension and instability in society.

Nevertheless the establishment generally feels uneasy about nationalism. Even its own pet projects are treated cautiously and there is a conspicuous lack of enthusiasm for them. In England, the jingoistic Last Night of the Proms is celebrated in the sort of furtive manner that befits an action one feels a bit guilty about enjoying. It almost seems as if the authorities are afraid that waving the flag may work too well.

When it comes to the association of nationalism with sporting occasions and other cultural displays such as musical performances, theatre, novels and films, etc., the establishment is relatively relaxed so long as its sporting and other cultural heroes remain mere symbols. By associating with such token nationalist gestures, the authorities can procure a passive respect for themselves in the process. In addition, it is still judged respectable for the intelligentsia to express their patriotic sentiments in a suitably elevated and cryptic form. On the other hand, the notion that cultural achievements performed in Britain might be accredited instead to universal humanity is entirely foreign to the intellectual élite. Cultural nationalism is about the only way that polite society is still prepared to express its patriotism openly.

In Britain, the transformation of nationalism from a long-standing patriotic tradition into a rather enigmatic cultural phenomenon has helped obliterate the involvement of the masses in political life. A diet of insipid cultural nationalism may be uninspiring for everybody outside of the intelligentsia, yet it is all that the authorities are prepared to tolerate because any further promotion of nationalism risks transforming the presently inert masses into an enthusiastic movement.

The major priority of the establishment these days is to avoid provoking any form of mass action. Nationalism has always contained an element of mobilizing mass appeal. In Britain, Mrs Thatcher's efforts to launch a nation-wide crusade around the Falklands' task force illustrates the benefits that the establishment can expect to derive from an outburst of patriotic zeal. Yet it is precisely that element that makes the establishment anxious about nationalism today. When nationalism moves beyond being a mere symbol into becoming a force in society it raises the unlovely spectacle – unlovely to the élites, that is – of providing a vehicle for mass involvement in society.

In the past, the establishment was confident that it had the capability to absorb every popular movement – no matter how radical. That confidence was hardly surprising in a country where the left viewed itself as the most patriotic section of society. Nowadays, however, the establishment no longer feels capable of co-opting even reactionary outbursts of national pride.

These days the establishment is working overtime to seek institutional solutions that will make it easier for it to get a better grip over a society that is unravelling. If nationalism could be monopolized by its own institutions, it would not be a problem. In that respect it is not so much afraid of nationalism as apprehensive of its expression among ordinary people. What the élite fears above all is the kind of lumpen xenophobia that parodies its own national traditions, but which it fears could get out of control and develop in a notionally anti-establishment direction. For example, this stance informed its reaction to the tiny right-wing British National Party (BNP) council victory in East London's Isle of Dogs in September 1993. Rather than viewing the extreme nationalist vote as a timely endorsement of the British way of life, every notable politician rushed to pour scorn on the local white electorate as a racist underclass incapable of upholding civilized standards. In America, the Michigan Militia arouses similar feelings of distaste even among right-wing politicians like Newt Gingrich and Pat Robertson. In Germany, Chancellor Helmut Kohl has backed demonstrations against neo-Nazi groups.

These days nationalism is likely to be regarded by the ruling élite as just as much a potential menace as an opportunity to cohere society together. Indeed, even the remotest association of nationalism with ordinary people makes the establishment feel distinctly uncomfortable. Shortly after the BNP's victory in Millwall the former

Education Secretary, John Patten, fashionably remarked that, 'The last place we want to see [the Union Jack] is wrapped round a shaven-headed British National Party storm-trooper or a drunken football lout besmirching the good name of Britain abroad'.[38] But when he went on to propose that the Union Jack be flown from civic buildings and schools so as to help reclaim it from the BNP, it triggered a backlash from critics who branded him jingoistic as well.

With nationalism, the key problem the establishment faces is that its considered promotion of national unity might backfire by instigating destabilizing nationalist outbursts. This dilemma has been compounded by its failure to create any original forms of nationalism suitable for the 1990s. For example, the 'politically correct' outlook that has now been adopted by the establishment frowns on both traditional patriotism as well as all expressions of national enthusiasm. In Britain, the essential absurdity of many of the recognized components of national unity – the monarchy, the Union Jack, the Church of England – has been amplified by the lack of any underlying rationale for them. Nationalism has little legitimacy in society, and few are prepared to suffer the ridicule that awaits those who dare champion its cause.

Although nationalism has been more or less repudiated intellectually, it continues to act as the operating basis for every state department from the Home Office to Customs and Excise. For many, the possession of an appropriate passport is an essential item to obtain access to social services. Through inertia these practices continue to exist by default, though on increasingly shaky intellectual grounds. The confusion in the establishment about nationalism threatens to exacerbate the disarray that already exists among its own institutions. The once familiar expression 'Great Britain' has almost entirely dropped out of use. The British army seems to feel happier flying the blue United Nations flag these days rather than the discredited Union Jack.

Western disenchantment with nationalism has been gathering pace since the beginning of the century. It first became apparent that jingoism was losing official approval when American President Woodrow Wilson called for national self-determination in his 'Fourteen Points' speech of January 1918. Wilson wanted to restrict self-determination to a couple of central European nations in order to undermine the Austro-Hungarian empire – Germany's ally in the First World War. Nevertheless, Wilson's own Secretary of State, Robert Lansing, reflected the disquiet felt by other Western leaders when he wrote in his diary later that year, 'The more I think about the President's declaration as to the right of "self-determination", the more convinced I am of the danger of putting such ideas into the minds of certain races'.[39] These fears seemed confirmed when most anti-colonial movements subsequently referred to Wilson in justifying their national struggles for liberation.

For the Western élites, fascism became a decisive nail in the nationalist coffin during the Second World War. Hitler had been democratically elected into power. A common intellectual criticism of his regime was that it represented 'the dictatorship of the scum'. For the intelligentsia, the evils of nationalism had been confined to what is now called the Third World and Eastern Europe until the Second World War. But if Western, civilized Germany could fall under the influence of the nationalist mob, who was to say the same could not happen to the rest of the West? After the Second World War, nationalism itself became increasingly discredited. Writing in the aftermath of the Second World War, Carlton Hayes pointed to a new threat to Western society:

> *Even in countries where personal liberties are still guaranteed, where a republican constitution still exists, and where liberal democratic government still functions, the 'masses' tend increasingly to evince a chauvinism, an intolerance, and a fanaticism strangely out of keeping with the individualism and internationalism which an older generation of patriots associated with liberal democratic nationalism.*[40]

For Hayes, the cure for mob nationalism was to educate the élite in all its ramifications of the nationalist threat, 'Clearly, the outstanding task before national education is to train among the coming generation a large number of men and women of character and reason who will perceive the dangers of integral nationalism'.[41]

The Nazi experience did not completely discredit nationalism. Like many of his contemporaries, Hayes still divided nationalism into two categories: 'Nationalism in many of its doctrines and much of its practice has undoubtedly been a beneficent influence in modern history. Unfortunately it has tended to endure a highly intolerant and warlike type which we have arbitrarily termed "integral".[42]

'Integral' nationalism was in fact a term coined by the French irrationalist intellectual Charles Maurras at the turn of the century. He portrayed nationalism as a substitute religion which culminated in a mystical cult of the Earth and the dead. Until the Second World War, 'integral' nationalism was solely applied to nationalists from outside the West. After the Nazi experience, however, Maurras's characterization of nationalism as mystical and arcane began to be applied to Western nationalism as well.

It was an effort to rescue Western nationalism that motivated Hans Kohn to shift German nationalism into the Eastern camp. He contrasted 'the rational and universal concept of liberty' that in his view formed the basis of Western nationalism with an Eastern nationalism which he claimed was founded 'on history, on monuments, on graveyards, even harking back to the mysteries of ancient times and of tribal solidarity'.[43] According to Kohn, Nazi Germany fell under the influence of 'tribalistic' nationalism because it had rejected the heritage of the Enlightenment.

Hans Kohn's concept of an 'Easternised' Germany could not come into its own until the cold war began. With the division of Germany in 1948–9, the finger of blame for Nazism was pointed at 'totalitarian' East Germany. Kohn's rather mobile definition of nationalism admirably suited the post-war order. Throughout the cold war period, Third World nationalists were labelled either 'democratic' or 'totalitarian' according to which side they backed in the Western/Soviet conflict. Indeed when Third World countries deposed regimes that were friendly to the West, the perceived nature of their nationalism would be inverted so that the Western defeat could be retrospectively accounted for.

With the awkward case of Germany removed, contemporaries of Kohn could differ over his characterization of Eastern nationalism, but everybody agreed that the divide in nationalism between East and West was still valid. Walter Kolarz held that Eastern nationalism was comparable to juvenile delinquency and that while 'some of the ethnical problems of present-day Eastern Europe were once problems in the West', the mature West had now grown out of nationalism altogether: 'Today, from the ethnical point of view, the West can be compared to an extinct volcano. On the whole, the process of the formation of modern nations is finished.'[44]

From right to left, the common characterization of nationalism during the cold war was that it was 'ambiguous'. Apart from cold war politics, this amounted to a recognition that nationalism could be tolerated so long as the masses were excluded from power and nationalist movements remained firmly managed by intellectual élites. Dictionary definitions faithfully reflected this ambiguity and therefore appeared somewhat contradictory to the non-expert.[45]

This attempt to divide nationalism into good and bad components is still evident today. For the Archbishop of Canterbury, Dr George Carey, 'national identity' can provide people with 'an important and proper part of how they understand themselves and their place in the world', whereas 'the logic of nationalism leads to repression and removal of those who do not share the national identity and to wars'.[46] Likewise, former British premier John Major emphasized a spurious distinction between patriotism and nationalism. When he addressed an audience of City financiers at the Lord Mayor's banquet in 1992, he told them that the collapse of communism had left a vacuum that could yet become a fertile breeding ground for 'extremism and unrest': 'The genie is out of the bottle and that narrow line between patriotism and nationalism is in danger of being overstepped in many countries'.[47]

The definitions of both the Archbishop of Canterbury and the Prime Minister express a greater concern with the dangers of nationalism than with its benefits. This reflects the shift in establishment concerns since the end of the cold war in 1989, which has seen fragmentation of multi-ethnic states in Eastern Europe and the unravelling of society in the West. In these conditions, anything that might group people together has become suspect – and this includes homegrown patriotism. Accordingly, even Western patriotism is now less likely to be viewed as ambiguous, but synonymous with ethnicity or fascism. A weakened Western élite instinctively reacts against any popular outlook. In a remarkable rejection of its own origins, the tendency has recently grown among Western establishments to denigrate nationalism in general and treat every popular expression of it with cynicism if not hostility.

Some, like LSE professor Anthony Smith, have tried to recast ethnic nationalism as the best way to inculcate loyalty to the institutions but it has had few takers. Smith emphasized the myths and memories of ancient ethnicity as positive, while downplaying the mobilizing potential of communal hatreds:

> The nation is embedded in a pre-modern ethnic past and by which it is thereby endowed with such warmth, energy and vitality. They are also the sources of those mobilising and purifying drives which can so easily degenerate into communal hatreds and wreak such havoc in ethnically mixed areas. The one seems inseparable from the other . . . But we must not mistake the part, however dark, for the whole.[48]

With the end of the cold war, nationalism has become a kind of codeword that sums up the lack of control that the Western élite has over modern society. From this perspective, it is hardly surprising that those institutions with not much going for them – such as the United Nations or the European Union (EU) – should try to highlight their supra-nationalist credentials. In a comment typical of the post-cold war era, Raymond Seitz, the former American ambassador to Britain, suggested that – in the light of developments in Eastern Europe – organizations like the EU should receive support because 'institutions which tend to attenuate nationalism are good to have around'.[49]

The establishment would be happy to have any institutions around that could replace its own dilapidated ones. According to political analyst Jack Snyder, ethnic nationalism is intensified nationalism which has attracted mass support: 'Nationalism typically intensifies when there is an increase in the proportion of people who have a voice in politics.'[50] In the absence of politically mature institutions, this could rapidly get out of hand. Snyder's concern was with the construction of institutions that would be sufficiently strong enough to withstand any mass ethnic upsurge: 'Ethnic nationalism appears spontaneously when an institutional vacuum occurs . . . It predominates when institutions collapse, when existing institutions are not fulfilling people's basic needs, and when satisfactory alternative structures are not readily available.'[51]

Snyder here exposed his lack of faith that Western institutions can restore stability. The search was on for new institutions that could replace those predicated upon defunct nationalism. Ironically enough, they are based upon a redefined ethnicity but that of the diminished individual rather than the bloodthirsty mob.

The panic-stricken forecasts of mob rule emerging to dominate the 1990s have proved to be largely inaccurate. It turned out that there was no need to repel ethnic mobs intent upon burning down London or Paris. Gradually, both the establishment and the intelligentsia came to realize that their fragile institutions were not in imminent danger from rampaging crowds. However, the experience did uncover a real problem that does confront the Western élite. Their inability to prevent the steady unravelling of their societies has been exposed. The end of the cold war revealed that it was the Western élite itself that was fragmenting. It is this despair at their own inadequate institutions that Snyder reflects so well. It was their own weakness that caused him to imagine that the disparate collection of isolated individuals that makes up much of modern society could transform themselves into a truculent rabble.

Primitive Democracy

The belated recognition that society is not about to be engulfed by the revolting masses, but is rather slowly deflating, has put a premium on primitivism as a celebration of modest humanity. When considering how to rebuild their bankrupt institutions, or 'capacity-building', recourse is made to the primitive political systems of Africa. Once the worry over mass involvement has been allayed, ethnicity can be introduced as a reorientation towards the local community. Nowadays every department of state or ministry – such as the police or the social security – keeps its national operations well in the background, while advancing itself as an integral part of the local community. In this way, elected local councils are steadily being replaced by quangos, which also distance themselves from national government by presenting themselves as 'independent' agencies comprised of appointees. This absence of democracy is not seen as an impediment. On the contrary, quangos credit themselves with the asset of not being subject to the whims of elected politicians, who cannot refuse the base instincts of the voting masses.

Radical philosopher of nationalism and ethnicity, Tom Nairn, goes even further and dreams of the day when all the 200-odd nation-states of the world are broken down into 'thousands of states'. For Nairn, such localism will both revivify the modern world and civilize it:

> We are likely to see a thousand or more 'states' after the year 2000, with revivified localisms functioning as the more effective vectors of a farther stage in world industrialisation . . . It will diffuse nationalism, but also change its profile – roughly speaking from an ethnic to a 'civic' mode more in tune with the formation of 'citizen communities'.[52]

In his excellent book, *Accountable to None*, *Times* columnist Simon Jenkins has detailed, however, how this ostensible promotion of local accountability and democracy in Britain over the last decade has in fact resulted in a substantial recentralization of power to the national institutions of the establishment (with the sole exception of the 'talking shop' of Parliament).[53]

Capacity-building is usually justified in the name of furthering democracy, but it is not always obvious that this 'furthering' means promoting a primitive notion of democracy. Primitive notions of democracy are increasingly being used to challenge the notion of mass democracy – not just in Africa, but in the West too.

In the early 1960s, during the heydays of the African state, premature attempts were made to try to belittle the achievement in African independence by presenting the local councils of the African tribal elders as being a more authentic version of democracy than the Western model that inspired the African nationalists. Harvard professor Rupert Emerson argued, for instance, that:

> Increasingly it has been contended in recent years that the Western assumption of the majority's right to overrule a dissident minority after a period of debate does violence to conceptions basic to non-Western peoples. Although the Asian and African societies differ vastly among themselves in their patterns of customary action, their native inclination is generally toward extensive and unhurried deliberation aimed at an ultimate consensus. The gradual discovery of areas of agreement is the significant feature and not the ability to come to a speedy resolution of issues by counting heads.[54]

This statement already betrays a significant disillusionment with Western political institutions. It seems that they could not easily be applied to Third World societies. For the West Indian political scientist Arthur Lewis, majority rule was 'totally immoral' compared to the consensual decisions arrived at by the 'original institutions of the people'[55]: 'The tribe has made its decision by discussion, in much the same way that coalitions function; this kind of democratic procedure is at the heart of the original institutions of the people.'[56] Emerson and Lewis never got anywhere with this theme because their assault upon majority rule was precipitate. Faith in the Western democratic method was still too pervasive at the time.

In the mid-1970s, the Dutch political scientist Arend Lijphart developed the notion of 'consociational democracy' that was very similar to the Emerson and Lewis stance. Consociational democracy is a sophisticated translation of primitive democracy. Lijphart argued that majority rule, or 'majoritarian democracy', was inherently oppressive because it repressed minorities. Consociational democracy, however, gave minorities a veto over every decision and thus put the onus upon arriving at a consensus with which all could agree. But what is to stop such a society disintegrating into a multitude of bickering minorities? Lijphart argued that minority leaders had to be trained to co-operate with each other: 'In a consociational democracy, the centrifugal tendencies inherent in a plural society are counteracted by the cooperative attitudes and behaviour of the leaders of the different segments of the population.'[57]

For Lijphart, 'elite cooperation is the primary distinguishing feature of consociational democracy'. Elevating minorities – and not even minorities, but minority élites – above the majority of people in reality means abolishing the influence of ordinary people. The object of consociational 'democracy' is to annul real democracy by replacing it with a mythical democracy, untainted by mass involvement. The real meaning of democracy is the rule of the people. To a large extent, consociational democracy is using semantics to lay siege to democracy in the name of minority rights.

This assault upon real democracy is presented as a rejection of Western culture in favour of indigenous systems of democracy. In the past, Western institutions with a feudal origin that have always been run in this supposedly authentically 'ethnic' manner, like the

British House of Lords, were denigrated as 'archaic'. The difference now is that there is a real effort to transfer its ethnically valid procedures to the rest of the Western polity.

Since the 1990s, the principles of this apparently ethnic consensual democracy are increasingly being applied to Western society as disillusionment grows. The elected politician is being replaced by the appointed representative of a minority (and everyone is a minority of one sort or another). Quangos are replacing local councils and even the supposedly sovereign House of Commons is being monitored by a judge. In Northern Ireland, the elections to the all-party talks in May 1996 were entirely conducted on the basis of consensual democracy. As a result, the Northern Ireland Women's Coalition (1 per cent of the poll) were given two seats as compared to the three seats allocated to each of the three parties who won 64 per cent of the vote. The result meant a massive decline in influence for the parties backed by the Loyalist masses. The party associated with anti-Western violence, Sinn Fein, was barred altogether.

To be blunt, primitive democracy means excluding the rude masses in favour of civil, that is polite, society. Deploying primitivist reasoning will be essential if such results are to win any respect in the West.

Africa: A Change of Image

Modern primitivism has been decisive in how African ethnicity is interpreted in the West today. The British establishment traditionally acclaimed the so-called 'martial' races, that is tribes such as the Zulus of South Africa and the Tutsi of Rwanda and Burundi. Though not as prominent, they also appreciate the Bushmen of the Kalahari for their services to the colonial armies as scouts and trackers. For the élite, these tribes can be distinguished from other Third World peoples because they typify the Western image of the 'noble savage'.

Thus the House of Lords has pressed the government to send a High Commissioner to Botswana to investigate allegations that the Gaberone regime was transporting – in 'cattle trucks' – peaceful hunter-gathering Bushmen out of their tribal homeland so as to develop the tourist industry there. Sir Laurens van der Post, a confidante of Prince Charles and author of a number of books and TV documentaries about the Bushmen, claims that the West can learn valuable spiritual lessons from them: '[The Khwe] are of great importance to understanding our own rejected selves. They are an example of our partnership with nature that we so badly need to renew in order to rediscover the world within us.'[58] The campaign to defend the Bushmen won the support of ex-premier Margaret Thatcher, former Tory party chair Lord Norman Tebbit and former Oxfam chair Lord Judd, among others.

Survival International – an NGO that is sympathetic to the tribal peoples of the world – initiated this campaign for the Bushmen, though these radical critics of the establishment are highly suspicious of top people's support for tribal peoples. In particular, they are hostile to the traditional conception of 'the Noble Savage' which they view as paternalistic. They are much more sympathetic to the Modern Primitive approach to technology which is steadily replacing the old-fashioned anti-technology of 'noble savagery'. Under the influence of Western primitivist ideas, NGO volunteers increasingly view such high-technology instruments as the internet and satellite telephones and video recorders as essential if diminished lifestyles are to appeal to ordinary people.

Conservationist groups like the Worldwide Fund for Nature (WWF) and the Royal Society for the Prevention of Cruelty to Animals (RSPCA) are intimately connected with the establishment, frequently through royal patrons. For Survival International campaign officers Barbara Gehrels and Aidan Rankin, these Western conservationists are in league with big business in Africa: mining companies, ranchers, loggers and the tourist industry. When these interests require land to be cleared of people so they can commence commercial operations, they call in bodies like the WWF to justify the expulsion of indigenous peoples on ecological grounds. Citing the case of the Bushmen, among others, Gehrels and Rankin argue that, where the aboriginal people are permitted to remain on their land, it is only under the strictest of conditions:

Usually the intention of such schemes has been to encourage tourism by pandering to Western ideas of 'noble savages'. The people concerned are thus dehumanised and presented as exotic species to be 'conserved' along with flora and fauna as long as they play by the rules.[59]

The Minority Rights Group have been objecting to the noble savage viewpoint for some time. In their report on the Bushmen written in the early 1980s, they remark how treating the San as spiritually superior transforms them into the human equivalent of zoo animals:

> *Our fascination with the San must not, then, lead us to conclude that the San must be preserved in all their pristine uniqueness merely so that we may continue to marvel at them. They are not, and do not wish to be, a human zoo; our approach must be based on more than our projection into them of what we imagine, from the viewpoint of materially more plentiful societies, to be the spiritual qualities they possess and we lack.*[60]

After investigating the Kenya Wildlife Service (KWS), George Monbiot has directly linked it to the development of the Kenyan tourist industry. Special Maasai villages – cultural *manyattas* – have been set up to attract tourists to the fantasy of 'the noble savage inhabiting the primordial wilderness'.[61] Meanwhile the KWS are clearing the Maasai from their traditional cattle grazing lands to create more 'Safari' space for tourists, thereby risking ruin of the environment. For Monbiot, it is the Maasai that are the best at preserving the land and the wildlife that lives off it:

> *By throwing out the nomads, the [KWS] conservationists are getting rid of the people who helped to shape the landscape, who are partly responsible for the complex pattern of forest, scrub, grass and swamp, that is so important to the wildlife.*[62]

Nevertheless, despite his reservations about tourist-orientated 'noble savagery', Monbiot believes that modern society has much to learn from the Maasai cattle herders of Kenya's Rift Valley, simply because they live where prehistoric man was located:

> *As these migrants disappear it is not only they but we who are diminished, for with them we lose what they may have to teach us about who we really are . . . Of the nomads, those who can tell us most about ourselves are surely the people following the trails of our ancestors: the migrants crossing the grasslands, the woods and volcano fields in the savannahs of East Africa.*[63]

In Wandsworth, London, Monbiot constructed a village community within an urban wasteland, to try to demonstrate to modern city dwellers that a sustainable, that is primitive, lifestyle is feasible even here.[64]

In a similar vein to Monbiot, two British anthropologists, Melissa Leach and James Fairhead, have written a study of the impact of local societies on forestry in West Africa. In it, they strenuously reject the conservationist viewpoint that demonizes local people by blaming them for the destruction of the rain forest there. Instead they point the finger at the activities of international logging companies and the modern world generally. According to Leach, 'Industrial and non-fallow farming, logging, plantations, urban sprawl, mining and industry, all destroy forests'.[65] Leach and Fairhead's researches have discovered that the traditional farming techniques of the local people increases forest cover:

> They know better than anyone how to increase forest cover. In the transition zone between high forest and savanna, where neither type of vegetation is entirely stable, farmers deflect the landscape from one to the other by their land management practices. [In Guinea] local people cultivate forest 'islands' around their villages. They plant trees that will protect the village from hot, dry winds and fire, give shade to people and their coffee and kola trees, and provide fruits, nuts, medicines or other useful products.[66]

Condemnations of the establishment's sympathetic pose in support of the 'noble savage' as racist in origin and exploitative in intent have become common in NGO literature. But, as we can see with Monbiot, the alternatives — which either stress that tribal societies are 'just like us', or argues that we can 'learn from them' — are no less backward-looking. This agenda assists the dissemination of primitivism as a role-model for modern society.

What we are being offered is a politically correct version of 'noble savagery', updated for the 1990s. Traditional 'noble savagery' believed the West to be modern, but despaired of it. The turn of the century Primitivist artists wanted to inject modern society with some authentic tribal humanity so as to revitalize it. But present-day modern primitives like Monbiot and others think that the West is also primitive, and the Third World is also modern; that is, there is little difference between the two. Modern primitives do not romanticize the past like traditional noble savagery did. Instead they view the past as a problem, from which a new start is required based on a recognition of mankind's truly primitive nature. Many welcome the use of technology, unlike traditional noble savagery, in so far as it helps reinforce this primitivist lifestyle by making it more attractive.

Gehrels and Rankin, for example, inform us that those Bushmen who opt to live in new houses, wear modern clothes, and inter-marry with other Africans, have been excluded from their lands by the environmentalists since they have become undesirable as a tourist attraction. Gehrels and Rankin object to these expulsions on the grounds that, 'Such changes were quite compatible with their sustainable, egalitarian way of life'.[67]

It is obvious that Gehrels and Rankin still retain a modified conception of the 'noble savage', albeit one that is perhaps more flexible than the conservationist one. Elsewhere in their article Gehrels and Rankin refer to 'sinister assimilationist agendas' where tribal peoples are encouraged to adopt peasant lifestyles. But what is so 'sinister' about peasant life, except that they are one step closer to urban life than nomads? The dividing line for Gehrels and Rankin is not what modern gadget an individual Bushmen may or may not use, but whether they begin to adopt the sort of 'mass' urban lifestyle that will encourage them to stand up aggressively for themselves.

Overall, the proposals by Survival International and others for a more realistic conception of what constitutes primitivism – living in modern houses, wearing modern clothes, using modern sewage facilities – seem to be better attuned to making the notion of a primitive, basic lifestyle more palatable to the existing denizens of modern society than the romantic tribal image (grass skirts, no shoes, thatched huts, dirt floors, and no electricity). If Western born and bred Modern Primitives are ever to identify with Africa's modern primitives like the Bushmen, then tribalism has to be redefined away from the mud hut and moved more towards the conception of the isolated individual in tune with nature. In that sense, the myth of noble savage is alive and kicking in the modern world, even if he is on the internet.

Barbaric Technicals

Not everyone in the West goes along with the Modern Primitivist ritualized worship of technology. For some, even the normal consumption requirements of a modern individual are the product of a reckless mania, the fulfilment of which could threaten global degradation. From this perspective, the global availability of high-tech merchandise only makes matters worse. The importation of modern arms and other Western technologies like radios and videos are regularly blamed for exacerbating trends towards barbarism in Africa.

For example, the article that right-wing American political analyst Robert Kaplan wrote in February 1994 for Boston's *Atlantic Monthly*, 'The Coming Anarchy', has rightly become infamous for its depiction of Africa as a cesspool emitting a stream of deadly plagues and tribal conflicts into the world – a global Pandora's box. Moreover, his 'Iron Curtain' solution to isolate Africa from the rest of the world caught the attention of Western policy-makers bent on constructing a 'Fortress Europe' or North American Free Trade Area (NAFTA) bloc designed to shore up their societies.[68] Less noticed, however, was Kaplan's use of African crises to make wider comments about the modern human condition.

After dwelling upon the troubles that tore apart the West African country of Sierra Leone in the early 1990s, Kaplan suggests:

> *Sierra Leone is a microcosm of what is occurring, albeit in a more tempered and gradual manner, throughout West Africa and much of the underdeveloped world: the withering away of central governments, the rise of tribal and regional domains, the unchecked spread of disease, and the growing pervasiveness of war.*[69]

Kaplan's aim is not to demonize Africa, but the world. Sierra Leone is his dystopia for the global future. The above passage continues, 'West Africa's future, eventually, will be that of the rest of the world'.[70] Regarding the plight of Third World regions like India, China and Africa, Kaplan has no hesitation in blaming modernization for their condition:

> *It is worth noting, for example, that it is precisely the wealthiest and fastest-developing city in India, Bombay, that has seen the worst*

> *intercommunal violence between Hindus and Muslims. Consider*
> *that Indian cities, like African and Chinese ones, are ecological time*
> *bombs . . . and it is apparent how surging populations, environmental*
> *degradation, and ethnic conflict are deeply related.*[71]

Kaplan cannot grasp that the problems of social squalor and environmental destruction that afflict Africa and the rest of the Third World are due to the failure of the market system to deliver. As a result, he accuses development, rather than the lack of it, for the region's predicament. Negative diatribes directed against modernism and technology abound in his article. When Liberian president Samuel Doe was tortured to death in 1990, Kaplan is offended when the spectacle is videoed and circulated around West Africa.[72] Côte d'Ivoire's modern road system is not an improvement in Kaplan's view. It 'only helps to spread the [Aids] disease'.[73] His conclusion has almost become conventional these days: 'Man is challenging nature far beyond its limits, and nature is now beginning to exact its revenge.'[74]

For Kaplan, it is humanity – and modern man in particular – that is his target, not particularly African savages. Indeed, the carefully regulated ritual tribal fights organized by African primitive societies are often positively contrasted to the evils of modern warfare. It is regularly claimed that ethnic conflicts in Africa were relatively harmless until modern technology began to be used by their participants, whether it be Somali-style 'technicals', radio stations in Rwanda or the ubiquitous AK 47 assault rifle.[75]

The stick fights of the Kichepo people in the Boma region of southern Sudan are a typical example of an African ethnic conflict that is entirely approved of in Western circles. Their heavily ritualized fights were last recorded on film in the mid-1980s. Organized between neighbouring villages, the fights were depicted as a rite of passage into manhood for the youth involved.[76] Strictly regulated by the tribal authorities, the whole exercise was presented as therapeutic for the community as a whole, despite the physical scars inflicted upon its young men, because it allowed individual frustrations to be exorcized in a relatively harmless fashion. The 'modern' civil war in the Sudan was presented in stark contrast to this modest tribally-regulated custom. The film-makers stressed a number of times that, 'within hours' of finishing filming, the Sudanese authorities banned foreigners from the region altogether due to the proximity of the war. Nobody has seen a Kichepo stick fight since (the unspoken implication being that the tribe has been destroyed by the civil war).

The reason why technology attracts such vituperation is not because Luddism is alive and well. Far from it. After all, people like Kaplan have to use technology to get their own views across. It is rather that machines – like cars, telephones, faxes, video cameras, internet computers and, yes, guns – have the potential of enabling ordinary people to participate as a decisive force in society, if only to a limited extent. So long as the West possessed a sense of mission, mass consumption of high-technology goods was not seen as a problem by the establishment. But now it has lost all sense of direction. If Africans only used modern devices 'in the privacy of their own homes', like Modern Primitivists advocate, then that could be tolerated too. What chills the hearts of the Western élite is the mass use of technology.

The Limits to Primitivism in the West

The development of primitivism is limited in Western society, primarily because of the presence of ethnic minorities there and the prevalence of racism against them. Indeed, the use of ethnicity was until recently almost exclusively applied to Western minorities. In America, 'ethnic' was a term of abuse. This old form of ethnicity stressed the marginality of ethnic victims as a racially oppressed section of society. Primitivism differs from this old form of ethnicity because it celebrates marginality and advocates that everyone is a victim, but a victim of modern society. Certain elements of primitivism can be derived from the presence of ethnic minorities in Western society. Occasionally, there are even opportunities to play at being an ethnic minority, such as at the Notting Hill carnival, in schools or on the media and other cultural platforms like the theatre, where identification with the ethnic roots of black society is actively encouraged. Outside of these restricted arenas, however, the ever-present fact of routine racial harassment and oppression makes the celebration of ethnicity difficult. Furthermore, the overwhelming discrepancy between the size of the white majority as compared to the ethnic minorities makes it problematic, but not impossible, to conceive of whites as a members of ethnic minorities.

It is otherwise in relation to Africa. Here white supporters of the *status quo* have a positive interest in promoting minority rights. Even the millions-strong white community of South Africa prefer to present themselves as an ethnic minority. Furthermore, most blacks still retain a latent sense of ethnic consciousness which can be worked upon.

For some time now the prime way the West relates to Africa has been through the large numbers of NGO personnel regularly sent out to the continent. Well before they reach Africa's shores, these people have been seduced by the primitivist milieu that pervades Western society. Once they arrive in Africa, they begin imposing this Western primitivism upon Africa. The ease with which Western perspectives can easily set the African agenda gives the lie to theories of sustainable development empowering people. First, it is because the West is the main source of power and resources in the world today, that it can impose itself upon Africa. This is why, for the moment, if Africa is considered civilized, then the West is a thousand times more civilized. Similarly, if Africa is barbarian, then the West is a thousand times more barbarian. In the same way, Western primitivism overpowers African versions since it derives its strength from the industrialized West. In the absence of any other alternative, Africans also are posing their demands in terms set by this Western primitivist agenda.

In Africa, NGO volunteers are not promoting African ethnicity but a sanitized version of ethnicity that has already gone through the mill of Western primitivism. Highly intelligent, well-educated and no doubt widely travelled too, what is it that makes the average NGO volunteer susceptible to primitivism? It is because they already view primitivism as morally superior compared to traditional Western mores that they wish to commit their superior abilities into making it even more influential.

Notes

1. Frank Furedi, *Mythical Past, Elusive Future*, p. 239. For example, despite the claims that the world wide web of the internet brings people together internationally, they meet only as isolated individuals stuck in their bedrooms, not socially.

2. National Lottery Charities Board, *International Grants Programme*, p. 47.

3. Ibid., p. 20.

4. John Carey, *The Intellectuals and the Masses*, p. 45.

5. More and more art forms are being subjected to censorship on the grounds of protecting people from stress, protecting children, etc. On the other hand, it is characteristic of the period that Minimalism is growing in influence. Originally an experimental product out of the mid-1960s, its bleak perspectives allegedly put us 'in touch with the essence of existence' according to John Pawson, the architect contracted to redesign New York's Madison Avenue along Minimalist lines. For Pawson, who peddles his barren interiors among a clientele that includes fashion guru Calvin Klein, Minimalism means 'the perfection an artefact achieves when it is no longer possible to improve it by subtraction' (*Evening Standard*, 6 September 1996, p. 27). Also see Pawson's *Minimum*.

6. As an artistic expression, 'Primitivists' was first used to describe the fifteenth-century painters Giotto and Masaccio, the predecessors of Raphael and Michelangelo. Of course, there is no connection between these medieval Italian masters and 'modern' art Primitivists.

7. Colin Rhodes, *Primitivism and Modern Art*, p. 133.

8. Thomas Eriksen, *Ethnicity and Nationalism*, p. 10.

9. Abner Cohen, *Two-dimensional Man*, p. 15. For Cohen, 'In many situations in modern society custom is as strange and as sovereign as it is in "primitive" society. Scholars are now "rediscovering" in modern society the existence and significance of an endless array of patterns of symbolic behaviour that have been for long associated exclusively with "primitive" society' (ibid., p. 1).

10. Ibid., p. 1.

11. Barbara Gehrels and Aidan Rankin, 'Conservation: Pandas before People?', p. 8. Survival is preparing a special book posing the question 'Are tribal peoples really primitive?' for publication in early 1997 (*Survival Newsletter*).

12. See ch. 9, 'Franz Boas and the Culture Concept in Historical Perspective', in George Stocking, *Race, Culture and Evolution*, pp. 195–233. Also see the discussion in Kenan Malik, *The Meaning of Race*. Malik employs the useful metaphor of a ladder to illustrate the continuity between Boas and the scientific racists he abhorred (p. 170). If the scientific racists supported a vertically-inclined hierarchy of races with whites at the top, Boas simply swopped it for a horizontal culturally demarcated society. Cultural relativism thus only implies the equation of social divisions rather than their eradication.

13. For a recent example, see Joao de Pina-Cabral and John Campbell (eds), *Europe Observed*.

14. Though the exhibition did cause affront to some post-modern sensitivities. Nancy van Leyden challenged its assumption that Africa is a single entity; 'Surely "Africa" as a unified and homogeneous entity is a stereotype that should have been

despatched long ago'('Africa 95', p. 237).

15. In the art world, a useful distinction can be made between nineteenth-century 'Orientalists', who portrayed the Exotic in an awkward demonstration of Western superiority, and the twentieth-century 'Primitivists', who believed that the West's abandonment of the mythic aspect of its everyday life was responsible for its *fin de siècle* sense of malaise, and sought in Africa and elsewhere authentic spiritual qualities capable of reviving their society 'by confronting it with its deepest memories'. By its co-option of primitive art, the contemporary establishment may seem to some to be signalling the demise of its traditional civilizing mission. Yet it is arguable that Primitivism – with its emphasis on Western spiritual revival – can provide a source of even more Mission(ary) Statements, and it is this which appeals to the establishment.

16. See V. Vale and Andrea Juno (eds), *Modern Primitives*. The blurb of this book describes itself as 'an anthropological inquiry into a contemporary social enigma – the increasingly popular revival of ancient human decoration practices such as symbolic/deeply personal tattooing, multiple piercing, and ritual scarification'. Also see Housk Randall and Ted Polhemus, *The Customised Body*.

17. Lisa Armstrong, 'Pretty Cool', p. 29. Another fashion critic, Sarah Doukas, comments revealingly 'The new girls don't work out. They're not interested in being Amazons'. 'Amazons' classically referred to a barbarian society of dominant women. But this image is too powerful now and the new androgynous, anorexic models look more like African famine victims.

18. In general, while middle-class youth celebrate fashionable primitivism, the working class are labelled the underclass for adopting the same lifestyle.

19. See John Gillott and Manjit Kumar, *Science and the Retreat from Reason*.

20. See Lynn Revell, 'The Return of the Sacred'.

21. In Africa itself, however, the churches are more ready to dispense with the formalities. According to one Roman Catholic priest in Western Equatoria, southern Sudan, in November 1994: 'Most of our Christians practice the traditional way of living': 'For example they will go to the witchdoctor [kujur]. It takes time to Christianize the culture, keeping the beautiful that is there. For instance, there is a beautiful rite for the introduction of a child to society . . . [It is akin to baptism] but if you go deeply into each symbol it is part of traditional religion. [We want] to preserve the old, and elevate it and perfect it.' (Quoted in African Rights, *Great Expectations*, [Insertions by African Rights]).

22. Sub-Saharan Africa Survey, p. 17.

23. 'Out of Africa: A Message', *Independent* (14 June 1996), p. 4.

24. Steven Mizrach, 'Modern Primitives: the Accelerating Collision of Past and Future in the Postmodern Era', Cyberanthropoly web pages at Http:\\www.clas.ufl.edu\anthro\ modern primitives.html (October 1996).

25. Cited in Jules Marshall, 'The Zippies'. Available on the web at www.southern.ac.com/mmm/zippies/w iredzip.html. Marshall claimed that the Zippies stood for the belief that 'technology can – indeed, should – be put to the furtherance of hedonistic and spiritual goals'.

26. Neal Stephenson, *Snow Crash*, p. 72.

27. Ibid., p. 26.

28. Steven Mizrach, 'Modern Primitives: The Accelerating Collision of Past and Future in the Postmodern Era', Cyberanthropoly web pages at Http:\\www.clas.ufl.edu\anthro\modern primitives.html (October 1996).

29. The Zapatista Indians in Chiapas, Mexico, have long had internet links. The Ogoni Community Association has its own web site. In the USA, Native American tribes like the Shoshone-Bannocks of Idaho and the Utes of Colorado have been using sophisticated carbon-dating and DNA tests on skeletons to substantiate their land rights (*New York Times*, 22 October 1996). Those American tribes who now operate wealthy gambling and casino franchises are reportedly using genetic engineering techniques to check the status of anyone claiming tribal fellowship.

30. FBI special agent Dale Cooper, star of David Lynch's TV series *Twin Peaks* (1990), prefigured at least Scully. He too encountered the paranormal – principally in the guise of 'Bob'. Given that the extent to which the FBI and its notorious founder J. Edgar Hoover have been exposed and discredited, the fact that the Scully and Mulder characters have successfully managed to rehabilitate the American national police organization is instructive. If you imagined the FBI building in Oklahoma that was blown up in April 1995 was full of Scullys and Mulders, with the fanatical nationalist J. Edgar Hoover types priming the explosion, you get the picture.

31. Robert Pirsig, *Zen and the Art of Motorcycle Maintenance*, p. 18.

32. Ibid.

33. Ibid., p. 121.

34. Ibid., p. 352.

35. Ibid., p. 284.

36. Ibid., p. 162.

37. Ibid., p. 284.

38. 'Britain is keeping its symbol tightly furled', *Sunday Telegraph*, 24 October 1993.

39. Cited in D.P. Moynihan, *Pandaemonium*, p. 83.

40. Carlton Hayes, *The Historical Evolution of Modern Nationalism*, pp. 224–5.

41. Ibid., p. 320.

42. Ibid.

43. Hans Kohn, *The Idea of Nationalism*, p. 543.

44. Walter Kolarz, *Myths and Realities in Eastern Europe*, p. 9.

45. A couple of definitions of nationalism from the 1960s: 'The ability of governmental and civic leaders to spread the ferment of nationalism among the masses is greatly facilitated by its highly irrational character . . . If kept within reasonable limits, a healthy patriotism is a great spiritual force . . . But nationalism that is narrow or egotistical is incompatible with any degree of progress' (*Encyclopedia Americana*, vol. 19, [1968], pp. 756–7); 'In the case of a citizen of a state who accepts that state as satisfying and representing his national feeling, nationalism denotes a devotion to the state and a nationalist is a person who feels and actively expresses such devotion. The words, however, are commonly used in a slightly pejorative sense, denoting an excessive attitude . . . By contrast with the admitted virtue of patriotism, nationalism corresponds to vanity and egotism in the individual and is at least halfway to chauvinism and imperialism' (*Chambers Encyclopedia*, vol. 9, [1969], p. 674).

46. 'Carey urges EC unity in face of nationalism', *Independent*, 12 February 1993.

47. *Independent*, 17 November 1992, p. 1.

48. Anthony Smith, 'Ties that Bind', p. 11.

49. Dominic Lawson, 'Bosnia is Europe's Problem'.

50. Jack Snyder, 'Nationalism and the crisis of the Post-Soviet state', p. 16.

51. Ibid., p. 12.

52. Tom Nairn, 'The Incredible Shrinking State', p. 3. For a fictional account of such a world, see Neal Stephenson's *Snow Crash*, where every American suburb has become a miniature nation-state called a 'Burbclave'.

53. See Simon Jenkins, *Accountable to None*.

54. Rupert Emerson, *From Empire to Nation*, p. 284.

55. W. Arthur Lewis, *Politics in West Africa*, p. 64.

56. Ibid., p. 86.

57. Arend Lijphart, *Democracy in Plural Societies*, p. 1.

58. 'Bushmen find few friends', *Daily Telegraph*, 17 May 1996. When Sir Laurens died later in the year, Jean-Marc Pottiez wrote in an obituary that Post's 'lifelong desire [had been] to root himself in the African experience and to make the history of the aboriginal African not only his own, but that of all mankind' (*Independent*, 17 December 1996, p. 10).

59. B. Gehrels and A. Rankin, 'Conservation', p. 8.

60. David Stephen, *The San of the Kalahari*, p. 15.

61. George Monbiot, *No Man's Land*, p. 116.

62. Ibid., p. 120.

63. Ibid., p. 3.

64. George Monbiot's Wandsworth community had the following note pinned up on a boundary post:.

PERMACULTURE
Ethics
    (1) EARTHCARE: On this site we hope to enhance existing wildlife habits, improve soil fertility, recycle our waste products, use renewable energy and generally minimise our impact on the environment
    (2) PEOPLE CARE: On this site we hope to provide some of needs such as food, shelter, community, skill and knowledge sharing
    (3) FAIR SHARE: On this site we hope to show how surplus land can really meet people's needs. As individuals we share our personal resources: – time, enthusiasm, skills, visions, ideas and toilet paper
New people stay one week – then they have to agree to the Principles.
(Personal communication to the author.)

65. Quoted in Kate de Selincourt, 'Demon Farmers and other Myths', p. 39.

66. Ibid., pp. 36–7.

67. Gehrels and Rankin, 'Conservation', p. 8. One is tempted to imagine what Gehrels and Rankin would think about those Bushmen who might take to driving fast cars, eating junk food and watching TV soaps.

68. According to Heather McHugh, a research analyst specializing in ethnicity under contract with USAID, Kaplan's article 'The Coming Anarchy' influenced the Clinton administration: 'Not only did Clinton read the article, but, in an unusual move, asked for an

assessment from National Security Council staff, CIA, State Department, and Pentagon' (*USAID and Ethnic Conflict*).

69. Robert Kaplan, 'The Coming Anarchy', p. 48.

70. Ibid.

71. Ibid., p. 60.

72. Ibid., p. 73.

73. Ibid., p. 54. One of the most fashionable panics today is that of epidemics spread via air travel. Like Kaplan, Richard Preston's popular novel *The Hot Zone* (1994) has an Ebola-type virus dispersing along a road, the Trans-African Highway driven through the Congo jungle, connecting Zaire with East Africa.

74. Kaplan, 'The Coming Anarchy', p. 54.

75. 'In recent years, conflicts in the region made the prized AK-47 more readily available and the spear was soon replaced by the automatic weapon as the weapon of choice. Inevitably the parameters of raiding changed . . . Tribes without rifles were overrun and the whole balance of the traditional rules of engagement was disrupted' (Sarah Errington, 'The Karamojong of Uganda', p. 6).

76. Richard and Julia Kemp, '*Kichepo Stick Fighting*'.

CHAPTER 2

Empowering the Victim

It would be a mistake to interpret the promotion of primitivism and ethnicity in Africa as a conspiratorial agenda by the NGOs and their volunteers to recolonize the continent. The vast majority of them are motivated by a genuine concern to relieve the plight of ordinary people. It is more that they are products of contemporary Western society and that means they really believe that ethnicity is most suited to enable African society to cope, if not the rest of the world as well.[1]

As we have noted, primitivism has its limits – particularly in the West. It is an ideology whose main effect is to provide an excuse why society can no longer go forward. Generally it is not about advocating that we all return to living in mud huts or consult witch-doctors.[2] Nevertheless a perspective that celebrates primitivism really fits the bill for a region like Africa where most people still live in either mud huts or shanty town shacks that surround most cities. Even so, modern ethnicity in no way entails that Africans must relinquish their meagre amounts of consumption goods. It means that, since Africans are considered to be closer to nature than Westerners, they should find it easier to accommodate themselves to a sustainable pattern of living. In other words, they are not as imbued with an attitude problem as Westerners.

Since NGO volunteers all tend to wear primitivist spectacles, every social phenomenon appears as ethnicity or as a phoney cover-up for ethnicity. Because the primitivist standpoint is based on Western criteria, whether the immediate environment is modern or backward is irrelevant. You meet an African airline pilot: he's a Dinka who can fly planes. You meet an African doctor: she's a Tutsi who can perform heart surgery. And so it goes on. The point being that, whenever you meet an African, you wonder what their ethnic identity is.[3] The primitivist mindset developed in Western conditions necessarily encourages NGO volunteers to probe into where people are coming from instead of thinking creatively about what people can do.

The privileging of primitivism reinforces the prejudice that a person's origins are determinant. This is not necessarily racist (though it certainly paves the way for racist attitudes to develop), because the assumption is that Westerners are motivated by their parochial sources too – their club, their family, their workplace, their sports team, their former school. As we have seen, in the West all these little local preoccupations are increasingly interpreted as ethnically inspired interests too.

The primitivist perspective has been greatly fostered by spreading notions of diminished or undeveloped individuals. Media preoccupations with the plight of African victims probably began with the launch of Bob Geldorf's Band Aid in 1985. Ever since, the African child famine victim has stood as an emblem for the continent. It has heightened the sense that Africans are childlike victims who are at risk from the modern world because they are so unfamiliar with it. To this day, Africa continues to be perceived as the victim continent of the world, if not a victim of famine then of ethnic conflict.

This perspective presents a completely distorted picture of Africa and Africans. The vast majority of Africans are dynamic people determined to succeed against all the odds. At best this majority is ignored, they are simply written out of history; at worst, their modernizing aspirations are suspected of causing many of Africa's problems in the first place. In his role as the diminished human *par excellence*, it is the African as victim that sets the moral tone for the rest of the world to follow. Hence the popular campaign to secure 'basic' human rights for Africans relies upon a degradation of the meaning of humanity to simply mean the right to food, the right to shelter, the right to life, etc.[4] If we are responsible, if we choose to make as little impact upon the environment as the ethnic African, if we diminish ourselves by reducing our consumption demands too, the Westerner can also acquire a measure of this morality, can also become 'basically' human.

It is in this *ethical* sense that the African victim has been empowered. The victim need never be referred to as such, moreover, because his status must be treated with 'respect'.[5] Only sad people wallow in their victimhood. It is much more cool to cloak the same victim status in the garb of 'indigenous knowledge'. The conception that indigenous knowledge, or rural people's knowledge, is superior to Western rationalism began life as part of the ecology or Green movement in the West. Eric Schumacher wrote his *Small is Beautiful* in the mid-1970s and went on to found the Intermediate Technology group.[6] R. Chambers's *Rural Development: Putting the Last First* was published in the early 1980s and it argued that 'Rural people's knowledge and scientific knowledge are complementary . . . outsider professionals have to step down off their pedestals and sit down, listen and learn'.[7]

According to Peter Walker in a recent collection of essays singing the praises of indigenous knowledge systems (IKS), African famine victims 'do not respond to stress from the point of view of ignorance, but from a position of knowledge . . . This traditional knowledge is neither fossilised nor stagnant. It is a means of survival'.[8] Again, the fact that many Africans still have to queue up at communal water-wells in the 1990s has been dressed up by NGO intellectuals with theories that celebrate the superior power of indigenous knowledge and the vital role played by traditional leaders in mobilizing free communal labour to drill bore holes.[9]

In this context, the idea of building a modern waterworks or a dam which can provide hot and cold running domestic supplies of water, a proper sewage system and decent irrigation for agricultural activities is considered absurd if not a positive risk to the environment. For Maryam Niamir, the possible opposition of local people to having 'indigenous' knowledge imposed upon them as an inferior substitute for modern living standards has to be allowed for: 'The attitude of the local people who are by now used to top-down projects may also be a constraint.'[10] These local people are no doubt imbued with the 'false consciousness' that living in the Third World should not also have to mean accepting the third rate.

With British-based NGOs like Intermediate Technology interpreting African dire necessity as a product of their ancient 'indigenous knowledge' rather than a product of grinding poverty, the concept of indigenism can then be served up to gullible Westerners as a 'sustainable' system that they should be proud to live by if the opportunity arises. Jeffrey McNeely wants to encourage 'design and implement research programs aimed at promoting the application of traditional wisdom to modern resource management' for the rest of the world.[11] Furthermore: 'Scientific investigators and researchers should include indigenous co-investigators in all phases of their research design and implementation.'[12]

Scientific development has always benefited from intuitive, non-rational insights. If 'indigenous' knowledge can provide some such input, then this is to be welcomed. But there is a world of difference between the occasional creative input and mixing up the methods of scientific investigation with that of 'indigenous knowledge systems'. Unlike in art, there can be no gradation between reason and irrationalism in science. The NGO intellectual viewpoint, however, profoundly influenced by Western primitivism, argues that 'traditional wisdom' can understand the world even better than rational science can. This elevation of the witch-doctor over the medical doctor is a result of a decline in belief in Western society, not because African healers have suddenly started working medical miracles.

Moral Ethnicity

Thanks to the Western perspective that primitivism should be respected, Africans are viewed as authentic by the NGOs only when they present themselves as victims. Moral ethnicity is the stunted individual aggregated into a community. Ethnic groups therefore comprise marginalized communities of African victims. Some NGO literature even champions the traditional community for its further suppression of individuality: 'How things are done is more important [to indigenous peoples] than what is done, with great emphasis placed on social relationships and preserving the harmony and integrity of the community and culture, more than on individual recognition or advancement.'[13]

Only ethnicity makes sense, everything else is bogus. The ready assumption is that true Africans must be proud of their ethnicity. It is not immediately obvious that the implication of this standpoint is that the integrity of any African who denies their ethnic interest is called into question. After studying one African society – Kenya – Cambridge professor John Lonsdale has tried to develop a moral conception of African ethnicity. For Lonsdale, it is ethnicity's commitment to seemingly authentic roots that makes it more effective than Western values in fending off abuse: 'Because native, [ethnicity] is a more trenchant critic of the abuse of power than any Western political thought'.[14] But what is it about ethnicity that gives it virtue, makes it moral? Lonsdale is evasive in answering this point, and his replies tends towards aphorisms that revolve around a mysterious 'inner logic':

- *'Ethnicity is universal: it gives the identity that makes social behaviour possible . . . It instructs by moral exclusion'.*[15]

- *'Moral ethnicity creates communities from within through domestic controversy over civic virtue.'*[16]

- *'[Ethnicity's] deep political language has followed an inner logic partly independent of the changing uses to which its key concepts have been put in high politics.'*[17]

Ethnicity can be considered as 'moral' because in contemporary society it is the diminished individual, the victim, who sets the moral tone. Ethnicity best encapsulates the marginalized communities of African victims and that is what makes it moral too. The implication is that it is through discovering their own ethnic identity that all Africans – indeed all humanity – can be similarly empowered.

We are now in a position to consider once again the National Lottery Charities Board's (NLCB) criteria for ensuring equality of opportunity in NGO projects designed for the Third World. The NLCB insist that the NGOs 'encourage equality of opportunity in all aspects of your project, irrespective of age, race, religion, ethnic origin, marital status, colour, nationality, gender, disability or sexual orientation'.[18] Furthermore, the project must be 'culturally sensitive, non-violent and respect social diversity'.[19]

There is an apparent contradiction between these two conditions. The first demands that there is equality of opportunity irrespective of ethnic origin. The second demands that social diversity, ie ethnicity, is respected. In the first, equal opportunity must be irrespective of – that is, without reference to – ethnicity. In the second, ethnicity must be respected. Ethnicity is not to be respected, and then it is. What is the explanation? The answer lies in Boasian cultural relativism. The existence of ethnic divisions in society must be respected, though no one ethnicity can be privileged over any other. In other words, specific ethnic groups cannot be privileged, but ethnicity itself must be.

In reality, the NLCB does not expect its NGO applicants to 'respect social diversity' without privileging any of them. Elsewhere in its document the NLCB asks grant applicants 'to empower women and/or girls where appropriate'.[20] Similarly, the NLCB do want to privilege particular ethnic groups. In its explanatory notes, the NLCB claims: 'We are likely to fund projects that strengthen the capacity of marginalised people to influence policy-makers . . . We will also support projects that get their messages across through the positive portrayal of disadvantaged people.'[21]

The NLCB then gives an example: 'Indigenous organisations producing publicity materials to promote their rights to ancestral land'.[22] The ethnicity that the NLCB wishes to promote is not the ethnicity of the savage, nor the ethnicity of the successful, but the ethnicity of the marginalized – the diminished victim, a moral ethnicity that is a peculiar product of purely Western concerns. This moral ethnicity bases itself solely among the most marginalized groups in Africa. It celebrates the mutual toleration of diverse ethnic identities. It is non-violent. It therefore has only the most tenuous link to any African experience of ethnicity.

The power of the NLCB's interpretation of ethnic identity and indigenous rights is not just derived from the vast sums that it has at its disposal, but from the cult of the primitive that already dominates the West. The NGO volunteers who queue up to obtain their grants from the NLCB feel it is only right that the 'poorest of the poor', the most downtrodden ethnicities in Africa, receive Western aid.

NGOs working in Africa creatively portray their projects as consistent with these moral objectives. For example, some clans in the northern part of Somalia that ActionAid is working with apparently uphold an entirely different code than that of the clan 'warlords' based around the Somali capital Mogadishu – such as the late General Aideed – that caused the Americans so much trouble in 1992–3.

ActionAid reports that, though the old regime had 'sought to impose a homogeneous "modernity" on the culture of clan and lineage' in the Sanaag region of the north, the clan elders nevertheless managed to survive 'more than 20 years of harsh centralised government' and are now thriving: 'There are now more than twice the number of sultans in "Somaliland" than at independence in 1960.'[23]

Indeed ActionAid has the sultans doing so well that they can even meet the NLCB's 'non-violent' criteria by abolishing the old and ancient tradition of plundering their neighbours. ActionAid has found that 'the return to tried and tested systems of governance has enabled Somalis in the north to break the momentum of war and opportunistic plunder' and, consequently, 'the establishment of modern political structures must take into account the moral authority of the elders'. ActionAid's research document on the squeaky clean sultans of Somaliland modestly concluded that, 'For the time being, external assistance must supplement rather than overwhelm the kinds of local grassroots initiatives that already exist'.

Unfortunately for ActionAid, this sentimental picture that they have painted of Somaliland has had a question mark placed against it by an authoritative source. According to a report by *Africa Confidential*, the Hargeisa government of Somaliland was at war on three fronts in early 1996: with Garhajis clan rebels sponsored by Mogadishu and Eidegalla rebels from Salahle region.[24] The Sanaag region may remain relatively peaceful since it is far from Hargeisa and is close to the coast, but cities like Burao have been left devastated and deserted by fighting between the pro-government Habar Jeclo clan and the Habar Younis clan over the last eighteen months.

The tendency to sanctify as morally pure particular African ethnic groups is a part of the noble savage tradition.[25] The most obvious recent example has been the canonization of Ken Saro-Wiwa and the Ogoni of Nigeria organized by Anita Roddick of The Body Shop. In the run-up to the execution of Ogoni activist Saro-Wiwa in November 1995 by the Nigerian military, a joint letter to the *Guardian* newspaper was signed by The Body Shop's Anita Roddick, Friends of the Earth UK director Charles Secrett, Green Party leader

Sara Parkin, Labour MEP Glenys Kinnock, and Liberal Democrat Party leader Paddy Ashdown.

In the letter, these prominent people claimed that Ken Saro-Wiwa's trial (on charges of murdering four other Ogoni leaders in May 1994) resulted from the Ogonis 'peaceful and effective campaign of protest against the environmental destruction and economic deprivation of the last 40 years perpetrated on them by the international oil companies and in particular Royal Dutch Shell.'[26] The pro-business *Economist* also agreed that the 500,000-strong Ogonis possessed 'a strong sense of identity' and their land has been 'raped by the extraction of oil'.[27] Furthermore, in January 1996, the august Fellows of the Royal Geographical Society voted by a large majority to remove Shell as their patron because of its responsibility for the 'exploitation, repression and suffering' of the Ogonis.

A leaflet published by Survival International pointed out that the Ogonis were only one of the many ethnic groups living in the Niger delta, each of which had a valid identity, even though they were only nominally Christian:

> *The roots of these communities go back for thousands of years. Each local group or clan has its own identity, and often its own language . . . Formerly people honoured many deities of earth, sky and water, under a supreme God. Today nearly all are Christians, though the old beliefs are by no means dead.*[28]

Survival International then went to claim that allegations that the Ogoni had been involved in ethnic clashes with their Niger delta neighbours were unfounded since these attacks were 'in fact' organized by the Nigerian regime:

> *Much of the violence [afflicting Ogoniland] has been attributed by the Nigerian authorities to 'ethnic' or 'tribal' rivalries. But there is evidence that these rivalries have been fomented from outside, and indeed that some of the attacks supposedly by local communities were in fact carried out by soldiers in plain clothes.*[29]

Since the letter to the *Guardian* was written, one of its journalists who is sympathetic to the Ogoni cause, Chris McGreal, has accepted that Ken Saro-Wiwa was complicit in the murder of the four moderate Ogoni leaders as well as encouraging attacks on neighbouring tribes.[30]

Saro-Wiwa's Movement for the Survival of the Ogoni People (Mosop) has been meeting with Body Shop officials at their headquarters in Littlehampton, Sussex, since at least November 1993. The sanitization of ethnic groups like the Ogoni has enabled Western NGOs and ethical companies like The Body Shop to establish a new relationship with an African élite on the basis of sharing a superior morality: both The Body Shop and Mosop allegedly care more about the environment and the oppressed indigenous peoples of the Niger delta than the Nigerian military and their cronies in Shell Oil. But the struggle to fit African ethnicity into the West's moral code has been problematic, none the less.

What does an NGO do when its African clients express weariness with traditional culture and curiosity about the outside world? In the case of the Nuba of war-torn central Sudan, the London-based African Rights NGO have painted a frightening picture that this 'array of diverse peoples with their rich variety of languages and cultures' will be transformed into a 'permanent underclass of deracinated people, condemned to second-class citizenship' if they ever abandon their traditions and give up their struggle against the Khartoum authorities: 'Cut off for so long, many Nuba tend to see themselves as a people who have much to learn from the outside world. They have less to learn than they might expect. Isolation has its advantages.'[31]

A recent report by ActionAid personnel in Ghana relates a discussion with the elders of the Ayakolia community within the Sapeliga chieftaincy. The basis of the discussion was the clash between the ideas of the NGO workers and the beliefs and traditions of the community. ActionAid claimed to be 'very sensitive' to local culture when working with such communities: 'Sometimes taboos and traditional practices can help the progress of development work' they contended. In addition, traditional respect for the land was seen as a good basis on which to discuss environmental issues. Issues raised over attitudes to women and health, however, were seen as another matter:

> It is more difficult, though, when staff see how certain taboos and practices can be detrimental, particularly to health. In some African

countries children are prohibited from eating eggs, even in the hungry
season when levels of malnutrition rise. A more stark example is the
practice of female circumcision which is widespread in many parts of
Africa and is surrounded by a number of taboos.[32]

The ActionAid report was coy about the consequences that this
difference of opinion over female circumcision has for the ethnic
communities: 'Knowing when to speak out and when to accept
practices can only be learnt over time.' This diplomacy is typical of
NGOs according to Oxfam fieldworkers Jenny Rossiter and Robin
Palmer: 'If partners should say something with which the agency
disagrees, there is a discrete silence – for example, on the gender
awareness of the Mujahideen'.[33]

An explanation for this 'discrete silence' by the NGOs can found
in the fact that raising objections to the ethnic practice of female
circumcision, or any other custom for that matter, abrogates the
NGOs own cultural relativist principles. Indeed it leaves them open
to the charge of racism for implying that Western cultural values –
which object to female genital mutilation (FGM) – are superior to
African ones, instead of being equally valid. Moreover it recalls the
days of empire, when Christian missionaries and colonial administrators insisted upon reordering traditional customs to suit their
prejudices, even down to instructions on how to have sex (the
notorious 'missionary position'). The necessity of promoting victim
culture is essential for the NGOs to distance themselves from this
infamous heritage.

The distinction of moral ethnicity from all previous versions is its
prioritization of victimization. African ethnic groups are feted and
sponsored only if they can show they are a victim in some sense. In
passing Thomas Eriksen remarks that sometimes 'in order to save "a
culture" one must lose it!'.[34] A creative approach towards victimization, such as claiming loss of culture, is often important in securing
NGO support.

It is the diminished individual, the victim, not the ethnicity itself,
that has priority here. Ethnic identity is only considered valid if it
represents a community of the disadvantaged. So as soon, therefore, as
an ethnic group is implicated in the victimization of anybody else then
it could forfeit its privileged status. This means, given that every ethnic

group is always victimizing somebody, that the privileged status of every ethnic group is always open to challenge for some infringement. By presenting themselves as the champion of Africa's victims, NGOs hope to avoid accusations of interfering in another culture.

The NGO community campaigns vigorously against the practice of female circumcision. Western officialdom is rapidly coming round to the same view.[35] For example, Sudan has been labelled as 'terrorist state' by Washington on some very sketchy evidence. But the fact that Khartoum has been singled out as complicit in FGM probably carries more weight these days. On the other hand, there has been very little Western reaction against the Ghanaian regime for disregarding FGM when practised there. Similarly, there is little objection to the Ewe ethnic group of Ghana for maintaining its 'Fetish slave' custom, whereby young girls – Trokosi – are offered as sex slaves to the Ewe priesthood in compensation for the misdemeanours of their ancestors.[36] But then Accra is considered a showcase for the structural adjustment policies of the International Monetary Fund (IMF) and the World Bank and thus far the NGO's protests have been ignored.

Cultural relativism's imprecations against interference have been so submerged by the rise of victim culture that many individual NGO volunteers happily criticize these bodies for not interfering enough, for example to protect girls at risk from FGM. They also admire whistle-blowers who expose the moral lapses of the higher bodies who ignore cases of FGM in friendly regimes, and call for a more consistent approach against all examples of victimization. But calls for a more consistent intervention by the West can only reinforce the degradation of African people.

The principles of the NLCB, for example, are not just to be adopted by the UK-based NGOs but by their southern partners as well. The NLCB insists that the NGOs 'encourage equality of opportunity in all aspects of your project, irrespective of age, race, religion, ethnic origin, marital status, colour, nationality, gender, disability or sexual orientation'.[37] Significantly, it then asks the NGOs: 'How confident are you that your partner organisations overseas can match your commitment? Why?'[38] The UK-based NGO must be able to demonstrate that its southern partner will not, say, discriminate against African lesbians or gays (cf., the clause on 'sexual orientation'), or it could lose its grant. The NGO is therefore obliged by the NLCB to police its African clients so as to monitor and evaluate their morals.

The pursuit of this politically correct agenda that has been entirely constructed in the West reinforces Murray Bookchin's pertinent point that such well-meaning Westerners have turned aboriginal people 'into a postmodern parody of the noble savage'.[39] For Bookchin, the problem with romanticizing ethnicity is that it imposes harsh ethical objectives on the indigenous peoples: 'Worse still, the "noble savage" myth obliges aboriginals to be superior beings, indeed almost angelically virtuous and exemplary in behavior and thought, if they are to enjoy the prestige of Euro-American recognition and the rights to which they are entitled.'[40]

From this perspective, the last thing that NGO fieldworkers have on their minds is advancing African ethnicity. It is tempting to imagine a scenario where NGO volunteers – eager to be accepted into the villages – initially bend over backwards to placate the rituals and traditions of the village elders, thus emphasizing their sympathy for ethnic rights. Once the NGOs are established, however, they can use their material wealth to create a new élite loyal to themselves among the village youth through launching a campaign directed against the elders on the grounds of gender abuse in order to oust them from power.

This view is too cynical, even conspiratorial. There may be instances of such Machiavellian deviousness occurring among NGOs operating in Africa but if they do, then they are best treated as irrelevant to the overall analysis of ethnicity. This interpretation falls into error through assuming that the primitivism promoted by the NGOs is merely a pose to ease their entry back into Africa to recolonize it. In reality, their primitivist approach is a product of the decline of Western society and would probably exist irrespective of what happens in Africa. Whatever the reactionary consequences of the NGO proto-primitivist agenda in Africa, the real crux of the problem lies in the degeneration of Western society, the milieu which is responsible for breeding NGOs and their volunteers in the first place.

Bearing this in mind, we can now proceed to consider the formation by the NGOs of a new élite based upon moral ethnicity in Africa.

Restoring the Broken Relationship between Africa and the West

Because of the backlash that developed against Keynesianism in the late 1970s, the West decided to reject its African offspring – the independent post-colonial state – and launch an all-out offensive against the structures that it had spent so much time and effort constructing during the decolonization process. Economically, through the privatization policies of the IMF and the World Bank, politically through the campaigns against the militarism and corruption of many African leaders, socially through the spread of media panics about African immigrants and Aids, the relationship between the West and the black African élite collapsed.[41]

From 1985 onwards, however, the potential of a new relationship between the West and Africa was created with the launch of Band Aid. This event generated a concern for the plight of Africans that inspired a generation of Western youth. The then tiny NGO community was swelled with a new influx of recruits who wanted to help. Unlike their missionary forebears, however, this generation of youth generally rejected the whole Western baggage of superior civilization, imperialism, Christianity, and improvement. Since they saw themselves as primarily victims of modern society and its politicians, it was relatively easy for them to transfer these feelings on to Africa, whose famine casualties were also seen as victims of modernization and interfering politicians. This NGO generation was going to be decisive in shaping Africa in the 1990s, but the framework they had adopted was unlike any previous Western effort to relate to Africa. Its principles were that Africans were victims of modern society and its politicians and, to save themselves, they had to be weaned away from dependence upon it.

Any Africans who shared these views were taken to be allies in the new cause. An élite was to be cultivated in Africa which would reject the legacy of the West and implement truly African cultural systems which could offer an alternative lifestyle that was at once practical and moral.

The New African Ethnic Elite

We have already established that the promotion of ethnicity by the NGOs did not mean that they hoped to force Africans back into mud huts, or even adopt tribal dress. Because it is felt that people like Ken Saro-Wiwa and the Ogoni were closer to their own concerns, such as protecting the environment, the NGO attitude is more that 'we can learn from them'. Moreover, the Africans that the youthful NGO volunteers tend to relate to the easiest are young African people like themselves – not at all the village elders, who were not particularly sensitive about the environment anyway.

African youth are generally a long way from being like the old men steeped in ancient rites and customs. In general, the African constituency who found the message offered by the NGOs most appealing were the young dynamic professionals of both genders who arose out of the reform movements that swept Africa briefly in 1989–90. They bitterly resented their exclusion from power by the old nationalist guard, though not enough to stimulate the masses sufficiently to bring down regimes, e.g. in Mobuto's Zaire or Abacha's Nigeria.[42] After all, only people who have been well educated can hope to grasp the Byzantine complexities of the politically correct jargon spoken by the Western NGO personnel. These people became the 'local staff' of many of the bright new NGOs operating in Africa from the late 1980s. They were employed to establish a constituency of support among ordinary Africans for the NGO agenda.

How can local NGO workers persuade Africans to adopt this moral agenda? Cambridge professor John Lonsdale believes that moral ethnicity is constructed through contest and debate: 'Moral ethnicity creates communities from within through domestic controversy over civic virtue.'[43] Such a 'contest' is certainly convenient for those NGO intellectuals who wish to blend their own moral standards into the African arena in order to appear organic. Writing in *Indigenous Organisations and Development*, a recent Intermediate Technology textbook, Norman Uphoff is cautious about these sorts of 'purely instrumentalist' views which assume that indigenous peoples will accept outsiders who try to 'mix and match' cultures. He advises that every Western goal must be based upon local institutions and customs, though they may have long fallen into disuse. Referring to his experiences in Sri Lanka, where the Shramadana custom of donating free labour for public benefit exists in the Gal Oya district, Uphoff comments: 'Our ability to activate more co-operative and altruistic behaviour was greatly assisted by the memories and positive valuation of *this indigenous custom, which made our modern local organisation at least partly traditional.'*[44]

Uphoff concludes that 'Formal modern organisations can thus be strengthened in their performance if supplemented by informal, more traditional structures of roles and behaviour patterns'.[45] The benefit of this approach for Uphoff is that, though the seemingly traditional NGO organization is a hybrid, it can expect to enjoy 'consensual support' rather than 'grudging acceptance' from the local community. Half the rest of *Indigenous Organisations and Development* is then taken up with accounts of NGOs persuading local African communities to work on their projects for free by reviving such customs: the Yoruban 'Egbe Olomo Ile' and 'Ogbomoso Parapo', the Isalu development union of Iseyin, all of Nigeria; the water-well projects of Upper East and West Ghana; and the 'Impandes' indigenous healer associations of South Africa.

This tendency to encourage blurring the distinction between Western NGOs and African traditional customs is not simply a ploy to secure a fairly mundane object, i.e., keeping within a tight budget. It is a consequence of fashionable Western thinking that celebrates the primitive and denigrates rationality, and which runs rife through NGO literature.

All this activity has exacerbated the difficulty of tracing where Western NGOs end and traditional ethnic organizations begin. Kingston Kajese rightly objects that the majority of African NGOs lack traditionalist roots:

> *The majority of Africa's NGOs have not come about as a result of a natural evolution and gradual adaptation of ancient traditional forms of association or organisation. Certainly, in East and Southern Africa, NGOs which can trace their rootage to the values, belief systems and organisational practices of pre-colonial Africa are rare.*[46]

Kajese argues that most African NGOs currently either have a 'foreign initiator' and a high dependence upon 'external funding', or can be viewed as little else than the unofficial arm of African government which can connect with 'people, situations and areas that the arms of the state may not readily reach'.[47] He then asserts the need for the local NGOs to 'decolonise' themselves of Western thinking by rooting themselves in their own 'cultures, traditions and values'.

Others, however, have pointed to the need to rejuvenate existing ethnic organizations by transforming them into NGOs. In the same journal as Kajese, Oxfam's Odiambo Anacleti declares for a much wider definition than Kajese's of what constitutes a non-governmental organization, and submits that it must now include traditional African institutions: 'One has to tread very carefully when talking of institutional building as though there was a situation of *tabula rasa* [in Africa]. There is a possibility for updating and modernising such institutions . . .'[48] For Anacleti, ethnic associations always were more or less equivalent to charitable organizations anyway:

> *These associations, most of them ethnically based, were formed with an aim of maximising whatever goods were provided by the state. They mobilised funds and other resources for education, built community centres, built feeder roads and provided social welfare needs to their communities . . . Recently, especially in Tanzania and other countries where the government capacity to provide such services has dwindled, such associations have taken the form of Trust Funds and assigned themselves the role of providing social services deemed necessary by the leaders of those communities.*[49]

Alan Fowler, an NGO consultant on Africa, has confirmed that approaches are being made to 'modernise' ethnic associations, or Community Based Organizations (CBOs), so that they duplicate NGO structures. He welcomes their role as 'legitimate' decision-makers:

> *There are increasing signs that traditional forms of social organisation, trusted by their members, are taking on a greater number of functions. For example, in Ethiopia during the power vacuum left by Mengistu, traditional leaders became responsible in certain instances for local security, and were recognised and accepted as the legitimate decision-makers for the community.*[50]

These examples of capacity-building or extending civil society do not stop at the local community level, however. The African state structure itself is increasingly being recast into the shape of numerous

NGOs. Joseph Hanlon, who made a comprehensive study of NGOs operating in Mozambique in the early 1990s, confirms that Western NGOs set up their own African NGOs out of the ranks of former state officials: 'NGOs strip people out of the state apparatus, which weakens the state.'[51] A second process is the complementary formation of NGOs by the African state itself:

> *Mozambique had already begun to create local NGOs on the Western model, from the top down and headed by the local equivalent of the 'great and the good' . . . Undoubtedly the most successful is the General Union of Cooperatives, which grew out of the Maputo green zones project.*[52]

Ian Gary on the other hand maintains the completely opposite opinion. Whereas Hanlon imagines the NGOs to be acting like white corpuscles ravaging the independent African state, Gary sees only bloated African bureaucrats 'high-jacking' previously independent NGOs. Citing the Ghanaian case of the 31 December Women's Movement, now led by president Jerry Rawlings's wife, Gary suggests that it used to be a revolutionary organization, but in the late 1980s it began to 'commandeer' development resources coming into the country. Finally it assumed shape as an NGO in its own right: 'As the political climate changed in 1992, "revolutionary organs" were no longer the norm in a "multi-party democracy" so the movement began to remake itself into an "apolitical" NGO'.[53]

Who is right between Hanlon and Gary? Are NGOs carving up the African state, or are the state bureaucrats hijacking the NGOs so as to be better able to feast off the aid flooding into Africa? In the case of Ghana, the state has probably got away with imposing discipline on the NGOs since it is the West's showcase for the region. In Kenya, on the other hand, Western NGOs faced down president Daniel arap Moi's attempts to regiment them because there they enjoyed the support of the American ambassador. In Ghana, Gary relates how foreign donors lined up behind Accra in 1993 to demand that the NGOs join its regulating instrument, Gapvod (Ghanaian Association of Private Voluntary Organizations in Development):

> *Coercion by various donors compelled many NGOs reluctantly to join and remain in a group which they felt was unrepresentative of*

the views of the bulk of the indigenous NGO community. The UNDP's [United Nations Development Project] resident representative in Ghana at the time explicitly told NGOs that if they did not join Gapvod they would be ineligible to receive money from any of their funding windows (such as Africa 2000). British Council scholarships, and other such opportunities, were only available if the organisation was a member of Gapvod.[54]

From the point of view of individual African politicians, civil servants or intellectuals, both routes – joining a foreign NGO or creating your own – represents a viable survival strategy. Equally, however, from the point of view of the survival of the African state structure as a whole, it is immaterial whether it is picked apart by foreign NGOs or whether it immolates itself. According to advisers to USAID, ethnic concerns are an important principle of capacity-building: 'The idea seems to be (at least in theory) that effective institutions, such as legal systems, constitutions, and schools, will provide outlets where ethnic community (*sic*) can express their concerns and provide systems to address those stated concerns.'[55]

Additional aid to improve the legal access of ethnic groups to be considered by USAID personnel are 'using public defenders, support for traditional legal aid efforts, legal literacy, nurturing paralegal networks, assisting legal advocacy NGOs, and alternative dispute resolution mechanisms'. Furthermore, USAID's Center for Democracy and Governance wants to increase ethnic access to the electoral system. Although not sanctioned as 'official agency policy', according to McHugh the CDG's 'Guidance on Electoral Systems Program' has become 'de facto' policy for the agency. The election guide first draws attention to the deep cleavages that afflict societies. It asserts that elections will not be effective if there are deep social cleavages and ethnic groups are excluded from participation. The guide notes that some governments preclude parties organizing on an ethnic basis. The guide advises that it might be problematic to press for the inclusion of ethnic groups in 'the first election' but thereafter 'the policy dialogue that accompanies democratic assistance should give attention to the fuller inclusion of the poor, religious minorities, etc'. Another USAID concept paper cited by McHugh mentions that 'ethnic groups that are denied political participation at national levels may more easily establish a significant political influence at the local level – where it is simpler for everyone to get involved for political matters'.[56]

The important point here is that the West, either indirectly through Western NGOs, or by directly funding African NGOs, is trying to transform the African state bureaucracy from a national agency into a localized one organized along ethnic lines. Moreover, for all the rhetoric about NGO 'voluntary service', the former patron/client ethnic relationships are being duplicated with the Western donors or NGOs becoming the new patrons for the various ethnic groups.

The fact that NGOs are trying to establish a new African élite to run new local state structures is not at all obvious. Establishing new 'states' is not the most popular activity these days, especially when being a politician is so unfashionable. These days, politicians the world over deal with anti-political sentiments by transforming themselves into community social workers, counsellors, or even soldiers, etc. Only rarely, then, do the new ethnically-based state structures try to imitate traditional state structures based upon localities and regions, as in northern Somalia. More usually, the new ethnic state structures adopt the guise of the NGOs – or quangos – and consequently the modern ethnic politician in Africa is more likely to appear in the guise of a NGO 'volunteer' than a traditional chief, emir or sultan.[57]

Though Western aid to Africa is being relentlessly cut back, a remnant is steadily being redirected away from the state bureaucracy and towards the NGOs and their African clientele instead.[58] These days it is often difficult to distinguish a multinational agency like the World Bank from radical NGOs. In its November 1989 report, *Sub-Saharan Africa: From Crisis to Sustainable Growth*, the agency repudiated its former orientation towards unlimited growth and called for the modern sector to support the traditional sector rather than aim to replace it:

> *Future development strategies need to recognise that, far from impeding development, many indigenous African values and institutions can support it. For instance the persistence of primary group loyalties, although often deplored by outsiders, has been a significant force for*

development. Communal culture, the participation of women in the economy, respect for nature – all these can be used in constructive ways . . . Many indigenous cultivation practices, such as mixed cropping, were once much criticised but are now seen to have technical merit. More generally, while the modern sector has been in malaise, the informal sector, strongly rooted in the community, has been vibrant.[39]

Examples of NGOs trying to reorganize important sections of African society along ethnic lines are becoming increasingly common. William Miles has noted in regard to Chad, for instance, that there has been a 'veritable explosion' of NGOs since 1991. They moved in there to fill the vacuum caused by the breakdown in state services, 'Three hundred new organisations were registered by June 1994, whereas in the entire period between 1963 and December 1990 there had been only ninety'.[60]

According to Miles, the voluntary organizations set up in Chad between 1963 and 1990 were chiefly religious and sports groups. From 1990, however, they tended to be members of the élite: professional bodies; gender/women's groups, language and cultural societies, student and development action groups. Following Kajese's analysis, Miles's assessment is that Civil Society – as he labels these 1990s' organizations – is engaged in an 'informal decolonisation' from the state by retreating into traditional, regional, ethnic or kinship structures.[61]

In regard to the interesting question as to who is financing this NGO 'explosion' in Chad, Miles is unfortunately vague. On the one hand, he claims that France is losing its traditional influence there and its support for the Chadian state is waning. Yet he also admits that 'Budgetary support for insolvent governmental ministries comes largely from Chad's foreign colonizer' and the NGO-backed Sovereign National Conference that established a provisional parliament in 1993 'was in large measure funded by the French government'.[62] Miles seems to have been misled into thinking that a change in the relationship between Paris and the Chadian nationalist élite is tantamount to a decline in French power in Africa.[63] A more prescient analysis might describe the process as a French-sponsored reorganization of the state bureaucracy along NGO-endorsed ethnic lines.

According to African Rights workers Alex de Waal, Rakiya Omaar and Michael Medley, sections of the Western church also organize along ethnic lines in southern Sudan at least:

> Significantly, the unity of the Church itself is fragile. Despite the best efforts of some Church leaders, the Church has ethnic and denominational divisions. For example the ECS [Evangelical Christian Society] Christianity of the Lakes Province and Bor is specifically a Dinka Christianity. It uses the Dinka vernacular and mobilises around specifically Dinka idioms and concerns (such as the burning of JAK [a Dinka deity]. Politically it is also Dinka . . . While ECS Dinka Christianity is acutely aware of the sufferings of the Dinka people, it pays little attention to the suffering the Dinka may have inflicted on other peoples.[64]

Southern NGO workers imitate the primitivist culture that is sponsored by the northern NGO institutions and literature. An 'African ethnic' agenda may make them look independent, even if the Western donors can pull all the financial strings. Yet the blunt fact is that that ethnic agenda is a sanitized product of Western society. As a result, a new African ethnic élite is attempting to cohere their society around the image of the individual victim that is established as an icon in the West, rather than any sense of ambition or advance.

Educating Africans to be Ethnic

Moral ethnicity assumes that Africans cannot be expected to cope with life in the chaos of the 'globalized' 1990s. This aura of paternalism is then augmented by the suggestion that careful and informed interventions are required to guide ethnicity in a more tolerant direction. This notion of the toleration of cultural diversity, of ethnic differences is also suspect. If the prime goal is never to offend another, but to be tolerant of them, then any aspect of ethnic culture that criticizes or offends any other ethnic culture must be eradicated. Only a sanitized mediocrity is acceptable. 'Toleration' is therefore transformed into a legitimate tool to educate and discipline Africans who deviate from the norm of moderation.

The idea that Africans need to be taught a lesson in these ethnic norms is tantamount to treating them like children. Consequently it is followed closely by a need for external facilitators to offer 'moral guidance'. Such interventions by NGO 'facilitators' makes a mockery of the notion that ethnic flexibility and political manipulation are fundamentally different from each other. The idea that Africans chose their own ethnic identity is a pleasant Western primitivist fantasy. The power of this agenda can be seen from the fact that it is beginning to transcend the popular conceptions of African tribalism in the West. Hence the irony that those people who celebrate the ethnic identity of the Ogonis also join in branding the Hutus as genocidal psychotics.

From the Western perspective of a moral ethnicity, there is no contradiction in treating one African ethnicity as saints while at the same time demonizing another. During the 1996 Eastern Zaire crisis, Oxfam published a full page advert in a number of national newspapers. This widely known and respected charity organization demanded that the UN force eliminate the Hutu militia in the refugee camps in Eastern Zaire in order to prevent 'more mass murder and more refugees'. Oxfam stated that it was not good enough just to send troops to ensure that food aid was distributed. The UN multinational force had to get to the 'root of the problems': 'Disarm the militias from Rwanda, to stop more killing. Help isolate those suspected of crimes against humanity. Sounds tough? Try genocide.'[65]

The continuity in the unequal relationship between the West and Africa stands exposed here. Historically, the West always explained its actions in Africa with some high falutin' justification: 'Christianity', 'progress', a 'civilizing mission', to 'stop communist dictatorship', etc. Today's excuse for whites to kill Africans is: to pre-empt ethnic 'genocide'.[66] This has nothing in common with real humanitarianism, but it is certainly has a high moral tone.

This agenda of moral and immoral ethnicity has been scripted in the Western capitals of London, Paris, Washington, Bonn, etc., though as often in the secret headquarters of the top NGOs as in the official corridors of power. Africans can therefore be differentiated into those who have accept the West's ethical agenda, and those who do not; those who are sympathetically treated like the Ogonis, and those who are branded with Hutu-like treatment.

Eriksen hits a topical note when he argues that those ethnic groups that revitalize themselves through creating a culture and a literature

– that is, become like NGO intellectuals and NGOs themselves – are more likely to survive in the eyes of the world than those minorities who remain illiterate, who 'may easily turn into underclasses' – in other words, end up like the Hutu.[67] Citing the case of the San of the Kalahari, Eriksen suggests two possible scenarios: assimilation as a 'low caste' in Botswana society, or they 'develop an elite of interethnic brokers', who can either be educated members of the indigenous group itself or 'foreign anthropologists, missionaries, or NGOs such as Amnesty International or Survival'.[68]

Attempts to shape ethnicity usually focus on the spheres of culture and education – the ambit of academics and the professions. Through promoting ethnicity as an aspect of culture rather than a political phenomenon, the masses are conveniently expunged from the debate.[69] Crawford Young decisively plumps for the intelligentsia as the originators of ethnic identity discourse, 'The ideologisation of identity depends upon the emergence of cultural entrepreneurs, almost always associated with the rise of a professional middle class and intelligentsia'.[70] Young makes a useful contrast here between the cultural entrepreneur who enlarges upon ethnic history and language, and the political broker who then acts to mobilize this 'capital':

> A distinction is worth making between the cultural entrepreneur, who devotes himself to enlarging the solidarity resources of the community, and the political broker, who mobilises ethnicity in a given situation, crystallising collective aspiration in the social and political realm. The latter archetype, the cultural politician, applies his skills to the optimum combination of the existing stock of factors of cultural mobilisation.[71]

For Young, though the cultural entrepreneur initiated the ethnic dialogue, the political broker very often finished it. For moral ethnicity, however, it is important that the cultural entrepreneur retains an authoritative influence over the debate.

These days, it is African politicians – Young's political brokers – that have been irrevocably associated with provoking ethnic conflicts. Those regimes who have escaped censure by the NGOs have generally done so by capitulating completely to the demands of the West, whether they originate from the major aid providers like the

World Bank or from the NGOs. Both Ghana and Uganda, showcases for the West in Africa, are pressing ahead with the measures that NGOs are introducing elsewhere in Africa.

Ghanaian leader Jerry Rawlings set about rehabilitating the traditional institutions of Ghana, like the Ashantehene, shortly after he seized power in December 1981. Secret talks with the IMF over an austerity budget began in August 1982. The Rawlings regime began moving to restore democracy well before the 1989–90 events that swept the rest of Africa, but it was to be a primitive form of democracy. In November 1985, the head of the National Commission on Democracy, Justice D.F. Annan, stated: 'We must measure the performance of the modern political system since independence against our traditional system and see whether the modern period could not have been improved by an interrelationship with the traditional system.'[72] In July 1987, his regime published draft proposals for 'restoring democratic rule' in late 1988. The Peoples' Defence Committees (PDCs) were abolished and replaced by district assemblies intended to 'democratise state power and advance participatory democracy and collective decision-making at the grassroots'.[73] Two-thirds of the assembly were elected by universal suffrage, but one-third were to be 'traditional authorities or their representatives' appointed by Accra in consultation with local dignitaries.

In 1990, the regime began to reorganize its regional bodies along similar lines, with the electoral choice being whittled down to one-third of the available seats. Simply the citation of a person's background is sufficient to justify the 'democratic' label and the 'representative' character of the regional fora, rather than the operation of the electoral ballot. Indeed the regime's electoral commission, the NCD, implies that such a selection method produces a *more* democratic representation than ordinary elections can produce:

> *It is true that as many as two-thirds of the members present at the [regional] fora were invited; but as the NCD argued, this was because it was anxious to ensure that they should be as representative as possible of the local community that they served . . . The clearest and most democratically-chosen representatives of each district were*

the District Assemblies, so delegates from each Assembly were invited. Similarly delegates from the Committees for the Defence of the Revolution and 31 December Women's Movement were invited as representatives of a large number of local people. In addition, the NCD invited chiefs and elders and representatives from a broad cross-section of recognised, identifiable bodies, which included teachers, nurses, farmers and trade unionists.[74]

Perhaps the best example of the Ghanaian regime following the Western NGO agenda is the 31 December Women's Movement. The organization was founded in May 1982 and is now run by Rawlings's wife, Nana – a member of the Ashante royal family. Its leadership comprises the top women in every town and village in Ghana. According to Shillington, the organization grew

because they used the established network of traditional society. In every town and tiny village there is a queen mother or prominent lady who is the traditional source of advice for women's marital, family or social problems. The 31 December Women went to the queen mothers first....with the approval of the queen mother, it was usually supported.[75]

Rawlings also sought to offset criticism directed at the IMF's Structural Adjustment Program (SAP) through implementing a 'Programme of Action to Mitigate the Social Cost of Adjustment'(PAMSCAD) in 1987. The 31 December Women's Movement began to receive foreign aid funds through the PAMSCAD programme.[76]

As Ian Gray has pointed out, the major donors have steamrolled Western NGOs into line behind the politically correct Rawlings regime.[77] Hence, in February 1994, when conflict broke in the Northern Territories of Ghana and 10,000 were killed as ethnic groups like the Konkombas and the Nanumba fought over access to government largesse – this outbreak of ethnic conflict, though severely embarrassing to the Ghanaian regime – never made the international news.[78] Two months later, however, the Rwandan Hutus were being denounced by all and sundry as genocidal maniacs. Ironically, despite its own ethnic clashes, Ghana was then invited by the United Nations (UN) to take over from Nigeria the leadership of the ECOMOG 'peace-keeping' mission to pacify strife-torn Liberia after the Ken Saro-Wiwa execution in November 1995.

In Uganda, thanks to close links between the government and the NGO community, the differentiation between 'cultural' ethnicity and 'political' tribalism has gone the furthest in Africa.[79] We have seen President Museveni reviving the 'Anglo-African' Kabaka of the Buganda as well as the other 'kingdoms' rejuvenated by the British. At the same time, he has barred political parties from electioneering – only individual candidates can stand – in order to restrain politicians engaging in tribal bargains during elections. Furthermore, ethnic groups which enter a dialogue with the Ugandan government are endorsed by the NGOs, whereas others who refuse to have any truck with Museveni are treated as outcasts by the same international community.

For example, in the Karamoja district, the Kampala government is implementing a major programme with NGO help to bring the area's previously unruly cattleherders to heel. When the Karamojong go on cattle raids and kill people, it is put down to the tradition that young men must raid cattle and kill a man as a 'rite of passage' to become an adult. Indeed, cattle raiding is even considered 'almost a sport'. With the influx of modern automatic weapons like AK-47s, however, 'the traditional rules of engagement are being disrupted' according to a BBC report. In April 1995, NGOs, government officials and the churches got together with Karamojong elders to organize a Peace Forum.[80] Rather than try to disarm them (which would directly provoke the Karamajong) the cattlemen have been asked to register their weapons and become paid 'vigilantes' at 10,000 Ugandan shillings (£3.50) a month. Cattle ownership disputes are to be negotiated by regular meetings presided over by officials. Rumours that the Karamojong are to be deployed by Kampala against their tribal neighbours persist, however, because the cattleherders refuse to leave their arms with the local police when they cross into Teso land, as has also been agreed.

On the other hand, after Museveni won power in 1986, he spent a number of years putting down the fundamentalist Christian Holy Spirit movement led by Alice Lakwena in rural northern Uganda. Now, in the countryside around Gulu, the Lord's Resistance Army (LRA) has also been causing the Kampala regime much grief. The army has been deployed to crush their revolt, but more unusually the NGO community has rushed to the support of the Museveni regime. The LRA has been painted in frightening terms. They are said to be made up of 'disgruntled Acholi tribesmen' – the rump of Lakwena's Holy Spirit movement – and they stand accused of resorting to bizarre tactics like deliberately targeting bike riders and villagers who own white chickens and pigs. 'Fundamentalism' must be strong stuff since, although the LRA are Christians, they are also alleged to be armed and funded by the Islamic 'fundamentalist' regime ensconced in Khartoum. Finally, the LRA seemingly delights in recruiting child soldiers to 'shoot, kill and burn down homes'. The American NGO, World Vision, has even opened a 'trauma centre' in Gulu for 'children who managed to escape the LRA'.[81] The Karamojong co-operate with Museveni in an NGO-inspired conflict resolution project and therefore they are received sympathetically by the West. The Acholis, also from northern Uganda, refuse to compromise with Kampala and they get tagged by the NGO community as 'fundamentalist' maniacs and child abusers for their pains.

None of these anti-democratic measures adopted by either the Ghanaian or Ugandan regimes has attracted as much international opprobrium, certainly not anything that can compare to the vituperative invective that has been directed against the Rwandan Hutus. This is because they are framed within the terms set by the NGOs for their own regulation of African society. The most significant feature of both the Accra and the Kampala regimes is their willingness to accommodate the major donors and NGOs.

The leaderships of Ghana and Uganda are remarkable in Africa because they are exceptions. Nearly every other African leader is under unrelenting pressure to capitulate to the NGO moral agenda. The main accusation against them is that they are responsible for causing the ethnic conflict that afflicts the continent.

The Threat of Ethnic Conflict

Early on in the 1980s, Goran Hyden, a Scandinavian specialist on Tanzania, predicted that the decline in Western aid flows to the state might result in an outbreak of ethnic struggles in Africa. He argued that, 'As the state closes its doors to the largesse . . . some ethnic groups may feel more directly deprived'.[82] Hyden expressed concern that there would be a greater risk of ethnic tension in these circumstances and even an inclination to raise demands for self-determination.

Three years on, however, Dov Ronen felt sufficiently confident to claim that, so long as the power of African state could be reduced, there would be less ethnic conflict:

> *The utilisation and manipulation of ethnic identities appears to be the single most important factor in political instability. This occurs when ethnic groups are mobilised by political leaders struggling to gain the centralised political power. If power were to be decentralised, the struggle for power would be bound to decline, and, with it, the intensity of political stability.*[83]

Back in 1983, Hyden had suggested a possible answer involving local NGOs. This decentralizing solution provided the basis for Ronen's audacious remarks. Hyden hoped that the substitution of NGOs for the state could avoid the prospect of ethnic conflict threatened by the decline in revenues, without jeopardizing the new financial stringency. It is worth quoting his seminal document at length because Hyden refers obliquely to a theme that would later become prevalent throughout the West – the concept of 'risk society':

> *Whether the issue is economic development or state coherence, support of nongovernmental organisations is likely to have a great payoff effect. Where such organisations are weak or non-existent, special efforts must be made to strengthen them. While ethnic tensions cannot be ruled out in these organisations, the probability that it will cause harm to society is much smaller than in the state realm because the organisations do not control more than a modest share of societal resources and, furthermore, the ideologies of these organisations often serve as a more effective restraint on 'parochial action' than a general political ideology with little immediate relationship to day-to-day issues.*[84]

This early statement goes much further than merely expressing the view that general politics are irrelevant to particular localities, that 'Society' is an abstraction compared to the practical and provincial. It contends that anything wider than the local might 'cause harm', is potentially dangerous or risky. Hyden thus justifies the redirection of funds to NGOs on the grounds that their modest application of resources helps prevent social expansion beyond the local. The assumption here is that ethnicity is dangerous only when it develops into a 'general' or national political direction.[85]

Similarly, in the writings of anthropologists Jane Guyer and Janet MacGaffey, we see the development of the theme that Africa would be better off without the nation-state, because alternative structures are already bubbling up in its localities. According to Guyer:

> The collapse of central administrative structures in some countries is almost bound to enhance the relative importance of all those other local leaders who can claim legitimacy to govern. The African countryside is not necessarily disorganised; it is simply that new forms of organisation may be appearing, using indigenous templates rather than ones encapsulated in the classic dyad [sic] of political thought about agrarian society, the peasant and the state.[86]

What gives substance to this dubious picture of a thriving parochialism is the powerful sense of Western weakness that all NGO workers experience in the face of the masses of Africa. Whereas a handful of empire-builders intimidated whole populations in the last century, today's mighty Western powers cannot imagine holding sway over anything greater than the population of a local district. Intellectuals like Hyden, Ronen and Guyer are desperate to persuade people that the local causes a lot less harm than the national.

In the wake of the collapse of the African state, an explosion of ethnic conflicts has been regularly predicted. Is it the African state, or its collapse, that increases the risk of ethnic conflict? And can moral ethnicity serve as a bulwark against ethnic conflict?

Western Africanist experts are sure that an African ethnicity based upon enfeebled individuals dependent upon guidance from the West will mean less conflict than an ethnicity based upon aggressive, confident societies. Our argument is that, on the contrary, the chief risk of ethnic conflict in Africa comes from NGO attempts to recast African society into ethnic moulds. Their predilection for local solutions derives from the primitivist milieu that they hail from in the West.

Notes

1. Furthermore, it is striking how identical modern theories of ethnicity – all flexibility, mobility and competition – are to modern theories of globalization, which highlight the rapid movement of commodities around a world economy uninhibited by national state boundaries. We will examine modern theories of ethnicity much closer in Chapter 5. It is permissible at this stage to note, however, that the adoption of this globalizing perspective by NGO volunteers helps reinforce the impression that African ethnicities are like commodities in the globalized market-place: trapped in a chaotic vortex they cannot hope to control, they aim to find a safe niche.

2. Though NGO volunteers are often in the right frame of mind to succumb to the powers of primitive healers too. A Dutch woman called Els, the Oxfam representative working in northern Mozambique, has recounted her experiences to travel writer Nick Middleton: 'The *curandeiros* (healers) here mostly deal in spells. They work. People often died without any medical explanation and the power of the *curandeiros* was a dangerous force to be reckoned with . . . I too was interested in this magic when I first came to Niassa but now I do not dig too deeply' (Nick Middleton, *Kalashnikovs and Zombie Cucumbers*, p. 137).

3. Western travel writers typically portray tribal Africa as the real Africa. Hence for Peter Hudson, 'I was not so interested in the nation of Mauritania as the country of Mauritania, the land of the Moors and African tribes, of camels and camps and culture' (*Travels in Mauritania*, p. 34).

4. Unlike the demand for democratic rights, which involve lifting humanity into collective struggles for the right to vote, the right to trial by jury, the right to association, the right of nations to self-determination, etc. It has been observed many times that basic human characteristics are no more than basic animal characteristics – eating, drinking, procreation, shelter. But while nature has provided for animals, it has been miserly to Man. Birds see better, dogs smell better, cheetahs run better. Even that miserable parasite, the tape-worm, spends its whole life in a state of continuous sexual bliss. A new-born foal can walk within minutes. But the human baby will *never* learn to walk, never mind talk, without society's help. If humanity means anything at all, it surely means transcending nature's meagre gifts to us. Transforming them into 'basic rights' not only degrades humanity, but pushes it far beneath the animal world.

5. Formerly the word 'respect' could mean the admiration of achievement, as in respecting a hero, a Noble prize winner, your elders and betters. Now to give respect simply means leaving people as they are, preserving the *status quo*, celebrating inadequacies as 'diversity'.

6. Eric Schumacher, *Small Is Beautiful*.

7. R. Chambers, *Rural Development*, p. 75. For a pro-market but interesting critique of this paternalistic 'respect the poor' Western approach towards rural Africa, see James Morton, *The Poverty of Nations*, pp. 41–3.

8. Peter Walker, 'Indigenous Knowledge and Famine Relief in the Horn of Africa', p. 148.

9. For an account that glorifies community bore-hole drilling, see Nancy Cosway and Steve Anawkum, 'Traditional Leadership and Community Management in Northern Ghana', pp. 88–95.

10. Maryam Niamir, 'Indigenous Systems of Natural Resource Management among the Pastoralists of Arid and Semi-arid Africa', p. 257.

11. Jeffrey McNeely, 'IUCN and Indigenous Peoples', p. 449.

12. Ibid.

13. Norman Uphoff, 'Preface', p. ix.

14. John Lonsdale, 'The Moral Economy of Mau Mau', p. 467.

15. Ibid., p. 328.

16. Ibid., p. 466.

17. Ibid., pp. 317–18.

18. National Lottery Charities Board, *International Grants Programme*, p. 47.

19. Ibid., p. 20.

20. Ibid., p. 23.

21. Ibid., p. 19.

22. Ibid., pp. 19–20. In South Africa, now that apartheid has collapsed, there are many cases of ethnicity being used to justify land claims. The Tsonga are claiming 50,000 acres of the Kruger National Park, from which they were evicted in 1969 ('Good and bad at game', *The Economist*, 6 July 1996, p. 105). Conservationists are objecting. The inhabitants of the Namaqualand reserves in the North-West Cape are debating whether a 'Khoikhoi' identity or a 'Baster' identity is the most effective way to secure land rights there (see John Sharp, 'Ethnogenesis and Ethnic Mobilization', pp. 95–8).

23. ActionAid, *The Roots of Reconciliation*, p. 3.

24. 'Somaliland: shrinking horizons', *Africa Confidential*, 16 February 1996, p. 5.

25. See, for example, George Monbiot on the Maasai of Kenya: *No Man's Land*;

and Laurens van der Post's book on the Bushmen: *The Lost World of the Kalahari*.

26. *Guardian*, 2 November 1995, Letters page.

27. 'Nigeria foaming', *The Economist*, 18 November 1995, p. 17.

28. Survival International, *Niger Delta Peoples*.

29. Ibid.

30. 'A tainted hero', *Guardian*, 23 March 1996. See also the allegations that he 'feathered his own nest' while working for the Federal Nigerian authorities in the oil port of Bonny, by environmentalist Richard North in London's *Independent*, 8 November 1996, p. 18.

31. African Rights, *Facing Genocide*, pp. 330, 340.

32. 'Talking taboo' at http://www.oneworld.org/actionaid/info/ghana.html, October 1996.

33. Jenny Rossiter and Robin Palmer, 'Northern NGOs in Southern Africa', p. 44.

34. Thomas Eriksen, *Ethnicity and Nationalism*, p. 129.

35. In May 1996, 17-year-old Fauziya Kasinga successively challenged the decision of the US Immigration Service to deny her asylum on the grounds that she was forced to flee her country, Togo, where she was being threatened with circumcision. In October 1996 the Kasinga case was influential in the decision of the US Congress to make female circumcision illegal in the United States, on the grounds that 168,000 girls of African origin or ancestry residing in the country are in imminent danger of the procedure. According to bill sponsor Senator Harry Reid (Democrat, Nevada), 'This cultural ritual that takes six adults to hold down a small girl

cannot be tolerated. These children cannot speak for themselves' (Norra Macready, 'Female genital mutilation outlawed in United States').

36. Emma Brooke, 'Slaves of the Fetish', *Independent on Sunday*, 16 June 1996, pp. 12–14.

37. National Lottery Charities Board, *International Grants Programme*, p. 47.

38. Ibid.

39. Murray Bookchin, *Re-enchanting Humanity*, p. 120.

40. Ibid.

41. These points are expanded upon in Chapter 4.

42. For a reasonably comprehensive description of the 1990 African events, see Michael Bratton and Nicholas van de Walle, 'Toward Governance in Africa'.

43. B. Berman and J. Lonsdale, *Unhappy Valley*, p. 466.

44. Norman Uphoff, 'Preface', p. x, my emphasis.

45. Ibid.

46. Kingston Kajese, 'African NGO Decolonisation', p. 11.

47. Ibid., p. 16.

48. Odiambo Anacleti, 'African NGOs – Do They Have a Future?', p. 281.

49. Ibid., p. 285.

50. Alan Fowler, *Institutional Development and NGOs in Africa*, p. 10.

51. Joseph Hanlon, *Mozambique*, p. 211. Hanlon adds that this weakened state body further 'justifies NGO claims that the state cannot help its own people'. Another justification is that NGO recruitment policy encourages 'popular participation and accountability', yet Hanlon remarks: 'this seems strange coming from NGOs which are accountable to no one, except the donor government which provides the contracts, and which rarely have any democratic structure of their own' (p. 215).

52. Ibid., p. 217.

53. Ian Gary, 'Confrontation, Cooperation or Cooptation', p. 161. Interestingly, the complete opposite situation was prevailing at the other end of the continent, where the international donors forced Kenyan president Daniel arap Moi to modify his plans to regulate NGOs (see Stephen N Ndegwa, *The Two Faces of Civil Society*, p. 51).

54. Gary, 'Confrontation, Cooperation or Cooptation', p. 160.

55. Heather McHugh, *USAID and Ethnic Conflict*.

56. Ibid.

57. This is not so bizarre as it first appears. In the heyday of the British monarchy, the state form that inspired indirect rulers was the African kingdom. During the decolonization process and the assumption of Labour to power after the Second World War, most ethnic leaders presented themselves as local councillors. During the nationalist independence period, they became nationalists – i.e. Zulu nationalists, Yoruba nationalists, Ashanti nationalists, etc.

58. American NGOs (or private voluntary organizations – PVOs) raised S7 billion in 1995, a third of which came from official sources. Britain's 400 NGOs working overseas raised S500m, of which more than 35 per cent came from Whitehall. Figures from an NGO survey in *The Economist* (London, 22 June 1996). The survey concluded; 'Most of the big agencies now get about half their income from governments' (p. 64).

59. World Bank, *Sub-Saharan Africa*, p. 60.

60. William Miles, 'Decolonisation as Disintegration', p. 48.

61. Ibid., p. 41.

62. Ibid., p. 50.

63. Unlikely, when it is remembered that Sub-Saharan Africa is about the only place in the world where both the French and the British can still act as Great Powers and get away with it.

64. African Rights, *Great Expectations*, p. 34.

65. 'No one ever said taking responsibility was easy', Oxfam advert, *Daily Telegraph*, London, 15 November 1996, p. 16.

66. The description of the Rwandan massacres of April 1994 as 'genocide' is debunked in Africa Direct, *Submission to the United Nations Tribunal on Rwanda*.

67. Eriksen, *Ethnicity and Nationalism*, p. 128.

68. Ibid., pp. 127, 130.

69. Thanks to Mark Ryan for this point.

70. Crawford Young, *The Politics of Cultural Pluralism*, p. 45. According to Oxfam fieldworkers Rossiter and Palmer, the intelligentsia who staff Southern NGOs are 'predominantly middle class, Western educated, and urban based (past or present)' whereas 'the poorest of the poor' recipients of aid 'are often excluded – save at a tokenistic level – from the debates NNGOs initiate or encourage' (J. Rossiter and R. Palmer, 'Northern NGOs in Southern Africa', pp. 45–6).

71. Young, *The Politics of Cultural Pluralism*, p. 46.

72. Cited in Paul Nugent, *Big Men, Small Boys and Politics in Ghana*, p. 140.

73. Nii K. Bentsi-Enchill, 'Steps at the grassroots'.

74. Kevin Shillington, *Ghana and the Rawlings Factor*, p. 167. This reminds me of the tired old justifications wheeled out for the preservation of the British House of Lords; that, though they are unelected, the Lords and Ladies have a greater representative background (from Dukes to dustbinmen) than the elected House of Commons (mostly lawyers, apparently). The democratic qualifications of unelected NGOs and quangos are legitimated in the same fashion.

75. Ibid., pp. 153–4.

76. Ibid., p. 155.

77. Ian Gary, 'Confrontation, Cooperation or Cooptation'.

78. 'North versus north', *Africa Confidential*, 7 July 1995, p. 4. According to the report, the fighting occurred because the regime was 'boosting the power of the paramount chiefs' by channeling resources through them, while other groups like the Konkombas lost out because they were acephalous (without chiefs). According to an anonymous Ghanaian journalist, however, the ethnic conflict could be put down to the activities of the 'Dzulekofe Mafia', a Ewe clique that includes Rawlings and which allegedly plans to seize parts of Benin, northern Ghana and the Ewe area of Togo in order to create a Greater Eweland state (see Anonymous, 'Dzulekofe Mafia to Create Greater Eweland Region in West Africa', pp. 34–5).

79. Paul Gifford is somewhat overstating the influence of Christian missionaries when he argues that the Ugandan government has withdrawn and left to them 'the survival, jobs, health, schooling, prospects, travel, advancement of ordinary Ugandans'

(cited in Donal Cruise O'Brien, 'A Lost Generation?', p. 64). It is more the case that Christian missionaries are transforming themselves into NGOs.

80. Sara Errington, 'The Karamojong of Uganda', p. 7.

81. 'A Rag-tag Army is Disrupting Recovery in the North of Uganda', *Financial Times*, 1 May 1996. This article explicitly praises Museveni, whose 'greatest achievement' is said to be 'the containment of a brutalised country's violent ethnic rivalries'. Its authors have apparently forgotten that, when Museveni's own National Resistance Army fought itself into power in Kampala in January 1986, it comprised considerable numbers of child soldiers. At the time, this was overlooked because the NRA said they were 'orphans'.

82. Goran Hyden, 'Problems and Prospects of State Coherence', p. 81.

83. Dov Ronen (ed.), *Democracy and Pluralism in Africa*, p. 201. Author's emphasis.

84. Hyden, 'Problems and Prospects of State Coherence', p. 81. For an extended discussion on 'risk society', see Ulrich Beck, *Risk Society*, and Anthony Giddens, *Beyond Left and Right*.

85. Hyden cannot be accused of racism against Africans for expressing these views. He explicitly condemns a return to colonialism and calls for the involvement of African NGOs in the decentralization process. In addition, fear of 'risk society' and the privileging of the local is applied throughout Western society.

86. Jane Guyer (ed.), *Feeding African Cities*, pp. 46–7. See also Janet MacGaffey's studies of *The Real Economy of Zaire*, where she has found that, 'The common cultural background and loyalties of those from the same ethnic group, and the mutual obligations and emotional bonds of family and kinship, all operate to promote the trust, accountability and sense of moral responsibility that is lacking in the official economy and that contributes to its irrationality and unpredictability' (p. 32). 'Trust', 'accountability' and 'moral responsibility' are all key concepts in the lexicon of the promoters of the new ethnicity.

CHAPTER 3

Privileging the Local

So far we have mainly considered African ethnicity from the point of view of its celebration by the West. But how can ethnicity be celebrated when there are so many terrible ethnic conflicts in Africa? The NGO answer to this stark contradiction is that the only solution to ethnic conflict is to emphasize the local even more.

The Western view of ethnic conflict in Africa has changed greatly from the explicitly racist images of African savagery during the 1950s' Mau Mau insurgency in Kenya and the Congo débâcle in the early 1960s, to blaming modernizing African politicians for stirring up ethnic animosities today. Ethnicity is now regularly shielded from accusations of savagery either by the assertion that ethnic conflicts negate genuine ethnicity, or by the substitution of another expression for ethnicity, such as 'indigenism' or 'survivalism'. Changing attitudes towards ethnicity have been reflected in a simultaneous change in approach towards ethnic conflict. This change also finds a reflection at the theoretical level, as theories of ethnicity have moved from being predominantly primordial-orientated, towards the instrumental and now to a moral theory of ethnicity (these theoretical reflections will be more fully addressed in Chapter 5).

Given that ethnicity is treated as sacrosanct, the solution to ethnic conflicts is always to emphasize the local. Most recently, blame for ethnic conflict in Africa is tending to shift from highlighting the manipulative role of nationalist politicians to focus upon the atomization of African society. The privileging of localism has therefore shifted priority from undermining the nation-state to constructing local élites and communities.

Sanitizing Savagery

As the cold war came to an end in 1989, the attitude towards examples of African barbarism and ethnic conflict began to shift. From treating every African as a potential savage, the same method was increasingly reserved for the modern African politician. A number of stories featuring uncivilized behaviour among African leaders began to circulate in the English liberal press. One story concerned plans by an eminent African stateman to build a cathedral that was even bigger than the Vatican's St Peter's in the middle of the jungle. In a report criticizing the waste of money that the president of the Ivory Coast, Felix Houphouet-Boigny, had spent on building the cathedral in his home town of Yamoussoukro, John Ezard imagined the place to be swarming with termites. Then he added: 'It is also possible to think of one of the occasional, furtive human sacrifices of Ivorian animism being performed on that central white marble altar'.[1] Earlier Gerald Bourke had filed another story from the Ivory Coast alleging that, despite the attentions of European missionaries, 'bizarre ancestral rituals still flourish here': 'Tradition dictates that the death of a tribal dignitary be marked by human sacrifices; the more powerful the personage, the more skulls he required.'[2]

No evidence is provided to substantiate this claim. Nevertheless Bourke helpfully adds that, 'Even the president, a staunch Roman Catholic, consults a marabout [witch-doctor]'. The liberal press has allowed its imagination to run riot at the alleged religious malpractices of this particular African leader who, when he died recently, managed to be buried without the sacrifice of any of the many European dignitaries who attended his funeral . . . or anybody else for that matter. Journalistic standards could go to the wall, apparently, so long as the reputation of African politicians like Houphouet-Boigny was successfully impugned. Similar rumours circulated about former Emperor Bokassa of the Central African Republic and President Mobuto of Zaire. The interesting point about these malevolent reports is that they accuse political leaders of being in tune with certain spiritual aspects of African culture. Within a few years, this debit set against African leaders would become a credit.

After one massacre during the Liberian civil war in 1993, the American *Newsweek* magazine ran a feature entitled 'Africa: The Curse of Tribal War': 'An ancient plague, whose outbreaks are often bloody episodes like the one in Liberia, continues to afflict the people of sub-Saharan Africa'.[3] Its writers referred to the 'wild profusion' of languages, religions and ethnic groups in Africa and concluded, 'such unparalleled cultural diversity brings with it a constant risk of conflict and bloodshed'.[4] It is interesting, therefore, that the report could also conclude, 'Ethnic awareness also has a place for Africans who recognise their people's ancestral customs and languages as a cultural heritage to be valued and preserved for its own sake'.[5] To the non-expert this made the whole report sound contradictory, but in reality it was simply transitional to a more constructive assessment of African ethnicity in the eyes of the West.

At that time, though, the most common response was that the unregulated masses were to held responsible for ethnic conflicts getting out of hand in Africa. In April 1993, all the speeches at the Rhodes University conference on ethnicity in Grahamstown, South Africa, still saw 'primordial ethnicity', that is, mass ethnicity, as the chief threat to Africa's future stability.[6] That conference was organized in the midst of the so-called 'black on black' violence in Natal between Zulus supporting the African National Congress (ANC) and Zulus backing Chief Gatsha Buthelezi's ethnic Inkatha organization. It was widely felt among the political élite that, if concessions were made to Inkatha, it would be taken as an object lesson by the masses to use ethnicity as a vehicle to exert a continuous influence upon the new South Africa regime.

In South Africa, the new thinking on ethnicity assumed that politics in general and political manipulation in particular confronted the country as a problem. On the other hand, an unsullied ethnicity was a cultural, non-political solution for all the communities that made up South Africa. Without any political restrictions imposed upon it, ethnicity could help generate a more decent South African society in the aftermath of apartheid. In a monograph attempting to assess the Inkatha/ANC conflict in Natal, Morris Szeftel writes:

> It's all too easy to assume that 'who says ethnicity, says conflict' and to forget to ask which forces and institutions politicise divisions and structure conflict and how they do it . . . Given the intensity of so many ethnic conflicts and the subjectivist nature of ethnicity this

tendency to collapse different layers of action together is understandable. Yet we need to remind ourselves that many people with different identities live together in varying degrees of tolerance and even generosity. People can be conscious of a particular identity without it having much relevance for the way they conduct their personal lives. They can also exhibit high degrees of prejudice against other groups.[7]

According to South African scholar Gerhard Mare, 'Democracy also necessitates that the boundaries of ethnic groups should be porous, allowing escape and entry. The tighter the definitions of membership, the more totalitarian an ethnic group becomes'.[8] Mare contended that ethnicity must be the norm around which a new South Africa must be constructed: 'Ethnicity should neither be privileged nor should it be granted a special status through prosecution or denial.'[9]

An ethnicity that is neither privileged nor denied means an ethnicity that is accepted as a routine, ordinary aspect of everyday local communities. Mare's response was echoed by Aletta Norval and others at the 1993 Rhodes conference on ethnicity, who sharply distinguished between the dangerous primordialism of Inkatha and the tolerant version now being advanced by the ANC government in its new constitution.[10] For Norval, a democratic post-apartheid society 'must always be open to contestation', but that requires that contested ethnic identities are not imposed upon others nor made to disappear:

[South Africa] must deal with ethnic identifications in a manner which recognises their fluidity and the possibility of their being articulated into a variety of political spaces. In this sense, a democratic politics would not negate the space of ethnic identification.[11]

Norval's conclusion is significant – only an ethnic orientation can enable people to make sense of their lives: 'To negate [ethnicity] will not make it disappear. It will only lead to bewilderment.'[12] South African president Nelson Mandela seems to have been listening to the anti-primordial message emanating from Grahamstown. Just before the elections that swept him into power, he wrote in the American periodical *Foreign Affairs*:

> *Ancient and long-dormant animosities have been unlocked by the ending of the Cold War, and these now threaten the very existence of some countries. Some suggest that an international divide is emerging between countries that tolerate diversity and those that do not. The latter will fall prey to internecine strife, sapping, if not destroying the potential of their people.*[13]

For Mandela, however, 'respect for diversity is central to the ANC's political credo' and furthermore 'a central goal of our foreign policy will . . . seek to make the world safe for diversity'.[14]

Taking heart from this ANC programme, Charles Tilly has claimed that the post-apartheid state can enable Inkatha supporters to make sense of their ethnic identity as Zulus and thereby engineer ethnic toleration in Natal. He notes that: 'States selectively confirm, co-opt, reinforce, or even create identity-bestowing social networks within which people organise work, sociability, and collective action; to some degree, all such networks come to depend on the state's backing, or at least its toleration.'[15] The people of KwaZulu can rely 'in part on the South African state's toleration of Zulu separateness'.[16] In passing, we can note Tilly's proposal that the new state reduces the risks posed by 'primordialism' in modern society by basing itself on local networks.

Even with a black face fronting the current regime in Pretoria, South Africa more closely resembles a Western society that its African neighbours. Modern South Africa retains an enormous industrial economy and a huge state bureaucracy left over from the apartheid era. Like its Western counterparts, it is the very opposite of parochialism. Yet, as we have seen first through apartheid, and then from Mandela's remarks in *Foreign Affairs*, the division of South Africa either into separate bantustans (homelands) or into a tolerant multicultural diversity of communities is considered essential for its legitimation. Whether South Africa's poorer neighbours to its north could duplicate its attempts to construct a new ethnicity remains to be seen.

The 1994 Rwandan Massacre

Kaplan's article, 'The Coming Anarchy', was published in February 1994 and was widely influential in casting Africans as hate figures and threats to civilization. After the April 1994 massacre in Rwanda, when an estimated 500,000 died, the whole world seemed to unite in agreeing that the Hutus of Rwanda were both mad and bad. How could African ethnicity and primitivism in general be considered to be a cause for celebration when Rwanda seemed to be a stark demonstration of its capacity to provoke so many barbaric atrocities? According to the Archbishop of Canterbury, George Carey, for example, their Christianity may be 'only skin deep':

> It's easy to talk about Rwanda being a Christian nation, but by their fruits you shall know them. Though the East African revival started in Rwanda in the thirties and forties, what happened since may indicate Rwanda is not as deeply Christian as we may think.[17]

The African Rights group, for its part, believed that the Hutus had become afflicted by a medical condition during the 1994 massacre in Rwanda: 'Genocide is such a pathological political condition that truly unusual motives are required for people to contemplate it . . . The Hutu extremists were able to tap deep currents of popular feeling.'[18] Award-winning BBC journalist Fergal Keane appeared to agree that the psychological balance of the Hutu was disturbed: 'Tens of thousands became infected – and I can think of no other word to describe the condition – by an anti-Tutsi psychosis'.[19] Beneath a strap reading 'the "victims" are the villains', *Guardian* journalist Chris McGreal commenting on the inhabitants of the Hutu refugee camps during the later Banyamulenge episode in Eastern Zaire in 1996, claimed, 'Rwanda's exiled Hutus are not perpetual victims of war. They are the ones perpetuating the conflict'.[20] Mary Braid of the *Independent* grouped the Interahamwe Hutu militia in Eastern Zaire together with the Nazis, 'Just as the Nazis disseminated propaganda against the Jews, the Interahamwe was fed – and fed others – a diet of anti-Tutsi propaganda'.[21] But others had gone further. For them, the African Hutus had proved themselves to be even worse than the wholly European Nazis. According to one account of the 1994 massacres, 'The dead of Rwanda accumulated at nearly three times the rate of Jewish dead during the Holocaust'.[22] On the other hand, a more radical version of the same massacre blamed the behaviour of the Hutus on

Rwanda's Belgian colonialists. The former Secretary-General of France's Médecins Sans Frontières has argued that:

> *Just as Hitler's grand plan was founded on an engrained European anti-semitism which he played on by singling out the Jews as the source of all Germany's ills, the Hutu radicals are the inheritors of the colonial lunacy of classifying and grading different ethnic groups in a racial hierarchy.*[23]

From the text, it is not clear why Destexhe sees only the Hutus as being susceptible to this particular colonial legacy.

But the way out for those who uphold ethnicity was outlined by the London-based Minority Right Group (MRG). The MRG did not directly accuse the Hutu ethnic group of responsibility for the 1994 massacre in Rwanda and the smaller-scale disturbances in Burundi. For MRG director Alan Philips, it was leading politicians who exploited the fears of the different communities in Rwanda and Burundi with the result that, 'the polarisation of the conflict and the use of indiscriminate violence have subordinated other identities and entrenched ethnic boundaries'.[24] In this way, the focus of responsibility for ethnic clashes is directed away from the NGOs' promotion of ethnic identity and on to ambitious and modernizing nationalist politicians.

The device that the MRG and others had hit upon was to assert that ethnic conflict was the negation of genuine ethnicity. The development of this approach towards ethnic conflict was preconditioned by the elevation of primitivist sentiments in the West and especially its assumption that it is unrestricted modernism that is responsible for the continuing barbarism of the African continent. As such, it is incumbent upon morally responsible Westerners to try to limit the impact of modernism on Africa.

Both the Hutus and the Ogonis are seen as victims of circumstance, but while the Hutus have been manipulated by ambitious African politicians into giving vent to humanity's capacity for brutality, the Ogoni – through their relationship with The Body Shop facilitators – have been able to articulate a more sustainable and therefore a less dangerous version of humanity. In this scenario, the local is privileged as the source of social harmony. The ambitious Hutu politicians were not content with what the local had to offer but the Ogoni are. That is all that is needed to distinguish between the sanctification and demonization of African ethnic groups nowadays.

Ethnic Conflict Denied: Sierra Leone

A new vogue of denying the concept of ethnicity has come about ever since ethnicity has been associated with 'ethnic cleansing' in the former Yugoslavia. The popular trend in the ideology of NGO intellectuals and Africanists is to replace ethnicity with the Latin American word 'indigenism' or with the North American 'survivalism'. After Bosnia, ethnicity has become more associated with its racist heritage. Through the influence of Boas and cultural relativism, most ethnicity theories propose that the differences between humans are more important than what we all have in common. The charge of racism is confined to those who believe that human differences demonstrate a difference in status. Cultural relativists stress, however, that humans are *equally* different. Even so, ethnicity has become tainted with the racist formulation through the widespread use of the term 'ethnic cleansing' in Bosnia and consequently some have prefered to dispense with it altogether. For example, it is denied that the conflict in Sierra Leone in the early 1990s was an ethnic one.

In his book, *Fighting for the Rain Forest*, Paul Richards is convinced that the Sierra Leone conflict is 'manifestly not ethnic'.[25] But why does he deny the veracity of the concept of ethnicity while at the same time filling his book with glowing references to ethnic institutions like initiation rites and secret societies, as well as committing himself to localism, survivalism and indigenous knowledge systems? These recommendations to glorify the primitive (without actually using the word) make all his denials ring hollow. We have already noted in our introduction the trend today to generalize ethnicity so much that it means anything to everybody and consequently nothing much in particular. The implications of this become clear in reading *Fighting for the Rain Forest*, because ethnicity is the silent assumption underpinning all the book's arguments though it nowhere puts in a definite appearance.

When Richards and others deny the concept of ethnicity, they are only denying the definition that maintains that humans are different in status. They still hold out, however, that humans are equally different and that is why they put such stress upon the need for toleration between cultures. Their emphasis upon the fluidity between cultures, the hybridization or 'creolization' of cultures, does not challenge this assumption either. The social determinant is still assumed to be where an individual is coming from – his different culture, rather than upon what individuals are capable of doing – whatever their cultural origins are – because what unites humans is more significant that what divides them. The notion that humans are equally different is the operating assumption that pervades Richards's book and this explains why it is full of praise for ethnic rites while never admitting to the existence of an ethnic dimension as a whole.

Over Christmas 1995 Médecins Sans Frontières (MSF) ran an advert based on the Kaplanesque portrayal of African ethnicity as a threat. Its ostensible aim was to raise funds to cope with the casualties of the conflict in Sierra Leone. Alongside a picture of a man with both his hands amputated, the text ran:

> *They're ripping out tongues, gouging eyes and hacking off hands. Christmas in Sierra Leone. We don't understand why men can become ruthless butchers, but in the city of Bo, Médecins Sans Frontières surgeons are dealing with some of the most horrific mutilations they've ever witnessed. Armed groups vying for control of the country's mining areas have found that maiming works better than slaughtering when trying to 'encourage' people to leave their homes.*[26]

Paul Richards challenges this way that NGOs like MSF have interpreted the conflict in Sierra Leone. In particular he challenges their Kaplanesque imagery that conjures up a barbaric Africa besieging the world. Richards argues that the conflict that engulfed Sierra Leone in the early 1990s was a consequence of its partial exclusion from the rest of the world. Referring to the popularity in the country of the first Rambo movie, *First Blood* (1982), Richards contends that the rebellion in Sierra Leone can best be seen as a desire to imitate Western values rather than those of African tribalism. For example, for Richards there is no evidence that the Rambo videos enjoyed by Sierra Leone's youth are a 'stimulus to half-forgotten barbarism': 'If there is barbarity in that experience it is the modern barbarism of the Vietnam war and anti-authoritarian backwoods survivalism, not reversion to the values of a violent African past.'[27]

Here Richards seems to place the blame for Sierra Leone's problems on the West. But closer inspection of this textual reference, as well as others in the book that celebrate the Rambo character, shows that Richards' sees a positive kernel in Rambo's 'modern barbarism', though he is reluctant to describe it as barbarism or primitivism when referring to Africa. Elsewhere in the book he makes clear his firm opposition to any form of violence, and his support for a peace process for Sierra Leone, but it is obvious that the real concern of the book is to buttress every primitive influence that the West can impart on Sierra Leone.

Richards's sympathy for the American survivalist movement is instructive. It is a good example of the modern primitivist trend that is sweeping that society. *Fighting for the Rain Forest* posits that a similar movement committed to non-violence could help revitalize Sierra Leonean society. In regard to high-technology like video recorders and satellite telephones, Richards welcomes their use in so far as they help improve the survivalist position. For Richards, a strategy that involves sticking high-technology gadgets on to African communities is still compatible with an overall perspective that views the systematic modernization of society as a problem for humanity.

Richards claims that the framework for the conflict in Sierra Leone: 'owes everything to the media flows and cultural hybridizations that make up globalized modernity'.[28] Yet, despite this formal commitment to modernity, he also calls for the recognition of the value of 'community indigenous knowledge'.[29]

It is obvious that Richards is intent on redefining the meaning of modernity. Significantly, he portrays localism as a 'healthy' alternative culture to the violent ideology of the rebels because 'increased globalization allows major re-thinking of the value of localism': 'Healthy government is first and foremost local government, and many of Africa's problems begin to appear where states sought to break such connections between people and resources.'[30]

Once again, globalization is being presented purely as an opportunity for local advancement. Richards defends his corner for his own brand of technological primitivism throughout his book.

As can be imagined from the book's title, it is full of reverence towards the rain forest, as well as ancient initiation rituals like the Poro and Sande that are used to maintain social coherence. For Richards, 'Bush knowledge is not barbarism. It is a way of making ends meet in harsh circumstances'.[31] But if bush knowledge is not barbarism, then what is? For Richards, barbarism seems to a feature confined to the modern world. As for Africa, Richards prefers to celebrate bush knowledge as a 'survival skill'.

Richards presents the actors of the Sierra Leone conflict as either victims or survivors. For example, he asserts that the rebel movement in Sierra Leone is mainly run by some 'disregarded' intellectuals who are 'victims' of social exclusion.[32] Richards views Sierra Leone as a society that is basically decent and non-violent and morally responsible – unlike the frustrated people who staff the rebel leadership.[33] He also interviews some video venders who like Rambo films because 'they teach skills and attitudes needed to survive on your own in a hostile world'.[34] For Richards, this basic survivalism is 'thoughtful, streetwise, post-modern'.[35] Yet it does not occur to Richards that, by peopling his account either with victims or with survivors, he is belittling the people of Sierra Leone.

The book follows convention in degrading the meaning of modernity by blending it with notions derived from Western primitivism. Richards wants the conflict that is ruining Sierra Leone to end, but the vehicle he imagines that can bring that peace is a strange one: a movement of victims committed to surviving. Ultimately, this convergence of modernity and indigenousness helps promote the wider idea that Sierra Leonean society has already arrived at all a modern society can expect to be. The message is: if you have survived, this is it. Don't expect anything more of our 'globalized' world than what is on offer for survivors in Sierra Leone.

Paul Richards's book, *Fighting for the Rain Forest*, purports to be a critique of Kaplan's remarks on the conflict in Sierra Leone upon which his article 'The Coming Anarchy' is largely based.[36] In fact Richards demonstrates a closer intellectual affinity to Kaplan than he thinks. The common ground between both commentators is that they turn African society into an exemplar for the West. For Kaplan the war in Sierra Leone is a negative object lesson, for Richards its indigenous knowledge is a positive example. Whereas Kaplan conjures up a ghastly vision of the whole world increasingly approximating war-torn Sierra Leone, Richards celebrates the same vision as introducing a potentially more civilized, moral society – committed to the values of indigenism, localism and survivalism.

Ethnic Conflict Denied: Rwanda

In a strange contrast to the immense barrage of propaganda that labels the 1994 Rwandan massacres not only ethnic conflict but also a genocide, the present Rwandan regime officially denies that ethnicity exists there.

The Tutsi-dominated regime in the Rwandan capital of Kigali was helped into power in 1994 by an Anglo-American alliance working through Museveni's Ugandan regime.[37] Various Western advisers have made strenuous efforts to ensure that the Kigali regime retains the support of the politically correct constituency in the West. As a result, the authorities take great pains to deny that ethnicity exists, though only to reintroduce it in a more politically correct form. For example, Kigali has introduced identity cards – funded by USAID – which no longer have a category for ethnicity. This is because, according to the official Rwandan government line, their country is a 'post-ethnic state' and there are no ethnic groups anymore. They view Tutsis and Hutus as an invented division imposed on the peoples of Rwanda by German colonists at the turn of the century and insist that a post-ethnic Rwanda is 'a restoration of traditional Rwandan norms' from before colonial times.[38] Interviewed by American journalist David Rieff, Rwandan Vice-President Paul Kagame argued for a moral divide to replace the colonially created Tutsi and Hutu division: 'Let's talk of right and wrong, not Tutsi and Hutu'.[39] The subtext here is that the Tutsi side is morally right and the Hutu side is morally wrong.

So-called 'post-ethnicity' in Rwanda really means moral ethnicity. But despite the frequent repetition of the term 'moral' by both Rwandese officials and the NGOs, it would be wrong to get the impression this means an increase in liberality in Rwanda. On the contrary, it means a more intense application of state authority. Even the very words you use identify your moral standards – or your ethnicity – and make you a target for state sanctions. One American NGO volunteer working in eastern Rwanda cautioned Rieff:

> *Don't say 'T' or 'H'. You'll get arrested. You can't use those terms*
> *anymore. It's a distinction that has been abolished. For the*
> *government, to use it is to talk like the people across the border in*
> *Zaire – in other words, the language of the* genocidaires.[40]

This 'language' refers to when ethnicity still meant something definite, when it was considered to be a dangerous primordial movement. Modern ethnicity is a moral code that confines you to your locality.

The African State Bureaucracy

From the localizing perspective of the NGOs, it is commonly regarded that African nationalist politicians manipulating genuine ethnic sentiments to retain a constituency of support are to blame for causing ethnic conflict. Increasingly, however, as the NGO concern has switched to the dangers of the atomization of African society, their localism has been concentrated on building up local élites and communities rather than destroying nation-states' structures. Even so, it is still important to dispense with the myth that African nationalism is responsible for ethnic conflict.

The message of anti-state localism is plain: whoever tries to wield the modern state risks unleashing a Pandora's box of problems on Africa. The blunt reality is that African politicians – whether democratic or dictators – never had much influence over the African state in the first place. That state machine was built by the colonial powers and their stamp was retained upon it throughout the four decades of African independence from 1957 onwards. If the African state machine is responsible for ethnic conflict, therefore, then African politicians cannot be blamed for it.

Mainstream analyses of the African state are, in general, obsessed with the particular individual or party at the top of the state and assign responsibility for everything that happens to them alone. As we shall see, the exclusion of the anti-imperialist masses from politics and the general clampdown on political activism in the aftermath of the independence period did lead to a growing concentration of power. An omnipotent figurehead usually emerged as leader of the nation, apparently unconnected with any specific class, who seemingly held all the reins of power in his own hands. As a result,

African leaders tended to assume an autonomous existence that floated above the rest of society. This phenomenon occurs when the indigenous capitalist class is too weak and divided to rule as a class, and has to offer to an individual or clique the exercise of state power instead. Though this phenomenon can occur sporadically in advanced capitalist countries (Hitler, Mussolini, de Gaulle, etc.) the endemic weakness of capitalism in backward regions like Africa gave personalized rule a degree of permanence during the period of independence.

It is ironic, therefore, how often these seemingly all-powerful leaders turned out to be not so strong after all. Their real power was derived from the state machinery and, at the end of the day, they ruled with the permission of those who ran this legacy of colonialism. That is why so many so-called strongmen who got carried away with the idea that they were omnipotent ended up in exile pondering what went wrong. While presidents and military leaders came and went, the state bureaucracies survived and continued to administer African societies throughout the post-colonial period of independence. Even relatively popular leaders found that they can do little without the co-operation of the civil service. Ultimately it was the vested interests of the state administrators who decided whether or not a particular policy was implemented or ignored.

Occasional military coups were the public reflection of the underlying tensions within the African political élites, but they did not usually challenge the pre-eminence of the state machine itself. Prolonged instability only arose in those struggles where the existence of the state bureaucracy was threatened. However, even in the case of the most thoroughgoing liberation struggle – like that of the Kenyan Mau Mau insurgents in the 1950s – land, not the state machine itself, was the central issue at stake in the conflict. This meant that even ostensibly radical African regimes took power with the former state machinery still intact.

For many on the left in the 1970s, the Zimbabwean struggle was the epitome of a progressive liberation struggle against reactionary white imperialism. Yet independent Zimbabwe's security service was for many years the same institution that operated for the Smith regime against the African freedom fighters. For example, in the light of the atrocities committed in Matabeleland by the Harare regime in the early 1980s, the Western media concentrated their criticism on Zimbabwe's North Korean-trained 5th Brigade, but this diplomatically overlooks the leading role played by those elements of the old Smith regime (preserved by the Lancaster House agreements) in crushing the Ndebele dissidents:

> The Central Intelligence Organisation (CIO) . . . had Ken Flower as its director from 1963 to 1981. His successor, Dan Stannard, similarly served the previous government. Minister of State (Defense) Sydney Seremayi is advised by, among others from the old regime, Deputy Secretary for Defense Colonel Malcolm Millar. Commissioner of Police Wiridzayi Nguruve has as his Commander of the paramilitary Police Support Unit Assistant Commissioner of Police Don Rowland. The unit has played a prominent role in recent operations against insurgents and civilians in Matabeleland, as has the antiguerrilla task force, led by former Selous Scout Colonel Lionel Dyke.[41]

Let us look in more depth at the example of Ethiopia. Today the members of the former Mengistu regime are on trial for their lives for executing members of the old empire after the 1974 coup. Yet the similarity between the old Emperor Haile Selassie and his Marxist successor, Colonel Mengistu Haile Mariam, is striking. It is wrong to conclude from this that African regimes naturally tend towards dictatorships, irrespective of their political hue. The point is that both Ethiopian leaderships were based on essentially the same state bureaucracy, and it is this that made the right-wing Negus and the left-wing Mengistu seem so similar.

The 1974 insurrection against Selassie has been interpreted as a popular revolt against a feudal monarch. In reality, Ethiopia's pre-1974 social relations were fundamentally the same capitalist relations as every other black African state. Its rural élite was no more 'feudal' and 'aristocratic' than that in northern Nigeria. From the Italian occupation in the late 1930s, but particularly since the Second World War, capitalist relations had increasingly penetrated the Ethiopian countryside.

What made Ethiopia stand out in the mid-1970s was the fact that its rural élite retained more formal political power than was the case elsewhere in Africa. Selassie's removal in 1974 was merely the climax of a long process that had commenced years before: the state bureaucracy's campaign to exclude Ethiopia's old rural élite from its traditional positions of power. Polish journalist Ryszard Kapuscinski's description of the pre-1974 court circle in Addis Ababa reveals the drastic measures that Selassie himself took to neutralize the influence of his rural élites over state affairs:

> The three principle factions in the Palace were the aristocrats, the bureaucrats, and the so-called 'personal people' . . . These 'personal people' of the Emperor, dragged straight from our desperate and miserable provinces into the salons of the highest courtiers — where they met the undisguised hatred of the long-established aristocrats — served the Emperor with an almost indescribable eagerness, indeed a passion, for they had quickly tasted the splendours of the Palace and the evident charms of power, and they knew that they had arrived there, come within reach of the highest state dignitaries, only through the will of His Highness. It was to them that the Emperor would entrust the positions requiring greatest confidence: the Ministry of the Pen; the Emperor's political police, and the superintendency of the Palace were manned by such people.[42]

Selassie acquired his autocratic reputation through these efforts to put pressure on his rivals. Yet the Emperor ultimately failed to put his rural 'nobility' in their place. This is the secret behind Selassie's removal from power in the mid-1970s. Ethiopia's US-trained army got the go-ahead to act when Selassie's main Western ally began to distance themselves from his regime. As Donald Petterson, the former American ambassador to Somalia, later admitted:

> The American-Ethiopian friendship had begun to wane in the very early 1970s, well before the Ethiopian revolution. There was growing political instability in Ethiopia in 1972–3, heightened by what was then viewed as the ineptitude and later as the criminal neglect of the Ethiopian government in failing to provide anything approaching adequate care for the victims of the drought that was ravaging parts of the country.[43]

Despite the chaos and the violence of the events that followed, the state bureaucracy and military survived the turmoil to get an even greater grip on Ethiopian society. And when David Aaron, President

Carter's deputy assistant for National Security Affairs, met Mengistu in February 1978 he could tell him that the United States was ready to help Ethiopia 'achieve the aims of the revolution'.[44]

French journalist Rene Lefort has indicated the active role the state administration was able to play even during the height of the mobilization of the masses after Selassie had been ousted, as it moved to obstruct attempts to implement decisions that were against its interests:

> Only one major institution had come through the first phase of the revolution relatively unscathed: the administration . . . The administration bent before all these changes and even managed to bury some of them in its nooks and crannies. Decisions of the Derg were not applied or not fully applied when they had to be carried out by civil servants alone. The executive was no longer executing.[45]

Like neighbouring Somalia, Ethiopia had all its cold war aid cut off after 1989 and the country quickly collapsed into factions. The opposition forces that had struggled for decades without success against first Haile Selassie and then Mengistu during the cold war quickly overwhelmed the regime, and the Eritreans seceded from the state in 1993. The Tigreans took over the country and introduced a new constitution in 1996 that split the remnant state into nine parts. Yet despite this constitution, according to Ethiopian expert John Cohen, the old Selassie machinery still operates, particularly in the west and south of the country.[46] Given this 'long stability', states Cohen, it should come as no surprise that the headquarters staff of the new regime wishes to continue the pattern of 'unintegrated prefectorial deconcentration that has existed since the mid-1940s'.[47]

The experience of independent Africa during the cold war, then, was an endless game of musical chairs, with African leaders moving in and out of power, but with the state machine remaining essentially intact. I have made the point that if the colonially constructed African state machine is responsible for ethnic conflict, then African politicians cannot be blamed for it. But it would be fallacious to insist that the state bureaucracy – or even the old colonial powers – are responsible for present-day ethnic conflicts in Africa.

Atomized Africa

The African state is changing today, not because of anything to do with the nature of African rulers, or even the African political parties, but because of the erosion of the state bureaucracy under the impact of Western pressure – initially economic pressure from the World Bank and the IMF, and then political pressure from the NGOs and the turmoil that followed the collapse of the Soviet bloc. Before only the African figurehead leader changed, now the state bureaucracy itself is crumbling into fragments. Given the intimate relationship that it has evolved with the state bureaucracy over the independence years, the African political élite is collapsing alongside the state. Its power and influence in society is thereby reduced (if only because it has not the resources to buy up the support of client constituencies as easily any more).

Nevertheless, it is presumptuous to conclude that African state fragmentation necessarily leads to a revival of ethnicity. To imagine this is to belittle the immense process of individualization that has gripped the world since the end of the cold war and the consequent collapse of institutions, East and West, North and South. Throughout Africa every institution is suffering from these forces of fragmentation, irrespective of their Western or African origin. It is only necessary to point to something as fundamental as the disintegration of the family as a core institution to highlight the extent of the atomization of society that is under way all over the world. From now on, we will all be truly individualized.

From this perspective, we can see how erroneous it is to imagine that the atomization of society in and of itself is a sufficient condition to recreate the conditions for African ethnicity to flourish. On the contrary, the project to establish a modern African ethnicity involves the building up of diminished individuals into local communities that can give society some semblance of stability and coherence. The privileging of localism may formerly have entailed an assault on the modernizing politicians of the African state, but now it is coming to mean the building up of society not its breakdown. Modern ethnic promotion does not involve the breaking down of nationalities into ethnicities, but the herding of individuals into local ethnic communities. A massive injection of dynamism is required to construct ethnicity these days whereas the African state can provide none at all, since it itself is in a state of prostration.

The creation of ethnicity in society therefore requires a definite force capable of inserting dynamism into it. Sponsors of ethnicity (and therefore ethnic conflict) must be able to exert some power to be able to instigate the successful realignment of social relations. A rapidly diminishing African political élite and a collapsing state bureaucracy cannot be the source of the dynamism that is necessary to create African ethnicity systematically. Their fall has been too far. At best, they have merely tried to use the mechanism of achieving an ethnic balance as suggested to them by their Western advisers (we will be investigating their 'Proportionality Principle' in Chapter 4). These efforts to obtain a measure of political stability have been dressed up as evidence of ethnic manipulation and used to blame them for all Africa's ethnic conflicts. This is an over-reaction because they have never had that much power to determine events in Africa. It is true that the sense of being under siege, a fear of others, of utter frustration, all these might engender sporadic outbursts of ethnic conflict, but this cannot provide a basis for a systematic and dynamic new ethnic order.[48]

That dynamism must come from elsewhere – an interventionist West, post-apartheid South Africa, and their NGOs – these alone possess the power and resources to restore some coherence to the broken fragments of African societies.[49] Indeed, 'society' in Africa is steadily atomizing into a myriad of individuals. If these individuals could be guaranteed to remain inert 'victims', that would present much less of a problem for the NGOs. The problem is that, though people are likely to respond to panics that affect them directly, there is no telling how they will respond. Moreover, there is a corresponding reluctance to pay attention to any authority figure at all. As far as the West is concerned, this makes ordinary people unstable and out of control. Rather than African nationalist politicians being blamed for ethnic conflict, this mass of atomized African individuals are increasingly seen by NGOs as the potential source of future ethnic conflict in Africa. The NGO concern to sustain local ethnic identities is therefore a project to restore a semblance of coherence to African society by ensuring the pacification of individual Africans in regulated local communities.

To cultivate ethnic identities systematically, however, requires an expenditure of resources well beyond the resources of most African politicians today, but potentially well within the reach of many NGOs operating in Africa.[50] For example, the West raised the funds to permit national elections to be carried out in war-torn Mozambique in 1994. Although many people participated in the elections, there was little enthusiasm about the parties involved and after the poll cynicism about the national parties if anything intensified. This is because there is little to separate politically the 'Marxist' Frelimo party from its former bitter rival Renamo. Incoherence and instability continue to afflict the country. On 29 October 1996, the Parliament unanimously approved a constitutional amendment 1996 to give more power to local councils, so they can carry out economic, social and cultural programmes as well as promote local development. The local councils and local mayors are scheduled to be elected in November 1997 (though this may be postponed until 1998).

According to the *Mozambique Peace Process Bulletin*, under the new amendment, 'local councils are regulated by the government only in a post hoc way, verifying that laws have been satisfied. Central government can judge the "merits of administrative acts" only if this is specifically permitted in national law'.[51] The *Bulletin* goes on to note that 'there seems to be no grassroots demand for autonomous local government' in the country, and 'In Mozambique, decentralisation is a fashionable donor demand and is largely driving both local government and land processes. Donors . . . are using their power to demand that Mozambique decentralise'.[52] The point is that this decentralization is designed to cohere the amorphous masses at a local administrative level since the attempt to cohere them at a national level failed.

The largest donor in Mozambique is the European Union (EU). It must have leant on the Frelimo government in Maputo to introduce the constitutional amendment because, as the bulletin notes, 'Frelimo's concern about losing local elections had led it to want to reduce decentralisation and to give local councils less power'.[53] NGOs are also critical of the donor agenda too, but from a completely opposite angle to Frelimo. They criticize the EU for not providing sufficient funding to enable them to monitor the local elections properly – i.e. because the roads and bridges that were damaged in the recent war have still not been repaired and therefore they will find it difficult to cover all the polling stations.

Where the West and its NGOs are influential, strenuous efforts are made to introduce structures that can sponsor moral ethnicity. At a conference, in the Zimbabwean capital of Harare in March 1989, to discuss humanitarian assistance to 'civilian victims of armed conflict', the 40 experts attending adopted six 'moral imperatives', of which the first is 'They should be careful not to challenge or undermine local culture'; and the third is 'They should make use of available, or help create indigenous, societal or other infrastructures for the management of aid'.[34]

For Oxford professor Terence Ranger, for example, ethnic conflicts broke out in newly independent Zimbabwe because there was insufficient flexibility where ethnic boundaries met. According to Ranger, in Ndebele-speaking Matabeleland after Zimbabwe had secured its independence in 1979, the dominant Shona guerrillas 'were not sufficiently flexible to be able to adopt the composite ideology which had served them so well throughout two-thirds of the country'.[35] They tried to force the local peasantry to speak Shona. The inevitable result was ethnic conflict in the area that has lasted on and off ever since. Ranger has since advanced another explanation for the continuing ethnic strife in Matabeleland – the outside interference of Buthelezi's Inkatha movement in the area:

> Some of the competing definitions of tribal identity are generous and inclusive while others are narrow and xenophobic. This is how I see the situation in contemporary Matabeleland where the argument rages between an exclusive and narrow Ndebele identity, which seeks to ally itself with Buthelezi's Inkatha, and a much wider idea of Ndebeleness, which includes all the various peoples of Matabeleland, and is perfectly compatible with the possession of a Zimbabwean identity as well as a Ndebele one.[36]

In his paper, Ranger warns the Zimbabwean government that its decision to send a delegation of Ndebele chiefs to Kwazulu to 'relearn' Zulu rituals is 'neither informed nor careful. Based on the notion of Ndebele/Zulu essentialism, it already had wide-ranging political repercussions'. Instead, Ranger calls for a 'nuanced' study of Ndebele identity since it is in a state of 'constant development', and makes an appeal for 'careful and informed interventions' – in so far as Ndebele identity 'can be influenced from outside'.[57] The implication here is that if local identities are vulnerable to outside influence for malevolent purposes, then they are also open to be influenced positively by others.

It is when the parochial in Africa has such a premium placed upon it by the West that ethnic identities can mushroom overnight. The problem with this Western sponsorship of local identity is that it celebrates the passive subordination of African people to the ethnically shrouded agendas and institutions of the Great Powers and their NGOs. At best, this will induce even greater cynicism among Africans about the necessity for social organization as a way to improve their conditions and thereby intensify atomization; at worst, it leaves Africans open to manipulation by rival Western powers.

Usually ethnic conflicts in Africa are violent but sporadic outbursts that quickly vanish. But the Nigerian civil war in the 1960s lasted all of three years because both sides had Western sponsors eager to get their hands on the Niger delta's oil wealth. Apartheid South Africa could build a tribal-based system that lasted decades because it had possessed an industrial powerhouse to back it up. The regular clashes between the Tutsis and the Hutus have been very violent but sporadic affairs on each occasion. In the intervening period between bouts, both communities intermarried with each other. But when the West intervened directly in Rwandan affairs from 1990, an international force arrived that possessed sufficient power to make Rwanda's ethnic divisions permanent.

African Rights, a leading British-based supporter of the Kigali regime, has been using moral ethnicity as a wedge against not just the Hutus in Zairean camps but against its NGO rivals too. It has directly accused the international NGO community of covering up its role in the 1994 slaughter, specifying its protection of Innocent Mazimpaka, an employee of the Netherlands Development Organization and chair of the League for the Promotion and Defence of Human Rights in Rwanda, whom African Rights accuse of complicity in the 1994 massacres: 'Highlighting this case is all the more important because several other members of human rights groups have been accused of direct participation in the genocide, but are being protected by the closing of ranks by national and international rights groups.'[58] According to David Rieff, African Rights' charges that some NGOs were covering up the crimes of their local employees or secretly sympathizing with the previous regime led the Rwandan authorities to expel all the French humanitarian agencies in December 1995.[59]

This is just a single instance, yet it reveals the potential that the hallowed codes of moral ethnicity have to become a vehicle for various Western powers to play out their rivalries in Africa – and all for the best possible moral cause. Plenty of moral justifications for conflict have been lined up. We have already referred to the clashes that have broken out between those NGOs who back African cattleherders like the Maasai and those conservationists who concentrate on protecting Africa's wildlife. Then there is the conflict between those Westerners who back pastoralists and those who want to help the African farmer survive. For example, the Canadian International Development Agency (CIDA) have been criticized for discriminating against the pastoralist Barabaig people of East Africa. According to one account, the CIDA 'has a dispiriting record of only recognising those grass-roots organizations which will carry out its policies':

> One of CIDA's more dismal moments, for instance, was the over-riding of Barabaig land rights in its pursuit of sustainable practices for a neighbouring group . . . Their ancient right to graze cattle was severely compromised by CIDA's attempts to initiate new settled farming projects for other land-hungry and displaced people within Barabaig territory. CIDA strenuously resisted any recognition of the pastoralists' rights.[60]

Privileging the local has been the common NGO solution to dealing with any risk – whether from outside agencies like the state or from internal atomization. But what this primitivist viewpoint blithely ignores is that the local is always a greater source of reaction than the national or the international. Privileging the local paves the way for rivalries to breed along ethnic lines. And when local ethnic communities are directly sponsored by the Western powers, a recipe for systematic reaction is being prepared. The thesis that the promotion of a moral ethnicity, based upon herding diminished individuals into marginal communities, will mean less ethnic conflict in Africa is therefore simply not true. On the contrary, it will leave African society more susceptible to ethnic conflict, not less.

We have now concluded our examination of the themes that shape the concept of modern ethnicity: modern primitivism, victimization and localism. Moral ethnicity amounts to the communal regulation of the inert individual. Political ethnicity, on the other hand, sought to mobilise or activate individuals to achieve definite ethnic goals. We will now survey the historical record of political ethnicity in Africa in order to distinguish it properly from moral ethnicity.

Notes

1. *Guardian*, 1 January 1990, p. 19. In his book, *Rome*, Emile Zola examines the architectural history of the Catholic Church in the Holy City to enable him to accuse the Vatican of being influenced by its pagan foundations (pp. 170–1). Besides St Peter's, Zola lists a large number of churches constructed out of the ruins of imperial antiquity. The statue of the Roman emperor on top of Trajan's famous column was replaced by a statue of St Peter in the sixteenth century.

2. *Independent*, 9 August 1989, p. 6.

3. 'Africa: The Curse of Tribal War', p. 9.

4. Ibid., p. 9.

5. Ibid., p. 13. The report also mentioned that, though tribal links could cause croneyism and graft, 'in other cases the social impact is thoroughly benign' (ibid.).

6. The key contributions are published in Edwin Wilmsen and Patrick McAllister (eds), *The Politics of Difference*.

7. Morris Szeftel, 'Ethnicity and Democratization in South Africa', pp. 190–1.

8. Gerhard Mare, *Ethnicity and Politics in South Africa*, p. 4.

9. Ibid., p. 109.

10. The new South African constitution provides for nine provinces and the current Senate is to be replaced by a Council of Provinces, 'which will give provincial premiers a direct say at national level' though not allow them either to levy taxes or run their own police forces ('South Africa's race to find a permanent constitution', *The Economist*, 4 May 1996, p. 61).

11. Aletta Norval, 'Thinking Identities: Against a Theory of Ethnicity', p. 67.

12. Ibid.

13. Nelson Mandela, 'South Africa's Future Foreign Policy', p. 88.

14. Ibid., pp. 88–9.

15. Charles Tilly, 'A Bridge Halfway', p. 18.

16. Ibid.

17. *Independent*, 16 May 1995, p. 5.

18. African Rights, *Rwanda*, p. 34.

19. Fergal Keane, *Season of Blood*, p. 9.

20. Chris McGreal, 'Export of Terror from Zaire', *Guardian*, 23 October 1996, p. 17.

21. *Independent*, 16 November 1996, p. 11.

22. Philip Gourevitch, 'After the Genocide', p. 92.

23. Alain Destexhe, *Rwanda and Genocide in the Twentieth Century*, p. 28.

24. Introduction to Filip Reyntjens, *Burundi*, p. 5.

25. Paul Richards, *Fighting for the Rain Forest*, p. xix. From the evidence of his own account, to describe the Sierra Leone conflict as ethnic would be to impute a degree of organization to it that is completely unjustified.

26. 'Life is a human right', *Independent*, 16 December 1995, p. 4.

27. Richards, *Fighting for the Rain Forest*, p. 111.

28. Ibid., p. xvii.

29. Ibid., p. xxv.

30. Ibid., p. 160.

31. Ibid., p. 85.

32. Ibid., pp. 25–7, 166.

33. Richards characterizes their actions as 'irresponsible destructiveness' (ibid. p. 27).

34. Ibid., p. 103.

35. Ibid., p. 104.

36. R. Kaplan, 'The Coming Anarchy'.

37. See Africa Direct, *Submission to the UN Tribunal on Rwanda*.

38. Ibid., p. 76.

39. Cited in David Rieff, 'Rwanda: the Big Risk', p. 76.

40. Ibid. Kigale's denial of ethnicity in Rwanda did not prevent their army making incursions into Zaire in October/November 1996 in order to protect Zaire's Tutsi minority, the Banyamulenge.

41. Ronald Weitzer, 'Continuities in the Politics of State Security in Zimbabwe', p. 85. South Africa is currently experiencing a similar transition as the ANC becomes absorbed into the former apartheid state machine.

42. Ryszard Kapuscinski, *The Emperor – Downfall of an Autocrat*, p. 30. The popular rumour was that Mengistu was the product of an illicit relationship Selassie had with one of these 'personal people'.

43. Donald Petterson, 'Ethiopia Abandoned?', p. 628.

44. Ibid., p. 632.

45. Rene Lefort, *Ethiopia*, p. 155.

46. 'Opposition and delay results from the fact that in many regions, particularly in the west and the south, deconcentrated government structures established under Haile Selassie and modified by military rule continue to function' (John Cohen, 'Ethnic Federalism in Ethiopia', p. 169).

47. Ibid.

48. Such violent mass outbursts provide the material for the horror stories of 'primeval' African tribalism. What these accounts ignore, however, is first their ephemeral character; and second the fact that they only take the form of ethnicity in the absence of more conventional vehicles for expressing mass demands.

49. NGOs are not the only Western sources funding ethnic factions in Africa today. A quick perusal of any handful of issues of *Africa Confidential* (London) is usually sufficient to acquaint a reader with the large number of foreign agencies funnelling resources to prop up regional warlords and/or ethnic factions within African political parties today. The existence of this flow of 'aid' and arms can come as no surprise to anyone familiar with the days when Africa served as the killing fields of the cold war superpowers as well as the apartheid state. This type of ethnic sponsorship still goes on even though the cold war is over, but it cannot be blamed for *causing* ethnicity because it simply manipulates existing ethnic tensions rather than positively creating ethnicity in the first place. In this book, we are concerned with the forces responsible for the re-creation of modern ethnicity in Africa, rather than those that are parasitic upon it.

50. For example, the income of Care, an American charity, was $294m in 1990 – roughly $1m more than Ethiopia's income for 1991 [Care figures from Ian Smillie and Henry Helmich, *Non-governmental Organisations and Governments: Stakeholders for Development*, p. 304. Ethiopian figures from Economist Intelligence Unit, *Country Profile 1993–94*, p. 45].

51. 'City Council Elections in 97?', p. 2.

52. Ibid., pp. 6–7.

53. Ibid., p. 3.

54. Thomas Weiss and Henry Wiseman, 'Delivering Humanitarian Assistance in African Armed Conflicts', pp. 124–5.

55. Ibid., p. 216.

56. Terence Ranger, 'The Tribalisation of Africa and the Retribalisation of Europe', p. 10.

57. Ibid.

58. African Rights, *Presumption of Innocence*.

59. D. Rieff, 'Rwanda', p. 70.

60. Neil Middleton, Phil O'Keefe and Sam Moyo, *The Tears of a Crocodile*, pp. 182, 218, fn. 10.

CHAPTER 4

Political Ethnicity:
A Historical Excursion

For a long time, Africa seemed to be immune to the nationalist 'virus' and the colonial powers could operate as if the people of Africa were an inert mass. Gradually, however, the gathering threat of nationalism elsewhere – India and then Arab nationalism in Egypt – was sufficient for the British authorities to introduce political tribal structures in Africa in an attempt to pre-empt the impact of nationalism there: these became known as 'indirect' rule. Even so, the nationalist tide was so strong when it came that it swept aside the tribalizing institutions, instigating a near panic among the imperialists.

From Slavery to Servility

The process initiated by the colonialists to tribalize African politics in the inter-war period delivered such a boost to the ancient customary traditions of Africa that it utterly transformed them. It is vital to dispense with the widespread misconception that precolonial Africa was dominated by some form of political African tribalism in order to grasp this point fully.

Both imperialists and radicals have argued that precolonial African society was tribally based. Colonial apologists justified imperial intervention as a mission to 'modernize' Africa and lift it out of its primitive origins. And, in *The Black Man's Burden: Africa and the Curse of the Nation State* (1992) radical historian Basil Davidson argues that modern African nationalism was perverted by Western 'nation statism', which should be held responsible for Africa's subsequent decline. For Davidson, nation-statism is a state based upon class privilege. True African nationalism is better represented by the precolonial tribalism of the Ashante people within modern-day Ghana because it was based upon mass participation:

> *The history of precolonial tribalism (by no means the same thing as later forms of tribalism) was in every objective sense a history of nationalism . . . However 'exotic' Asante might appear in its African guise, it was manifestly a national state on its way toward becoming a nation state with every attribute ascribed to a West European nation state, even if some of these attributes still had to reach maturity.*[1]

The history of Africa since its first contact with the West has been the constant remoulding of its social relations once it became integrated into the world market through the ever tightening grip of capital. As Davidson has admitted in his previous work, even African tribal states like the Ashante and the Zulu were products of foreign encroachment into Africa rather than representing examples of authentic African political tribalism.

The Europeans' initial relationship to Africa was based upon equality – primarily trading guns for slaves with Guinea Coast communities from the sixteenth to the nineteenth centuries. In this, they merely copied the Arabs of North Africa or the eastern seaboard, who sought both slaves and gold. The European slave–gun trade came to dominate completely these societies once the Atlantic slave 'triangle' became established in the eighteenth century. For example, the great African state of Benin tried to avoid the trade but only fell into dilapidation when others began to prey on it. According to Davidson, Dahomey grew into a powerful slave state to avoid Benin's fate:

> *Dahomey's power to resist [Western encroachment] . . . depended on delivering slaves to the coast: the drastic but inescapable alternatives were to enslave others – in order to buy firearms – or risk enslavement oneself. This indeed was the inner dynamic of the slaving connection with Europe; and it pushed Dahomey, as it pushed other states, into wholesale participation in slaving. No single state could possibly withstand this combination of slaves and guns.*[2]

The Atlantic slave-trade – supplanting the traditional Arab traffick – had a vast impact on African society. Through their participation in it, a few African societies like Dahomey were able to grow into state formations. The Ashante state flourished on the basis of the gold trade with Arabic North Africa as well as slaving. But this experience was still relatively restricted. Only with colonialism was tribalism generalized throughout Africa.

During the nineteenth century European capital developed into the industrial form and began to accumulate in its own right. Consequently, slavery and slave-trading with the coastal African states lost its importance to European (but not to the American) powers. Europe came to look upon Africa in a new light: as a source of raw materials and a market for its manufactured products. Rivalries between the European powers provoked a scramble to grab the largest slices of the continent for themselves. It was carved up among the various European powers at the 1885 Berlin conference. Here, the various African colonies were treated as so many chess pieces to be manoeuvred across the diplomatic board: 'Their value was basically instrumental inasmuch as they represented counters which could be used to strengthen a state's position in Europe or in imperial strategy.'[3]

The European powers had been unable to agree at Berlin on how to show the 'effective occupation' of the African territories they each claimed. Consequently, they were obliged to stake their claim by conquering those inland states which refused to submit to them by treaty. The Europeans were confronted with two main types of society in inland Africa – hierarchical slave- or gold-trading states, and 'acephalus' communities – that is, those without a chief. The greater power and resources of the inland states attracted the attention of the colonialists, who sought to tame these societies first. Ironically, the colonialists now turned to good use the hostility these states had acquired among the acephalus communities through their reputation as slavers for the Arabs and Europeans in the past.

By campaigning against the enslaving of the acephalus communities by the inland rulers, the colonialists struck a twin blow at their opponents. They could readily recruit troops among the communal villagers by promising to liberate them from their slaving neighbours, while at same time depriving the inland cities of an important source of their wealth. The inland states of the African interior put up considerable resistance to imperialist occupation, but they were eventually subdued by the newly invented machine-guns of Richard Gatling and Hiram Maxim.

The Times advised the leader of the first British expedition against the Ashanti state (inland from the 'Gold Coast') in 1874 on the most suitable conditions for using the new weapons:

> *If by any chance Sir Garret Wolseley manages to catch a good mob of savages in the open, and at a moderate distance, he cannot do any better than treat them to a little Gatling music . . . Altogether we cannot wish the Ashantis worse luck than to get in the way of a Gatling well served.*[4]

'Making the Map Red', chapter four of the Ellis book, contains an illuminating survey of how the new-fangled machine-gun helped the European powers abolish the curse of slavery in Africa.[5]

Western intervention into the African heartland had the effect of ending the isolation of rural Africa. Yet many of the more isolated villages remained peripheral to the capital accumulation process even up to the time of independence in the 1960s. However, in those regions disturbed by the white invasion, measures had to be taken to ensure that, as far as possible, the rural masses were lulled back to sleep. It was to ensure this object – together with the secondary object of achieving 'cheap government' – that the colonial victors set about restoring the deposed emirs and monarchs to their overturned thrones.

Lord Frederick Lugard was responsible for subduing inland Nigeria, which had been under constant pressure from the surrounding French territory. He had conquered Northern Nigeria for the Crown by 1903, and put down the Satiru revolt in Sokoto in March 1906. Lugard began to call for a policy of 'rule through the chiefs' shortly after Satiru. In 1893, in his 'The Rise of our East African Empire', he had written in reference to his previous post in Uganda: 'The object to be aimed at in the administration of this country is to rule through its own executive government . . . the [British] Resident should rule through and by the chiefs.'[6] 'Rule through the chiefs' was not a particularly original idea and Lugard's proposal was quickly adopted by Whitehall.[7] According to the editor of the *Cambridge History of Africa*, the urgency was inspired by fear of the African 'educated native':

Both in London and Africa officials were keen to strengthen the powers of chiefs as a way of restricting the influence of educated Africans. Official nervousness, indeed, was such that in 1913 Lugard, in Nigeria, was allowed to discourage schools from teaching the Stuart period of English history, since this might foster 'disrespect for authority'. African rulers by divine right were judiciously cultivated.[8]

The fear was that the 'educated native' would adopt the nationalist ideas advocated by the Indian National Congress (founded 1885). The Abyssinian (present-day Ethiopia) crushing of the Italian army at Adowa in 1896 as well as the Japanese defeat of the Russians in 1905 also did their bit to concentrate the imperial mind on the prospect of rising African nationalist resistance to colonialism. As a result, there was an explosion of European interest in African ethnography. Between 1905 and 1914, 80 books recounting tribal histories were published in Europe, mostly written by administrators serving in the field.[9]

Indirect Rule

The British introduced indirect rule into Africa at a seemingly leisurely pace. From the decision to initiate indirect rule to its implementation there was much hesitation and procrastination. Before the First World War, indirect rule was almost totally confined to the West African colonies. According to Lugard, the first step in implementing indirect rule was to 'induce those who acknowledge no other authority than the head of the family to recognise a common chief'.[10] Groups of these acephalus communities could then be brought under the control of a single administrative unit: the Native Authority. The British district officer would then educate those chiefs who made up the Native Authority 'in adapting the new conditions to the old', while 'avoiding everything that has a tendency to denationalization [ie, Westernisation]'.[11] As the Native Authority showed itself capable of conducting its own affairs, then 'direct rule, which at first is temporarily unavoidable among the most backward of all, will decrease and the community will acquire a legal status'.[12] At this point taxation is introduced. Elsewhere, Lugard makes clear that this tax is 'the basis of the whole system, since it supplies the means to pay the Emir [or chief] and all his officials'.[13] As a result, chiefs of communities, who before the British arrived did not recognize any authority, began receiving up to half of this tax as their 'salary'. According to West African scholar Margery Perham, indirect rule is merely:

> a kind of inversion of the constitutional trick we have learned in England; the autocratic Emir retains nearly all his powers in theory while in practice, behind the curtain, he is checked and propelled, not by a ministry, still less by a democracy, but by an unobtrusive, kindly, middle-aged Englishman who derives his authority from the military power and wealth of Great Britain.[14]

But there was more to indirect rule than a 'constitutional trick', however inverted. To sustain it required systematic state intervention by the colonial authorities to preserve the social relations that had propped up the *ancien régime*, principally the indigenous systems of land tenure.

From 1908 to 1912, the mandarins of the Colonial Office were much exercised by the problem of land tenure in northern Nigeria. How could market relations – specifically, the right to sell your own land – be introduced when the legitimacy of the Native Authorities rested upon communal land? They eventually agreed to introduce a completely new principle: 'that in countries acquired by conquest or cession, private property, whether of individuals or communities, existing at the time of the cession or conquest, is respected'.[15] This new concept of 'community private property' formally preserved the traditional form of communal land tenure while introducing the concept of land as private property.

Lugard himself acted to obscure further the real relationship. His experiences of indirect rule were codified in his book *The Dual Mandate in British Tropical Africa* (1922). In it, he argued that 'The restriction on alienation matters little, I think, to the African cultivator, provided he enjoys fixity of tenure in perpetuity. This indeed is "ownership" in the native sense of the term'.[16] Accordingly, the African peasant was verbally transformed into an individual proprietor, and the awkward fact that he could not sell what he supposedly 'owned' was placed on one side. Lugard was quick to draw out the political rationale for this so-called 'African' form of ownership: 'Individual proprietorship . . . makes for individual progress, thrift, and character. It is the strongest inducement to good farming, and politically an asset to the Government, to which the peasant owes the security of his holding.'[17]

To preserve this set-up, Lugard argued that it must be protected from capitalist social relations (always encapsulated in the form of the dreaded educated 'native' from the coast, never in the sterling British entrepreneur).[18] Since the end of slavery, the coastal areas had become completely submerged under world capital relations. As a result, this 'élite' of so-called educated natives on the coast developed on the basis of market relations that emerged outside the immediate control of the colonial powers. As a thoroughgoing capitalist and land speculator, the coastal 'native' could be portrayed as a 'stranger' likely to prey upon the unsuspecting peoples of the interior. Lugard to the rescue of the underdog!:

> *In this case it is the native authority, and not the stranger, who requires protection – and, indeed, in some cases the community has been disintegrated by the acquisition of land by such 'strangers'. The new rule recites that by native law no stranger can acquire an interest in tribal land except by consent of the native authority, nor can he permanently deprive the community of the use of the land.*[19]

This system was so successful in preserving the authority of the northern Nigerian emirs that they gratefully proved their loyalty time and again to the British colonialists. They backed Britain to the hilt during the First World War and helped put down 'Madhis' – religious fundamentalists who raised revolts to try to throw out the British. There was good reason why they proved so subservient. According to Perham, by 1932 the Kano emir and his staff 'were terrified of the administration and their one idea was to do everything they were told lest they should lose their jobs'.[20] This system of land tenure that Britain introduced before the First World War was later incorporated into the constitutions of independent Nigeria.

Once the Muslim emirates of inland Nigeria had been domesticated, it was the turn of the 'liberated' acephalous communities to benefit from the fruits of European civilization. District officer Charles Arden-Clarke frankly described how he carried out in practice the necessary preliminaries among the Mama villagers in the foothills of Nigeria's Plateau region before they were introduced to Lugard's theory of indirect rule in 1925. He led his patrol into each village, and then:

> We settle down and smash to pieces all the compounds in the village except those of people I know to be really friendly and doing their best to help me. As far as I am concerned there is no such thing as neutrality; a man is either an active friend of the administration or he is an enemy. If an enemy, his compound is levelled to the ground and the grass roof burnt . . . It's rather a piteous sight watching a village being knocked to pieces and I wish there was some other way but unfortunately there isn't.[21]

Once the village had been pacified in this way, Arden-Clarke organized the collection of taxes – two shillings for each male per annum and one shilling for each female in a village. According to Rooney, the collection of taxes was unpopular, but 'it created an effective link between the District Officer and the village headman, who had to collect the money. Later . . . this helped to bolster up the position and authority of the headman'.[22] Taxation also obliged the villagers to appreciate the 'value' of money.

Sir Gordon Guggisberg, a Canadian engineer, was Lugard's director of public works before being appointed Governor of the Gold Coast [modern Ghana] in 1919. Conditions in that colony were less favourable to indirect rule than in Nigeria: 'The problem of Guggisberg and his successors was that, unlike Nigeria, there were few outstanding chiefs and they therefore had, in a fashion, to be invented.'[23] Lugard mentions a certain Captain Armitage, who said in reference to the northern territories of the Gold Coast:

> The powers of the chiefs had largely lapsed, and it was the custom to put, one might almost say, the village idiot on the stool [throne]. Our policy has been to re-establish the powers of several big chiefs, and it has been a remarkable success.[24]

The colonial powers could not hope to accomplish the efficient operation of capitalist exploitation without the co-operation of the chiefs, who therefore had to be 'bought'. Hence, through such measures as the subtraction of 'rebates' from hut taxes that the chiefs collected, rural class differentiation proceeded apace alongside the colonial invention of tribes. For example, Sierra Leone's chiefs used their traditional positions to enrich themselves

> both by marketing their share of agricultural produce secured as tribute and by selling the produce they obtained from diverting customary labour contributions into cash-crop production . . . In 1937 chiefs supposedly relinquished these rights in return for regular salaries but in practice they continued to exploit this source of wealth for some time longer. They also manipulated their crucial position as custodians of the system of communal land tenure . . . Some chiefs expanded their own holdings and turned such land over to cash-crop production. Later on, in the 1930s, when gold and diamond mining became one of the mainstays of the economy, along with export agriculture, the chiefs were able to claim rents or royalties from mining companies in return for land concessions.[25]

In return for the privilege of occupying their newly lucrative positions, the domesticated traditional rulers were expected to provide 'voluntary' recruits for work in plantations and mines, and later on, the army.

After the First World War the indirect rule system began to spread over to Britain's East African colonies. In 1920, colonial secretary Lord Milner confirmed in a dispatch on the use of 'native' labour to the Governor of East Africa that 'the principle of working through the native chiefs is right'.[26] In April 1925, a memo written by Sir Donald Cameron, the Governor of Tanganyika (present-day Tanzania), is worth quoting at length as an illustration of the application of indirect rule to East Africa, where, once again, the 'educated native' stands as a metaphor for the threat posed by African nationalism:

> If we set up merely a European form of administration, the day will come when the people of the Territory will demand that the British form of administration shall pass into their hands – we have India at our doors as an object lesson. If we aim at indirect administration through the appropriate Native Authority – Chief or Council – founded on the people's own traditions and preserving their own tribal organisation, their own laws and customs purged of anything that is 'repugnant to justice and morality' we shall be building an

edifice with some foundation to it, capable of standing the shock
which will inevitably come when the educated native seeks to
gain possession of the machinery of Government and to run it on
Western lines.[27]

In Tanganyika, Cameron's task had been made more difficult by
the fact that the colony had been controlled by German imperialism
between 1890 and 1915. The British were at a total loss over who
merited entitlement to chieftaincy, an issue critical to the successful
implementation of indirect rule policy. Hence, Cameron was first
obliged 'to find out what their system was'. In the event, as Iliffe
points out, 'Much effort was devoted to "finding the chief" by
recording the genealogies which African contestants invented'.[28]
One district officer explained what had happened. He wrote that
while Africans had enthusiastically participated in this quest for the
descendants of the former chiefs, those they had found turned out
to be 'the imbecile, the leper, the syphilitic, ex-convicts, ex-rickshaw
boys, ex-domestic servants and so on. Any one in fact who was
incapable or unlikely to exercise authority'.[29] To operate their indirect
system in East Africa, the British were obliged time and again to
intervene and invent their own candidates for chieftaincy.

The eventual successful establishment of indirect rule in East Africa
provoked the wry comment from Cameron in 1928 that 'Paradoxical
as it may seem, although indirect has replaced direct administration,
there is a great deal more administration than there was before'.[30]
Cameron noted that the remotest African peasant was now linked
into a chain of command that reached up into his own office. Jan
Jorgensen has demonstrated the extraordinary lengths that the colonial
authorities went to in Uganda (apart from Buganda) in order to
obtain a suitable ethnic framework:

> *In much of Uganda, the colonial state created* ex nihilo *[from*
> *nothing] 'traditional' chiefs to administer territorial units that were*
> *often equally artificial . . . First the traditional chief would be*
> *recognised as a chief within the terms of the Native Authority*
> *Ordinance of 1919, which defined the duties and powers of chiefs*
> *and confirmed the colonial state's authority to appoint, transfer and*
> *dismiss chiefs and to regulate their conditions of service. Second,*
> *the traditional chief would be retired and replaced by a mission-*

*trained son or relative chosen by the colonial state. Third, the new
chief would be transferred to a post other than the traditional one.
Fourth, having separated the chief from his traditional political base,
the original post would be made appointive rather than hereditary.*[31]

The position in Kenya was complicated by the presence of
substantial numbers of white settlers as well as Indians (and Arabs
on the coast). Even so, in 1923 the Duke of Devonshire, the colonial
secretary, issued a White Paper asserting 'Native Paramountcy' in
order to undermine the white settlers' campaign for self-government
along South Africa lines:

> *Primarily Kenya is an African territory, and His Majesty's
> Government think it necessary to definitely record their considered
> opinion that the interests of the African Natives must be paramount,
> and that if and when those interests and the interests of the immigrant
> races should conflict, the former should prevail.*[32]

The White Paper continued by spelling out Britain's role:

> *In the administration of Kenya His Majesty's Government regard
> themselves as exercising a trust on behalf of the African population,
> and they are unable to delegate or share this trust, the object of which
> may be defined as the protection and advancement of the Native
> races.*

Besides preserving a role for Britain in Kenya – as Defender of the
downtrodden Natives – protecting African interests also meant the
further promotion of tribal traditions in Kenya (in other words,
protecting Africans from the nationalist virus).

In the Sudan, the source of this nationalist virus was generally
seen as being Egypt rather than India. As far back as 1918, the
Governor of the Sudan, Sir Reginald Wingate, had called for the
societies of the southern region to be investigated so as to improve
colonial administration there:

> *I refer of course chiefly to those parts of the country untouched by
> Islamic culture – the superstitions and the folk lore of primitive
> tribesmen which are subjects of the deepest interest in themselves and,
> apart from their anthropological and ethnological values, of importance*

as contributing to that sympathetic comprehension of the people and their mentality which is so essential to a successful administration.[33]

After the 1919 Wafd revolt in Cairo, British officials based in Khartoum worked overtime to counter the influence of Arab nationalism seeping down the Nile to threaten Britain's prosperous East African colonies.

In 1924, Sir George Schuster, the Sudan government's Financial Secretary, wrote a paper arguing that the black southern region of the Sudan should be turned into a 'buffer state' to prevent Arabic influence growing there, and also 'insure that the influence brought to bear on the African tribes in the southern part of the Sudan are harmonious with British influences spreading up from Kenya and Uganda'.[34] Four years later, Sudan's Civil Secretary Sir Harold MacMichael warned of the dangers of Arabs sympathizing with the plight of black Africans in the South, and called on the British authorities in Khartoum to preserve the 'negro' language and customs in the South for purely self-interested reasons:

> *In time we shall reap our own advantage, for a series of self-contained racial units will be developed with structure and organisation based on the solid rock of indigenous traditions and beliefs . . . the sense of tribal pride and independence will grow, and in the process a solid barrier will be created against the insidious political intrigue which must in the ordinary course of events increasingly beset our path in the North.*[35]

But before people like the Nuer were allowed to develop their 'sense of tribal pride' however, they had to made more docile by RAF bombing. The Nuer's magicians were identified as the source of resistance and the RAF successfully argued their planes should be used rather than foot soldiers, since 'no magic survives a good bombing'. The Nuer and other recalcitrant peoples in the South consequently had to endure three years of bombing until the 'air policy' was terminated in March 1929.[36] On 25 January 1930, MacMichael officially promulgated the 'Southern Policy' and the use of the Arabic language was all but banned in the southern provinces of Sudan. Khartoum then sought to employ anthropologists of the calibre of Professor Evans-Pritchard to research into the culture of southern peoples like the Azande and the Nuer. In his 'Sudan notes and records' written between 1933 and 1935, Evans-Pritchard confirmed that the Nuer system of kinship was in decline thanks to 'frequent feuding' and generations of war (and the attentions of the RAF?). Definite lines of descent were giving way to more territorially-based political relationships.[37] Such researches justified the British policy of fostering tribal leaderships to cohere the acephalous southerners.

French Native Policy in Africa

The British had no problem in framing the image that their African indirect rulers should take: the British monarchy. All over Africa, they set up their chiefs as little kings and queens to reign over their towns and villages. For the republican French, however, African monarchies were not an option. Any African élite had to dress according to a Parisian image of an élite. The French set out to crush the 'aristocratic' chiefs that had sprung up as result of slaving or ivory-trading. As Lugard's thoughts were turning to indirect rule in Nigeria, the French Governor-General of French West Africa, William Ponty, implemented an ambitious programme to abolish the chiefs. Raising up the spirit of 1789, he advocated the need to 'fight the influence of the local aristocracies in such a manner as to assure us of the sympathy of the multitudes, suppress the great native chiefs who are nearly always a barrier between us and the administered masses'.[38] In France, according to William Cohen,

> Local rule, was considered a centrifugal force threatening the unity of the nation. In its history, the French people found ample evidence to show that local rights were upheld by feudal and regressive forces, whereas progressive forces were represented by central authority.[39]

Under French rule, former African kingdoms like that in Fouta Djallon (Guinea) were carved up into several cantons, the ruling house was destooled, and amenable chiefs were installed as direct agents of the French. The 'French' chiefs were seen as lowly instruments of Paris, not as authorities in their own right – as the British painted them. Governor-General J. van Vollenhoven was opposed to the British policy of establishing native authorities: 'There are not two authorities in the *cercle*, the French authority and the native authority. There is only one; the *Commandant de Cercle* commands, only he is responsible. The native chief is only an instrument, an auxiliary.'[40]

Van Vollenhoven spelt out the French idea of whom should comprise the African élite – those who the British despised as 'educated natives':

> *This elite was ostracised from the native society because it no longer lived in the native manner, and could not return to it. Proud of their effort, presumptuous and sometimes unbearable in their vanity, this category represents the young, the avant garde, the example.*[41]

For van Vollenhoven, while the masses could be left to stultify under their own traditions, this élite 'must evolve more and more in our environment'.[42] These so-called *evolues* were eventually granted French citizenship and some even sat in the National Assembly in Paris.

Once this Frenchified élite began to take on board all the ideals of the French Revolution and began to press for all their people to benefit from liberty, fraternity and equality, then the French were not as capable of dealing with this nationalist challenge as well as the British, who always retained the option of playing off 'their' native authorities against 'their' pro-nationalist educated natives. From the 1930s onwards, French colonial administrators increasingly began to regard Britain's African colonies – and, in particular, their policy of indirect rule – with a mixture of envy and regret. But it was too late to do anything about it. As Governor-General Brevie put it in January 1931, 'To want to transform from one day to the next the Amewokal of Ouillmede into a perfect collaborator of our administration would be equivalent to trying instantaneously to change the Sire de Couch into a prefect of the Third Republic'.[43] As a matter of fact, however, the British were beginning to discover in the 1930s that indirect rule was encountering difficulties in trying to cope with the nationalist challenge.

The Challenge of African Nationalism

With the onset of the Great Depression in the 1930s, British officials became concerned that a system that relied upon the traditional chiefs alone for stability was becoming redundant – especially as urbanization proceeded apace. In 1931 in the important Copperbelt district in Northern Rhodesia [present-day Zambia] the copper companies established a system of courts staffed by tribal elders in the mine compounds to try to maintain tribal customs among urban workers. The courts arbitrated in minor disputes and served as an 'avenue of approach' between mine management and their employees. In 1935 the consensus collapsed and serious rioting broke out in the important Copperbelt in Northern Rhodesia. According to J. Clyde Mitchell, the strikers rejected the tribal elders as their leaders: 'During the disturbances on the Copperbelt in 1935, we learn, the mine policemen, tribal elders, and some of the clerks took refuge with the European officials in the compound offices'.[44] The contemporary growth of the rural 'Watch Tower' Christian millenarian movement also prefigured the shape of things to come in the countryside. It was considerably hostile to the chiefs as well, banning them from councils and in some cases, like the Ila chiefs in 1934, deposing them altogether.[45] An offshoot of this movement spread to the Katangan mines in Belgian Congo where it was known as Kitiwala. A number of Kitiwala adherents went on to become nationalist leaders in the 1960s.[46]

Given Christianity's implacable hostility towards African religious traditions, the missions inevitably came into conflict with the colonial administration's drive to promote African tribalism.[47] Of course, the silence of the missions on racial discrimination, exploitation and the general atmosphere of colonial repression, limited their influence among Africans to a certain extent. Nevertheless Lugard banned missionaries from entering Northern Nigeria and General Kitchener also barred them from the Muslim areas in the Sudan. Lugard dutifully recorded an important reason for the proscription: 'among Christian converts any attempt to repudiate the authority of the chiefs [is] prohibited'.[48] For Lugard at least, there was nothing incompatible between Western Christianity and African tribalism.

Anthropologists Turned Apologists

The publication of *The Dual Mandate* in 1922 sparked off something of a debate over the usefulness of indirect rule to colonialism. In 1924 J. F. J. Fitzpatrick condemned the institution for propping up corrupt emirs in Northern Nigeria. On the other hand, according to one colonial officer touring Nigeria in 1926, '"Self-Government" in Nigeria, if it ever comes, will be the self-government of the country by the Native Authorities and not by any elected Council in Lagos!'.[49] More cautiously, the anthropologist Bronislaw Malinowski was concerned that the impact of the West on African societies was primarily negative. In 1929, he concluded that indirect rule was the best way to mitigate the effects of the 'culture clash':

> The real difference . . . consists in the fact that direct rule assumes that you can create at one go an entirely new order, that you can transform Africans into semi-civilised pseudo-Europeans within a few years. Indirect rule on the other hand recognises that no such magical rapid transformation can take place, that in reality all social development is very slow and that it is infinitely more preferable to achieve it by slow and gradual change coming from within.[50]

Though many anthropologists ended up working for the colonial administration in Africa, there are few clearer instances of them bending their science into an apology for imperialism.

Anthropologists like Malinowski viewed Western products like radios, aeroplanes and medical science as potentially dangerous for African societies since they undermined the authority of traditional institutions.[51] However, in recognizing that it was impossible to return to the past, they instead sought to foster what they called 'acculturation', the easing of the adjustment process to ensure that the best features of Western 'civilization' were disseminated without disrupting local social organization unduly.

In 1934, both Sir Donald Cameron and Margery Perham joined Malinowski in his defence of indirect rule. A former district officer, W. R. Crocker, fought back. He was joined by Lord Hailey, who pronounced that indirect rule 'had passed through three stages, first of a useful administrative device, then that of a political doctrine, and finally that of a religious dogma'.[52]

After a conference with his senior officials in October 1939, Malcolm MacDonald, the then colonial secretary, articulated his reservations that Britain may 'end in difficulties' if indirect rule proved unable to cope with the growing problem of the educated, or 'detribalised', natives:

I am anxious that we should pursue a slowly but surely developing policy of training the Africans to look after their own affairs. This policy is being followed amongst tribal natives according to the principles of Indirect Rule, and we have reached a stage in which Native Authorities in various territories do control much of what in this country would be called local government. The question now arises, what next in those territories? Moreover, the problem is complicated by the existence in some colonies of large numbers of detribalised natives, living in towns or other centres of European influence. They are often represented on Legislative Councils. So the two different machines for native government exist side by side: and we are likely to end in difficulties unless we can think out very carefully how they are to be co-ordinated in future developments.[53]

For 'large numbers of detribalised natives, living in towns' read the 'working class'. Here the usual scapegoat for Britain's problems in Africa, the nationalist 'educated native' who sat on the Legislative councils, is replaced by the emerging African working class.[54] This injection by the masses into politics gave an added urgency to plans for a political settlement with the 'educated natives'. But the real crisis was the dire economic straits in which Britain found itself during the Depression. Britain needed to intensify the exploitation of its colonies, but was concerned that the Native Authorities would not be able to hold the line alone in maintaining stability, particularly as the African working class was beginning to make its presence felt. Far from dispensing with the 'educated native' and his nationalist creed, the new direction instigated by MacDonald was to take him on board.

The truth seems to be that the world economic depression of the early 1930s was in large measure responsible for converting the official classes from a development policy which showed confidence in Britain's trading position – the 'dual mandate' of Lord Lugard – to one which combined a protectionist outlook with the doctrine that economic development should precede the granting of self-government.[55]

The symbolic acceptance by Lord Lugard of Lord Hailey as the chief researcher of the African Survey project of the late 1930s signalled the change in official policy. Hailey had plenty of experience as an administrator in the Punjab, and he was well known for his pro-'educated native' views. Around that time, Lugard also abandoned his project to bring out a second edition of *The Dual Mandate*.[56] The Colonial Office did not find a solution to the problem of how to coordinate MacDonald's 'two different machines' – that is, the two different African élites – until after the Second World War. Nevertheless, this commencement of a search for an alternative to 'indirect' rule was tantamount to admitting that the colonial policy of 'directly' confronting nationalism with the tribal alternative had failed. It would be some time before the colonialists could develop – much less implement – a coherent new strategy. This aimed to undermine the nationalist threat indirectly, that is, by converting nationalism into tribalism.

Decolonization of a Kind

Contrary to popular sentiment, Britain required its African empire more, not less, during and after the Second World War. It was really only with its entry into the European Economic Community (EEC) in the mid-1970s that Britain entirely released its grip over its former African colonies.

The Second World War ruined Africa's traditional colonial powers, France and Britain. Britain's gold and dollar reserves did not match its dollar deficit with America. The need to acquire dollars became paramount for London and it looked to the empire to provide them. As a consequence, the empire seemed to be more dynamic than decadent Britain:

> The late 1940s and early 1950s were the heyday of the African empire, when it seemed to have a coherence and dynamic of its own. This coherence and dynamic was merely the reflection of the passing utility which Africa appeared to have for western Europe in its struggle for post-war economic survival; by the mid-1950s the appearance had faded . . .[57]

When the war ended, wartime controls on sterling were strengthened not loosened and, in May 1947, a policy of dollar discrimination was introduced which *departed substantially from the requirements of the post-war US-dominated economic order, the Bretton Woods system . . . The core of the dollar discrimination policy was the establishment of the dollar pool. The colonies were encouraged to earn hard currency to make up for the large dollar deficit of the sterling area. Britain and the independent members [the Dominions and non-empire sterling members] were the heaviest dollar users. Africa supplied about half of some twenty products imported by America: cocoa, coffee, tea, iron ore, non-ferrous metals, diamonds, wood, rubber, hides and skins. In addition Africa exported significant quantities of manganese ore, chrome ore, asbestos, beryllium, columbium, sisal, pyrethrum and whattle extract.*[58]

Between 1948 and 1957, only the African colonies, and Malaya and Ceylon [present-day Sri Lanka] out of the entire empire showed a positive balance of trade with the USA. The UK had a massive deficit throughout. As a result, colonial Africa accummulated large amounts of sterling reserves. But British intentions for Africa initially went far beyond merely paying off their war debts. In March 1948, British foreign secretary Ernest Bevin explicitly sought to use the mineral wealth of the African colonies as one part of a three-prong plan to restore Britain's former position in the world – by organizing 'the middle of the planet – W. Europe, the Middle East, the Commonwealth'. True to his reputation for arrogance, Bevin held that if Britain 'only pushed on and developed Africa, we could have US dependent on us and eating out of our hand in four or five years . . . US is very barren of essential minerals and in Africa we have them all'.[59]

Kent points out that Bevin accepted the defeat of his ambitious project in 1949 (and therefore turned to the NATO [North Atlantic Treaty Organization] idea) because the Americans refused to back London's plans to restore their Middle Eastern empire; Western Europe rejected British plans to become a Third World force and Britain by itself lacked the means to embark on major development plans in Africa. Even so, Africa remained central to Britain's plans for post-war recovery.

Throughout the period of political decolonization in the 1950s, there was next to no 'monetary decolonization' for the former colonies – even after sterling convertibility into dollars was restored in 1958. In the following year, Harold Macmillan became 'ruthlessly determined to shed the colonial albatross' once the application to join the EEC was made.[60] When de Gaulle blocked this option, the sterling bloc had to be stretched to last even longer. It began to break up with Harold Wilson's devaluation of sterling in November 1967, but did not finally die until 1974 – the eve of Britain's full integration into the EEC. It is impossible to understand Britain's post-war decolonization strategy in Africa up to the 1970s without bearing this imperial dependence upon Africa in mind.

Making Africa Pay

Towards the end of 1947, Britain's Labour chancellor of the exchequer, Sir Stafford Cripps, informed the governors of the African colonies that

> the whole future of the sterling group and its ability to survive in my view depends on a quick and extensive development of its African resources . . . We should increase out of all recognition the tempo of African economic development. We must be prepared to change our outlook and our habits of colonial development and force the pace so that within the next two to five years we can get a really marked increase in production in coals, minerals, timber, raw materials of all kinds and foodstuffs and anything else that will save dollars or sell in a dollar market.[61]

Charged with supervising this imperial expansion, the Colonial Office was inflated in size. From a staff of 400 in 1938, it grew to over 1160 by 1947. Specialist departments increased in number from five to over twenty during the same period. Britain's need to step up the exploitation of Africa depended upon the colonial office's dexterity in reshaping its relations with the two African élites.

This need to expand their stake in Africa had posed a number of awkward problems for the colonial powers. The new dominant world power, American imperialism, wanted to remove all barriers to free trade and capital flows and this was viewed as a threat to their colonial interests by the Europeans. However, with the Marshall Plan of June 1947, a *modus vivendi* was reached with Washington where the European powers continued to exploit their African colonies as America's gendarmes in return for a commitment towards eventual decolonization. From then on, Washington limited its pressure on the European powers to decolonize to the forum of the United Nations (which it controlled via its grip on the Latin American member states).

How to get the African élites to accept the intensification of Western exploitation became the central question of colonial policy in Africa in the immediate post-war period. The problem that confronted the colonial office in intensifying the exploitation of Africa was that the whole political structure that they had installed in the inter-war period – indirect rule – was designed to extract the maximum amount of surplus value at the minimum expense in terms of administrative and military resources. On the other hand, they also had to bear in mind the burgeoning African nationalist movement that sought inspiration from such events as the British surrender of Singapore to the Japanese army in February 1942.

Given the economic plight Britain found itself in as a result of the Second World War, it became necessary to expand the extraction of surplus value throughout the African countryside by drawing in as many smallholders as possible and converting them into labourers for capital. Indirect rule, based as it was on lulling the masses to sleep, was inadequate to remould a new, more dynamic relationship between imperialism and the African people.

It is a common misconception that political independence for Africa became inevitable after the Second World War. It is true that the European powers were being pressed in this direction by American imperialism during the war. But they themselves preferred the more ambiguous term 'self-government', which merely implied autonomy under the Crown. The decisive factor that swayed the balance was the eruption of African nationalism as a major force on the political scene in the dying days of the Second World War. Despite strenuous efforts, the indirect rulers proved incapable of stopping urban nationalist intellectuals from stirring up the rural masses with their agitation for 'freedom from the whites'. If the modern élite had succeeded in attracting the support of the rural masses for this programme, imperialism's days would be numbered in Africa and all London's plans to use the colonies to support its own sickly economy would be dashed.

After much prevarication, the Colonial Office sought to utilize the ambitions of this class as a vanguard to open up the African interior by offering them the prospect of an unopposed route to independence. At the same time, a substantial political price would be extracted from them for this concession: the status of the traditional rulers was to be guaranteed in the constitutions of the new independent state. Through a series of piecemeal constitutional concessions, the colonialists hoped to make tribalism more palatable to the nationalists. In this way, they hoped to disintegrate nationalism while at the same time granting its objective of political independence.

With its modern élite already well-developed before the war, the decolonization of the Gold Coast is a good example by which to study this strategy.

The Ghana Case

After the British had forced the Ashante state into submission at the turn of the century, they encouraged the growing of the cocoa tree imported from Latin America. The elders treated cocoa separately from their traditional subsistence crops and charged a rent on the land it occupied which they disguised as 'tribute':

> Access to land for cocoa-planting was obtained within existing legal forms that had not previously been used for commercial agriculture. Subjects of each stool [throne] exercised their right (hitherto applied to primarily-substance food farming) to plant its land. The chiefs extended to cocoa beans the principle, previously used only of natural products such as gold and wild kola, that the stool should receive a share of the proceeds, usually amounting to a third . . . this so-called 'cocoa tribute' was 'actually a form of rent'.[62]

The Wall Street crash of October 1929 and the world slump that followed dramatically hit primary product prices, which 'led to more extensive and ambitious schemes for controlling commodity production, and the beginning of a more or less systematic development of marketing regulation aimed at securing high prices and stable demand'.[63]

During the 1930s, Ghana became the world's biggest producer of cocoa and the Ashante chiefs prospered:

Rich farmers practised money-lending as a means of investment; debts were often paid off in cocoa crops or in usufruct of the debtor's land, enabling the rich farmer to increase his own saleable product. The rich farmer was often a farmer-cum-chief, or even a farmer-cum-chief-cum-broker. His object might be to control as much cocoa as possible in order to sell it to the Europeans . . .

The cocoa broker with his advance, and the rich farmers [sic] with his loans, were figures of no little power in the rural Ghanaian community. By lending money to poor peasants in return for a pledge on their crops, they could keep them in perpetual debt. Rural society began to differentiate between a petty bourgeoisie and ordinary peasants, both groups tied into the system of cash-crop production for the external market but the former successful both in production of its own crop and in the expropriation of the crop from others, while the latter often succumbed to debt and poverty.[64]

Between October 1937 and April 1938, all Ghana's cocoa farmers and urban 'brokers' united to oppose a price-fixing ring operated by the British processors like Cadburys and Rowntrees. They organized a 'hold-up' or ban on cocoa sales, plus boycotts of Western products, to defeat the British price ring.

When the Second World War broke out, chocolate (and cocoa) ceased being a luxury product. It became a strategically important commodity to the British who needed it to purchase American weaponry. In a new version of the Triangle Trade, British convoys sailed from America carrying munitions, off-loaded them in Britain, set out for the Gold Coast to pick up a cargo of cocoa beans, and then crossed the Atlantic again.[65]

After the war, the British were anxious to continue this money-making system. Ivor Thomas, the Parliamentary Under-Secretary of State for the Colonies argued, in a memorandum for the Labour cabinet, that: 'we should try to re-establish, and indeed improve upon, the pre-war position in which exports of primary produce from the Colonies to America were among our principal earners of dollars'.[66] Malayan rubber was the most important dollar-earner, but West African cocoa came a close second. The colonial office in London was confident that the war years demonstrated that a cocoa marketing board could 'achieve a stabilization of fluctuations in supply and demand'. The official functions of the new Cocoa Marketing Board set up in 1947 were: '1) to fix the seasonal prices payable to producers; 2) to determine purchase arrangements and issue licences to buyers [the cocoa processors]; 3) to set up and maintain the necessary executive machinery for purchasing, shipping and selling all purchased cocoa.'[67]

The cocoa farmers of Ghana were led to believe that, in high price years, they would be paid less than the world price of cocoa, and the difference would be placed in a reserve fund. In this way they could be compensated out of this fund in low price years, and so the price for their cocoa would be 'guaranteed'. In reality, the Board made a handsome profit every year from the 1940s to the 1960s and, instead of the reserves being made available to invest in the Ghanaian economy, they were held in London and used to help prop up the British economy. In 1953, cocoa exports earned Ghana £25 million, but only 21 per cent of this was sent back to Ghana. The following year, cocoa earned Ghana £20 million, but only 16 per cent was returned. According to Basil Davidson, 'Ghana was in fact helping to finance Britain's banking system'.[68]

As far back as the pre-war cocoa 'hold-up' the British had been working overtime to protect their stake in this vital commodity. At that time, the cocoa processors and the British press had blamed the hold-up on 'abuses, such as undue advances to native brokers'.[69] The urbanized African brokers mediated between the processors and the cocoa farmers, to whom they advanced credit with the crop as collateral. As 'middlemen', they served as convenient scapegoats for the British.

Worried at this indication of embryonic unity between urban and rural élites, the pre-war Colonial Secretary Malcolm MacDonald had sent Lord Hailey off to survey Britain's African colonies and make an assessment of the indirect rule policy. Hailey reported back in his 'Native Administration and Political Development in Tropical Africa' during the height of the war. He concluded that the dynamism of the modern African élite should be channelled through the institutions of the Native Authorities. This would 'invigorate' those bodies and at the same time guard against the new élite setting themselves up in opposition to them. Hailey argued that elections would serve to strengthen the Native Authorities by giving them a new source of legitimacy that would not have to rely upon either African traditions or the British.

The colonial governors, on the other hand, bitterly resisted Hailey's conclusions and fought a rearguard action to uphold the old system of indirect rule that relied solely on the chiefs. Governors like Sir Alan Burns of the Gold Coast argued that – rather than democratize the Native Authorities – stability could be best ensured if indirect rule was extended in scope by appointing two or three Africans, including a paramount chief, on to his advisory Executive Council. He wrote on 8 July 1942:

> *I assure you that I am not an alarmist, but each day I get fresh evidence of the increasing feeling of Africans against Europeans, and against the Government which the Europeans represent . . . It would be disastrous for the future, and dangerous in existing circumstances, if we lose the goodwill of the Africans which did exist and probably still does to some extent, by failing to make a gesture which I am convinced would have an immediate effect on public opinion.*[70]

The debate over the best way to manipulate the African élites to suit Britain's interests was rapidly overtaken by events, however. The price of the war was threatening the continued existence of the empire itself. Coming under intense pressure from Washington and its 1941 Atlantic Charter (which endorsed the principle of the right of 'all peoples' to choose the form of government under which they will live); then the fall of Singapore in February 1942 and the Indian Congress's 'Quit India' campaign that same summer; the imperial question acquired a new urgency in the corridors of Whitehall. In relation to a colonial office discussion in May 1943 over how to deal with a US-inspired declaration on the colonial territories, one official – Christopher Eastwood – suggested they do the 'decent thing' and tell the truth:

> *It seems to me utterly wrong to set independence as the general goal for the greater number of the colonies and even if we have said something of this sort in the past (which I do not think we have) it would be a great mistake to say it again.*
>
> *I do not think the phrase 'self-government' is really much better. I suppose it does leave a loop-hole for argueing that what we really*

*mean is only local self-government, but that would not be a very
honest interpretation of the phrase.*[71]

Two months later, Oliver Stanley, the new Colonial Secretary,
pledged to the commons that the government would 'guide the
colonial peoples along the road to self-government within the
framework of the British empire'. According to Pearce, Stanley used
the phrase self-government: 'for precisely the reasons stigmatised by
Eastwood as not very honest. The Secretary of State thought only
the larger colonies could ever reach Dominion Status, and as a loop-
hole was using the ambiguity of the term'.[72] British strategy, then,
depended upon hiding behind diplomatic phrases so as to buy time.
For Stanley self-government did not mean independence. It did not
even mean home rule (political autonomy within the empire).
Instead, the programme of extending local 'indirect rule' system was
to be intensified.

The Colonial Office had bowed to Burns and the other governors,
and by 1944 there was an unofficial majority of African chiefs on
the Gold Coast's advisory Legislative Council. Burns' 1946
constitution ratified the role of the chiefs, and excluded the so-called
'young men' who represented the modern élite in Ghana. This layer
of the African élite were subjected to intensified harassment by the
colonial governors as the war drew to a close.

The Labour government that swept to power in 1945 had little
impact in Africa at first. Indeed the pigeon-holed Colonial Office
option to democratize the Native Authorities was a more
'progressive' position than that taken by the new Labour ministry.
For example, when Labour's Colonial Secretary George Hall stated
in June 1946 that 'they [the colonies] shall go as fast as they show
themselves capable of going', he was welcomed with applause by
the Opposition benches as voicing 'Tory colonial policy'.[73] A few
months later, Hall was replaced by his junior minister, Arthur
Creech Jones.

Creech Jones had been a national secretary of the TGWU, and
therefore a former colleague of the transport union's leader Ernest
Bevin. There the connection ceased, however. Creech Jones
followed the radical Liberal tradition in Labour's foreign policy and
had been inspired by the radical anti-imperialist Liberal E. D. Morel

in his youth. Before the war, Creech Jones was given to making speeches condemning the 'feudal' system of indirect rule in Africa. When the Webbs' Fabian Society set up a 'Colonial Bureau' in 1940, Creech Jones became its chair. As such, he introduced a collection of essays published by the bureau in early 1945, where he argued that socialists could not renounce responsibility towards the colonies 'because of some sentimental inclination to "liberation" or international administration'.[74] Creech Jones favoured adopting a more positive approach towards the colonies.

In the Fabian Colonial Bureau, Creech Jones had become influenced by fellow Fabian Leonard Woolf's criticism of Lugard's 'indirect rule' policy, who argued in his essay 'The Political Advance of Backward Peoples' that it was a misguided attempt to 'mummify' African society:

> *In its extreme form it leads to an effort on the part of the administrator to preserve each native or tribal unit . . . intact like a museum piece, insulated as far as possible from any of the disturbing and disintegrating influences of western or European civilization.*[75]

Before entering the 'Bloomsbury Set' through his famous marriage to novelist Virginia, Leonard Woolf had been a district officer in Ceylon [now Sri Lanka] in the early 1900s and was secretary of the Labour Party Imperial Advisory Committee. His contribution to the Fabian essays on the colonial question did not advocate abolition of indirect rule, however. In 'Political Advance . . .' Woolf refers to Lord Hailey's work and develops his concept of 'democratized' Native Authorities. Woolf's insight was that indirect rule could be used not just to legitimate the *status quo*, but also as a school for training 'a sufficient number of educated Africans to make self-government possible'. In other words, for inculcating in them tribal values – in the guise of the English municipal socialism that radicals like Woolf held dear to their hearts:

> *The system of indirect rule can be used as a highly efficient instrument for training Africans in self-government, but only on one condition. It is not enough to use, develop, or create tribal or native institutions and authorities and then hand over to them power or the simulacrum of power. A native authority which in fact consists of an autocratic*

> *tribal chief or emir, discreetly impelled by a District Officer to establish a police force and drains, is not an emblem of democratic self-government. There is everything to be said for developing and creating native authorities as the organs of local government, but if they are to be instruments of training Africans in the art of self-government, they must be fundamentally democratic in the western sense. That means that the organs of indirect rule, the native 'Authorities', must themselves be directly responsible to the native peoples; they must be democratized.*[76]

Accordingly, Creech Jones sent a letter to the Colonial Office in April 1945 in which he suggested that the old 'feudal' system of indirect rule should be abandoned in favour of training the educated African nationalist élite in local government procedures:

> *an increasing place for the educated and able men and women in government and administration and an adaptability which eliminates the feudal character of indirect rule and finds representative people (by democratic machinery) instead of hand picked chiefs and others who conform to 'official' needs.*[77]

Creech Jones was appointed Colonial Secretary in October 1946 and supervised the introduction of the new approach. As he put it a few months later in a letter to the Governor of Nyasaland [present-day Malawi]: 'In its social repercussions, the problem of increased productivity is closely connected with the development of an efficient system of African local government.'[78] In the midst of a fuel crisis that had all but paralysed Britain, Creech Jones sent a Local Government Despatch to the African governors in February 1947. In it he emphasized that the 'Native Authorities' must become 'efficient, democratic and local'.

It was by giving the 'educated natives' a stake in the Native Authorities that the British hoped to secure African compliance with their financial plans. They also hoped to alleviate pressure from the modern élite to move quicker on the national question by buying them off with local half-measures. In response to the demand for independence, the British would only acknowledge that 'self-government' might mean autonomy at some unspecified time in the future. Furthermore, the experience of working with locally minded politicians could be expected to exert an ethnic influence upon their radical nationalism.

Under Creech Jones, then, Colonial Office policy was designed to make the indirect rule system – if not the indirect rulers – more palatable to the modern élite along the lines suggested by Hailey and Woolf during the war. And, unlike Lugard's pre-war informal indirect rule arrangements, the scheme that Creech Jones planned was to be systematically introduced in all the African colonies from 1947. Moreover, the Colonial Under-Secretary responsible for Africa, Andrew Cohen, even anticipated a situation where the chiefs might disappear entirely from the African political scene – a circumstance which Lugard would have regarded with horror. At a summer school for Colonial Office staff in August 1947, Cohen argued that the chiefs may retain their political privileges in the short term:

> Taking a longer view, however, a time may come when . . . chiefs will no longer be in a position to make an effective contribution to the development of local government. It is suggested that the evolution of native administration must be conceived in the light of this possibility.[79]

Cohen obviously envisaged here at time when the educated nationalists had entirely transformed themselves into ethnic politicians. It is well known that, through Africanization, the modern élite came to be integrated into the 'modern' state structure of the colonial administration. For example, a Colonial Office committee of Britain's African policy made the point in May 1947: 'Africanisation [recruitment of Africans] was essential if the Colonial Service was to become in time the civil service of new self-governing states.'[80] But not so well known are the British efforts to 'educate' the modern élite in the rites of indirect rule.

Cohen was able to draw out the reactionary logic of Woolf's intertwining of education with 'indirect rule', while keeping the progressive gloss implanted by the Fabians' socialist imprimatur. Cohen's 1947 summer school report concluded: 'We regard it as urgent that African local Authorities should be stimulated to introduce as great a measure as possible of democratic representation into their system', only to add significantly: 'while retaining their good traditional elements'.[81] Cohen adapted Woolf's proposals so as to strengthen the influence of the most reactionary elements in African society upon the 'educated' newcomers, while ensuring that imperialism's tracks were kept covered at the same time.

Under Cohen's scheme, members of the modern élite were first to be nominated to the Native Authorities by either the British district officers or the chiefs themselves, with direct elections only being introduced later. The Native Authorities would then serve as electoral colleges for Provincial Councils, which would then elect representatives on to the national, but still only advisory, Legislative Council. While the introduction of elections, direct or otherwise, were to add legitimacy to the Native Authorities, these 'reinvigorated' bodies were then, in turn, to thwart the aspirations of the nationalists towards independence from the colonial power.

> The 1947 plan was designed to secure the collaboration of the nationalists and at the same time to slow their political progress by making representation at the centre dependent on the support of the rural, illiterate majority. The use of Provincial Councils as electoral colleges would tend to exclude the 'ballot-box' politicians.[82]

As a result, the nationalists could only achieve any progress towards power in the new system of 'democratized' Native Authorities, or 'Local Government' as they were increasingly known as, by being forced into alliances with the rural élites.

In the event, the popular uprising in Accra in February 1948 obliged the Colonial Office to abandon the attempt to implement Cohen's scheme in full (the Eastern region of Nigeria was later to be targeted for Cohen's 'local government' treatment). After February 1948, the modern African élite acquired a greater share of national power than had previously been anticipated by the Colonial Office planners. Yet the apparent 'concession' that they no longer had to construct electoral alliances with the elders to win power only signalled a change to a more aggressive posture on behalf of the British. After the fuss had blown over and much steam had been let off during the Watson Royal Commission, the Colonial Office began working to set the modern and rural élites in opposition to each other. The British had decided to stir up resentment between the two African élites to get their way. The changes were codified in the 1949 'Report by the Committee on Constitutional Reform'. Later known as the Coussey commission after its chair, it was the first ever British body composed entirely of Africans. It was a sign of things to come, however, that several of its members appointed by the British were from the Ashante royal family and there was barely a nationalist among the rest:

> *Of the forty members of the Coussey Commission, not one was prominent in the [nationalist] CPP [Convention People's Party] and all were members of the intellectual 'middle class' which expected to inherit the political mantle when the British handed over a large measure of self-rule.*[83]

Naturally, the Coussey commission firmly rejected the earlier Watson Report's conclusion that the chieftaincy was 'doomed'. On the contrary, the commission held that the disappearance of the chiefs would be a 'disaster':

> *Contrary to the view expressed in the Watson Report, we believe that there is still a place for the Chief in a new constitutional set-up. The whole institution of chieftaincy is so closely bound up with the life of our communities that its disappearance would spell disaster . . . We cannot, therefore, accept the status which the Watson Report would assign to them.*[84]

The Coussey committee then suggested proposals for a constitutional 'bulwark' against the 'charlatan and the demagogue' of the nationalist CPP in the areas outside the major towns:

> *There is a popular cry throughout the country for universal adult suffrage. Our recommendation is for universal adult suffrage but by indirect election . . . We have weighed the risks involved most carefully and by recommending election in two stages, except in the municipalities of Accra, Cape Coast, Sekondi-Takoradi and Kumasi, we have provided a means for the exercise of responsible judgement in two stages, in the election of members to the Assembly. This process of election should minimise the dangers inherent in the wide and rapid extension of the franchise before the development of that full political sense which is the true bulwark against the charlatan and the demagogue.*[85]

Creech Jones accepted this 'sound' recommendation of the Coussey Commission. He warned the cabinet that in the Gold Coast 'no system would be workable which did not provide, for a very considerable degree of African participation in the control of policy, while preserving the Governor's ultimate responsibility':

> During the past eighteen months there has been considerable political agitation in the Gold Coast and the extremists have been conducting a campaign for immediate responsible government, which has attracted support among the less responsible elements. There is, however, a large body of moderate opinion which, while recognising that the country is not yet ready for full responsible self-government, is convinced . . . that immediate constitutional change is necessary. I think that the Governor should be placed in a position to rally behind this moderate opinion. The Coussey Committee is recognised by the public in the Gold Coast as having being a widely representative body and its report is undoubtedly a considerable victory for moderate opinion.[86]

If the cabinet rejected the report's proposals, Creech Jones believed 'moderate opinion' would be alienated and 'the extremists given an opportunity of gaining further and weightier support and making serious trouble'. In other words, there was a danger that the chiefs might be pushed into sympathizing with the radicals. Indeed, Creech Jones already felt that the chiefs had been too advanced in suggesting that elections to the Regional Councils should be direct. The same month he told Sir Charles Arden-Clarke, the new Gold Coast governor, that they must be indirect too: 'I am inclined to the view that it would be preferable for the members of the Regional Councils to be elected from and by the Local Authorities themselves.'[87] The recommendations as a whole were inserted into the 1951 constitution that Nkrumah and the CPP bound themselves to observe after they had overwhelmingly won the elections that year.

In his response to the Coussey committee report Creech Jones, the former campaigner against 'feudalism', had shown that he thought the chiefs were being too democratic. In fact, the tendency among the elders to be influenced by the nationalists was something that had been worrying the British even before the February 1948 riots. In the autumn of 1947, the leader of the pro-chief United

Gold Coast Convention, Dr Joseph Danquah, invited Kwame Nkrumah to be their general-secretary. According to Geoffrey Bing, the Labour MP who became Nkrumah's attorney-general, 'Dr Danquah called in Dr Nkrumah because he believed that through nationalism he could save the chiefs . . .'.[88] Hence, besides fear of anti-imperialism among the young nationalist élite, there was an additional reason why Britain had sought rivalry, rather than electoral collaboration between the élites, to become a feature of the new system. They were afraid that the indirect ruling chiefs would be swept along in the rising tide of African nationalism too.

When the Gold Coast authorities reacted to the spread of swollen-shoot disease among cocoa trees at the end of the war by cutting out the ineffective ones and burning them down, the Ashante cocoa chiefs responded in an aggressive manner that added fuel to the February 1948 riots. Cocoa trees take five years to mature, and as the chiefs saw their only capital go up in smoke they rebelled vigorously by embarking on another boycott campaign:

> *The government therefore faced what appeared to be a united opposition of farmers, urban dwellers and chiefs; the chiefs, at the moment of test, had failed to provide what had been the core rationale of Indirect Rule – effective political leadership which kept the population loyal to the government. As is well known, the riots and emergence of the nationalists eventually frightened the chiefs back into more or less supporting the government. But the damage had been done.*[89]

Britain's trusted 'Indirect Rulers' were developing anti-imperialist tendencies themselves and were therefore unreliable as the sole prop of colonialism. Furthermore, an anti-British alliance between the chiefs and the modern élites was definitely not on the Colonial Office's 'self-government' schedule. The fate of classical 'indirect rule' had been sealed by the political realities that confronted Britain after the war. The attempt to form a chieftaincy-dominated alliance had been made redundant by events. After February 1948, even though the brief alliance between Danquah and Nkrumah had quickly broken, the permanent isolation of the elders from the influence of the nationalists became the main objective of the Colonial Office. Accordingly, under the Coussey proposals, indirect rule was virtually revived as the 'local government' of the country areas dominated by the rural élites.

The local councils were no longer to be the first rung of a unified political system that reached up to the capital. But in compensation for this loss of access to national power, the British offered the elders the local councils as a constitutional power base from which they could defend their former 'indirect rule' privileges against encroachment from the modern élite. At the same time, through the so-called democratization process, the councils acquired the 'typical English local council' stamp of approval from London and were integrated into the machinery of the new states.

In the post-war period, British colonial strategy in Africa became fixated by the need to buy time to reconstruct a new system to replace indirect rule, which had been sidelined by African nationalism. This required that ministers had to obstruct and procrastinate whenever they were asked to set a date for the implementation of the long-awaited 'self-government' for the colonies. According to Andrew Cohen, head of the Colonial Office's Africa Department, in May 1947, even self-government for the Gold Coast 'was unlikely to be achieved in much less than a generation and elsewhere it would probably take longer'.[90] Over two years later, in October 1949, the cabinet still concurred with Creech Jones when he advised them against setting against a date for full self-government for the Gold Coast because:

> such undertakings were undesirable in principle: they were apt to have an unsettling effect on the local population, who were encouraged thereby to press for further constitutional reform instead of applying themselves to the task of getting the best of the constitution currently in force.[91]

While African nationalists and the US-dominated United Nations pressed the British to 'set a date', the other European colonial powers were pressuring Britain to slow down. In a brief Cohen prepared in November 1951 for the 1952 Anglo-French negotiations over their respective African territories, he alluded to French criticisms that the British were 'moving too fast' on 'constitutional reform'. Cohen rejected this allegation if the French meant the British have gone too far. Instead, he conceded that:

If on the other hand what is meant is that reform started too late and has therefore had to move more quickly than we should have liked, then we can agree, since it would certainly have been better if the changes which have taken place during the last three years could have been preceded by more adequate preparations.[92]

The Colonial Office was obliged to 'move more quickly than we should have liked' because it was forced to improvise when its former 'indirect rule' system collapsed when confronted with African nationalism. Between 1948 and 1951, however, the British succeeded in reconstructing a modified system within which nationalism could be contained from the earliest stages of the decolonization process. Cohen reassured his ministers that the Colonial Office had taken this into account in preparation for the constitutional 'reform' of the other British West African colonies like Sierra Leone and the Gambia 'where nationalism has hardly developed at all'.[93] To crown his accomplishment, Cohen pointed out that French officials had lately become increasingly aware of the inadequacies of their own 'assimilation' policy in tackling the growth of African nationalism. He concluded that, sooner or later, the French would be forced to adopt the British system, and that therefore the British should use the 1952 talks as an opportunity to encourage them in this direction.

Débâcle in the Congo

In the early 1960s, the Congo became a byword for everything that could go wrong with African decolonization. In many ways, it appeared to be the complete opposite of the prolonged process of decolonization that the British Colonial Office was able to organize for its African colonies on the Ghanaian model. Yet both colonial authorities had resorted to sponsoring tribalism in order to deal with the nationalist threat in both the Congo and Ghana.

In the Congo, the words 'crisis' and 'tribalism' almost became synonymous.[94] In Ghana, however, though the British had panicked in 1948 over the collapse of indirect rule, by procrastinating they were able to buy enough time to modify nationalism by introducing a much more sophisticated ethnic agenda.

The Congo was granted independence by Belgium on 30 June 1960, but the moves to thwart its freedom had began eighteen months before. In October 1958, the Confederation des Associations Tribales du Katanga (Conakat) was founded in Elizabethville in the heart of the copper-producing Katanga Province of the Congo. Fronted by Moise Tshombe, son of one of the few wealthy African plantation owners and a Methodist-trained wholesale merchant, Conakat was in reality sponsored by European settlers to fight the Congolese nationalists that came to be led by Patrice Lumumba in Leopoldville (present-day Kinshasa). By mid-1959, it had accepted the affiliation of the main European settler group and gave it a monopoly of European recruitment and organization.[95] Katangan separatism was a colonial invention fronted by Africans:

> In case the 'extremists' from Leopoldville should decisively influence the Belgium governmental declaration on the future of the Congo, anticipated for late 1958 or early 1959, the Elisabethville settler group felt it indispensable to give Katanga a 'moderate' African spokesman. The moderate voice had to appear as the expression of a common front of all the local ethnic groups and in this way claim the role of the sole party and negotiator to exert effective pressure on the colonial authority.[96]

In July 1959, after allegations that Conakat's sole role was confined to chasing other Congolese out of the province, it issued a programme which admitted to broader objectives:

> a. Union of all the original residents of the province of Katanga, black and white, without racial discrimination, who by their behavior have shown that they have been integrated in the province;
>
> b. Protection of the legitimate rights of the original residents of this province;
>
> c. Reciprocal benefits in the moral, material, physical and intellectual evolution of the province and its inhabitants;
>
> d. To struggle henceforth against seizure of any power in this province by a non-Katangan;
>
> e. To cooperate actively with Belgium toward the goal of accession to independence, but with order and calm and above all without precipitate haste.[97]

While the European settlers were creating Conakat, the Belgian authorities in Leopoldville were hastily moulding their own African front, the Parti National du Progres (PNP), formed in November 1959. This was no more than an amalgam of local chieftaincies with little else in common except they received 'substantial financial backing' by Brussels, and the colonial administration gave it 'virtually overt support'.[98] Its biggest base was among the Bayaka, whose paramount chief, the Kiamfu of Kasango Luanda, was held to be 'one of the most powerful traditional chiefs in the entire Congo'.[99] The principle effect of the PNP was to be confined to being a spoiling exercise against the main nationalist parties. Since the PNP was so intimately linked with the colonialists, many of the chiefs associated with it steadily lost much of their former influence and Brussels was then obliged to come out in defence of the openly secessionist settlers' front, Conakat.

When the paramilitary Force Publique police began to mutiny against its white officers, Brussels sent its paratroopers into the Congo 'to protect European lives' barely two weeks after independence had been granted. Tshombe declared Katanga independent of the Congo the following day, requesting Belgian assistance at the same time. The Belgians worked overtime to shore up Tshombe's shaky rebellion. Lumumba appealed to the United Nations to eject the Belgians. By August the UN troops arrived, but only to replace the Belgian troops in their positions and clamp down on the Congolese. According to Weissman, 'The United Nations was the transmission belt for American policy' and that policy was to co-operate with Belgium.[100] The following month, Lumumba was dismissed from office in a CIA-backed coup led by the Congolese army chief of staff, colonel Joseph Desire Mobuto, a move ratified by the UN in November. Lumumba shifted his base to Stanleyville, but was captured making his way there by Mobuto's forces who delivered him up to Tshombe. He was eventually murdered by the Katangans in January 1961.

The next two years witnessed the prevarication of the UN – and American imperialism – over what to do about the Katangan secession. Eventually, UN troops occupied Elizabethville when America, fronted by the UN and its Leopoldville allies, persuaded the Belgians and their confederates that the West had created a viable regime in Leopoldville. In addition to Brussels, Katangan nationalism had won support from Britain, France, South Africa and Rhodesia, and mining interests in the United States. In January 1963 Tshombe accepted the reintegration of Katanga into the Congo after a shabby compromise was agreed. The last UN troops did not leave until mid-1964, by which time insurgency had broken out again.

To quell the 1964 revolt – which spread to over half the country – Tshombe was offered the leadership of the Congo by the West, which he accepted. With its predominance of Third World member states by the mid-1960s, the United Nations had lost much of its usefulness to the West as a cover for its activities. For them, there was no alternative to Tshombe and direct intervention. With the help of American B26 bombers and transport planes, Belgian paratroops and South African and Rhodesian mercenaries who had fought in Katanga, plus token units of the Congolese army, the rebel centre at Stanleyville was captured in November 1964. The insurgency continued, however, and Tshombe was overthrown in another coup organized by the CIA and replaced by Mobuto in November 1965.

The European-inspired Katangan movement only had the effect of inspiring the coherence of the Congolese nationalist movement. Yet ethnic tendencies were present among leaders of the Congo independence movement from the very beginning. The point is that they were then an embryonic form of resistance to Belgian colonialism that matured under the leadership of intellectuals like Lumumba into full-blown nationalism. Crawford Young acknowledges that ethnicity transformed itself into nationalism as the anti-colonial movement reached its crescendo in 1959: 'The historic sequence in the emergence of the nationalist expression is of great importance. The precursor of nationalism was an ethnic awakening which took in several parts of the Congo, mostly notably among the Bakongo.'[101]

Ethnicity as embryonic nationalism was progressive in that it was directed at removing the colonial presence in Africa. Ethnicity that was solely concerned with defending the interests of a particular group, on the other hand, only made headway once the anti-imperialist movement in the Congo began to falter. This reactionary form of ethnicity had been submerged by the overwhelming anti-imperialist aspirations of the masses, but appeared as soon as the masses became disenchanted with the failures of the nationalist project.

In its submerged form, ethnicity took the form of a concern with ethnic equality, ethnic rights and 'balance'. Hence, according to Weiss, even the radical Parti Solidaire Africain (PSA) were taking account of ethnic proportions in the run-up to the independence elections of May 1960: 'Every party appointment, every committee, was now scrutinized for ethnic favoritism or a lack of an appropriate ethnic balance. Once this measuring stick was accepted it was inevitable that many segments of the party should find something to criticize.'[102]

Yet there is nothing 'inevitable' about the triumph of ethnic division in the Congo. At that stage, the outcome of the anti-imperialist struggle was still unclear. Later, for instance, the PSA would become one of the leading forces behind the 1964 revolt – which Weiss was to describe as 'the greatest post-independence revolutionary movement in Africa'. It is unclear how the PSA could accomplish this feat in 1964 if it was being torn apart by factional bickering four years earlier. The PSA struggle certainly did degenerate into ethnic squabbling once the momentum against the imperialists was lost in November 1964: 'After about a year of activity the tension between the Bambunda and Bapende became so great that there was a split, numerous defections, and a considerable weakening of its elan'.[103] Apologists for the West no doubt were highly relieved at this result. But it is to invert reality to argue that the movement was troubled by ethnic strife all along. To reiterate, tribal enmity could only gain ground as the general movement against the West faltered in the Congo.

The lesson that the colonial powers did draw from the Congo débâcle was that confronting nationalism with tribalism (in this case, in the form of Katangan separatism) was counter-productive since it provoked the nationalists even more and, worse, painted the West as diehard reactionaries in cahoots with primitives. Encouraging nationalists to become tribalists, on the other hand, was much more effective because it left the West looking comparatively progressive. To this end, the West had every interest in promoting into an obsession the ethnic balance of every African nationalist movement.

Ethnic Equality in Independent Africa

The confusion remains considerable over what constitutes the real relationship between African nationalism and ethnicity. The fashionable view is that nationalists dismissed or, at best, ignored ethnicity and all their subsequent difficulties are put down to this 'arrogance'. From this perspective, ethnicity is so powerful and persuasive that it easily undermines all the modern trappings of the African state. Thus for M. G. Smith, even urban educated Africans can be considered to be 'automatically' ethnic:

> *Even within the new educated national elites, intense loyalties to one's natal group normally take precedence over all others except self-interest, and are so powerful and pervasive that almost everyone automatically gives priority to the claims of interests of his group over those of other units and the state.*[104]

All of which does not explain why African nationalism managed to win out against the colonial sponsorship of tribalism in the first place. Far from ignoring tribalism, a cursory survey of the literature indicates that African nationalism evolved a complicated approach to tribalism. African nationalism formally opposed traditional tribalism – which it tended to portray as an imperialist plot – but it accepted milder forms of ethnicity.

There are many examples of the notorious nationalist antipathy for ethnicity. The radical Guinean nationalist Sekou Toure is generally recognized as being the African leader most hostile to tribalism. He turned the nineteenth century local hero Samori Toure into a nationalist cult figurehead because he fought the French. In December 1957, he abolished the institution of chieftaincy.

Despite these principles, however, most African nationalist regimes came to accept ethnicity during the independence period. We will examine this process in detail. It involved the urbanization of ethnicity and the widespread adoption of tribalism in the form of ethnic proportionality or ethnic rights. This discussion will help prepare the ground for the evolution of modern African ethnicity, which has almost entirely removed itself from its rural origins.

In order to examine this process properly, however, we must first look at the key elements of the post-independence context in Africa which pressurized the African nationalist élite into accepting ethnicity

---

The African Nationalist Tradition on Tribalism

- *'The educated nationalists saw in [indirect rule] nothing but an imperialist device on the part of the governing power by which the subject races might be kept down for ever, or at least indefinitely.'*[105]

- *'Any difference, any kind of fissure among Africans is seized and turned to the imperialist and cold war interests. The Congo offers perhaps the most striking example of how tribal dissensions and political careerism are exploited in order to fragment united territories and exacerbate divisions.'*[106]

- *'[In the anti-colonial revolt] tribal dissensions weaken and tend to disappear; . . . When they remain – as in the Congo – it's because they are kept up by the agents of colonialism.'*[107]

- *'Colonialism has often strengthened or established its domination by organising the petrification of the country districts . . . Ringed round by marabouts, witch-doctors and customary chieftains, the majority of country-dwellers are still living in the feudal manner, and the full power of this medieval structure of society is maintained by the settlers' military and administrative officials.'*[108]

- *'The racist whites in South Africa had worked out a careful plan to "develop" the oppressed African population as Zulu, as Xhosa and as Sotho so that the march towards broader African national and class solidarities could be stopped and turned back.'*[109]

---

as a 'right' instead of a 'foreign plot'. These were the failure of the nationalist project, the manipulative use of foreign aid flows, and the persistent Western cultivation of ethnicity in both rural and urban Africa after independence. We will look at each of these in turn.

The Failure of the Nationalist Project

The winning of African independence represented a great blow to the West in general and the European colonial powers in particular. The whole world needed Africa's agrarian produce, but now they had to negotiate terms with independent African regimes. London and Paris actively sought to restore their pre-eminence through playing their ace card – ethnicity. The eminent Africanist, Crawford Young, concludes that the independence period was the prime era of ethnicity:

> Students of African politics have not, until recently, been especially preoccupied with this issue. One obvious reason was that ethnicity as a norm of political behavior was largely obscured in the colonial period . . . until the metropolitan power had irrevocably committed itself to departure it could not be clear just how significant an element ethnicity would be.[110]

In reality, ethnicity merely took on a new appearance. The Western powers had learnt that by directly confronting African nationalists with tribal movements it only provoked them – as in Ghana, the Congo, South Africa, etc. Instead, from the 1960s onwards, they worked overtime to convert the new African regimes into tribalists as a vital step towards dispensing with African independence. Ironically, to dispose of African nationalism, it was first necessary to strengthen the African state.

Though granted formal political independence, the African state remained linked with the West through the fusion of the new African élites with the old colonial state bureaucracy. The survival of this new regime depended on the political defeat of the African nationalist movements and the integration of its leaders. How was this to be accomplished?

In every colonial struggle the imperialists tried to separate the modern nationalist leaders from the masses. Some could be flattered or bought off – like Banda, Kenyatta, Houphouet-Boigny. If this did not work, the authorities cracked down on the mass movement, detaining the activists. Through these methods they hoped to isolate the nationalist leaders. But imprisonment could always embellish a leader's credentials (Kenyatta, Mandela). In those cases where this option failed as well, the leaders were exiled (Seretse Kharma, Nkrumah) or eliminated (Lumumba, Cabral and Mondlane) in the hope that their successors would prove more malleable.

The objective of this strategy was based on the assumption that it was easier to deal with a group of isolated leaders than a volatile mass movement. As individuals cut off from mass pressure, the leaders would be more inclined to compromise and co-operate. It is far easier to make concessions to an individual leader's desire for status and power than it is to meet the demands of the mass movement for real change. The aim of the exercise was to turn the nationalist leaderships into negotiating partners.

In general, this strategy ensured a successful transfer of power from colonial authorities to the new African nation because the negotiating partners were immunized from mass pressure. By the time independence negotiations were completed many of the African leaders had become more dependent on these colonial institutions than on mass support.

This colonial legacy throws light on the problems that every new African regime – even those radical leaderships who barely negotiated with the colonialists at all – faced when confronted with state power. In every case the nationalist leadership had a fundamental choice to make. Would it rely on the energy of its mass support or would it look to the existing state institutions for the exercise of its authority? For the more moderate leaders the choice was clear from the outset – the masses were unpredictable while the civil service and the army were there to serve. In practice most African leaders attempted to combine governing through the old colonial structures with a degree of political mobilization.

Before long, therefore, the new leaders became either willing or unwilling prisoners of the state administration. It was easier to follow the tried and tested methods of the past than to innovate with new popular institutions. The civil service was well-trained and educated in administration and the exercise of power and the anti-colonial movement was not. A ready-made, all-purpose institution with a worked-out routine and clear procedures seemed a preferable alternative to the unknown. As a result African leaders became more and more reliant on the state machinery and political innovations simply consisted of setting up one public enterprise after another. The anti-imperialist leadership had begun to fuse with the old state bureaucracy.

The dependence of African leaders on the institutions of the state was necessarily at the expense of their mass base. As the political leaders lost touch with their grassroots supporters the role of state institutions became more important. Slowly, the attitude of the leaders began to change. Whereas before, the anti-imperialist movement was seen as a source of authority it increasingly came to be defined as a problem.

The new leaders became accomplices in the exclusion of the mass movement from politics. The new leaders did not need such movements, but political institutions that were only accountable to them. Repression and political control got rid of the hotheads, and once the anti-imperialist movement was demobilized the African governments could set about redefining the meaning of political participation. The African leader dependent on the state looked upon political activism with suspicion. He needed political institutions not to activate the masses but control them. These were the conditions in which the one-party system emerged and came to characterize independent African politics.

Foreign Aid and Ethnicity

Political independence did not just mean power passing solely to the African nationalist leaders. As we've seen, two African élites had been groomed by the departing colonial powers, the rural traditional chiefs – known by the colonialists as Native Authorities, and the urban nationalist élite.

The products of African agriculture attracted the interest of all the major powers at this time of decolonization. The rural élites had control over production of the marketable crops and minerals as well as a grip over the political loyalties of the large rural masses (plus the sympathy of imperialism); with the dynamism of nationalism behind them, the urban élites had control of the sale and income of the world commodity products, connections with friendly foreign powers – such as the Soviet Union, and access to international aid flows. By playing them off against each other, the imperialists attempted to manipulate the divided African élites. At the same time, the African leaderships also tried to improve their position and fend off the West by playing it off against the East, as well as their former colonial power against its rivals. To assert themselves in this situation, the West made full use of their immense material resources.

With most African states achieving their independence from 1960 onwards, they became eligible for foreign aid from the various multinational agencies that had been set up after the Second World War. Until then, the decolonized colonies were supposedly in receipt of development aid from the colonial power. Britain set up its first such fund in 1929, which was strengthened in 1940 with the passing of the Colonial Development and Welfare Act. However, by February 1945 only £1,037,575 had been paid out to the African colonies alone. This all changed in the immediate post-war period, however. After independence, the African regimes tried to use their political status to play off rival Western powers against each other – and in some cases, against the Soviet Union and China – to get the best foreign aid projects.

The provision of foreign aid by the West to the newly independent African regimes became a highly sophisticated operation. The expansion of the IMF and the World Bank from their original focus on Eastern Europe to include the Third World was largely undertaken to reduce the vulnerability of the West to African manoeuvrings. Of course foreign aid was also good public relations for the former colonial powers, as well as the 'anti-imperialist' United States of America, but foreign aid also helped to ensure that the rural masses previously out of reach of the capitalist system could be reached and subjected to exploitation.

Our concern, however, is the way in which foreign aid helped further the political goals of the Western powers. It was channelled only through the modern élite who formally controlled state power, so the rural/traditional élite had to approach the new regimes for the largesse to buy up the political support of their followers. The promise of lavish amounts of foreign aid was held out to them to ensure their co-operation. The success of this strategy depended on the fact that, apart from the sale of their monocultural products, these rural élites had few alternative sources of funds. Meanwhile, rumours emerged from the West that the urban élite who controlled the various marketing boards, crop subsidies and aid dispensing were 'dipping their fingers in the honeypot'.

Senegal's Mouride Brotherhood

An Islamic Sufi brotherhood, the Mourides were founded in 1886 by a mystic, Amadu Bamba, after the French colonialists had broken the power of the Wolof states. Religious mystics reorganized the former Wolof region into a system that combined the worst features of ancient Africa and the worst features of imperialism. In the 1970s the Mourides were 500,000 strong, and controlled one-quarter of Senegal's main export cash crop – groundnuts.

According to Donal Cruise O'Brien, there were specific barriers which prevented the Marabouts from developing into fully-fledged capitalists. He argued that it was the need to anticipate the reactions of Marabout followers which ensured that élite incorporation into capitalist social relations remained partial:

> *a religious clientele can only be maintained where the followers receive a real return for their loyalty in occasional subsidies, and where the power and wealth of the leader is conspicuously displayed: the American and other limousines which glide along the roads and tracks of the Mouride region are not valued principally for the comfort which they ensure on bumpy surfaces, but for the impression they make on the peasant followers. . . .*
>
> *There is reason to doubt that the Marabouts can easily be transformed into a capital-accumulating bourgeoisie, for they do not at present save or invest any substantial proportion of their receipts . . . [it] tends to be dissipated in unproductive ways: American cars, perfumes, clothes, luxurious beds, food, numerous wives and concubines, the 'entourage', etc.*[111]

This analysis avoids the evidence that the patrimonial lifestyles of these rural African leaders was a function of foreign aid and, as such, was regulated by colonial agents. For delivering the vote he controlled in the 1960 Senegal election, the Mouride leader received £112,000 from the capital – the equivalent of several years of harvest of peanuts, the cash crop that forms the main source of income for the Mouride movement.[112]

The Mouride religious movement was a rigid hierarchy based upon the submission of follower to their marabout, or religious leader. While most Mouride followers had a few acres to scratch a living from, the marabouts – numbering 300 to 400 – were Senegal's biggest landowners. They relied upon the unpaid labour of their followers to work their fields, which amounted to as much as 9000 acres. Lip-service was paid to the religious reasons for this and the many other obligations that the Marabout's followers carried out for him. However, the real reasons were more material: the Marabouts controlled the distribution of the land. When Senegal, France's leading African colony, became independent in 1960, the Mourides came into their own. The Khalifa–General alone controlled 400,000 votes of his followers. The nationalists were obliged to make a great effort to get those votes.

Leopold Senghor, the first nationalist president of Senegal, was a Catholic who won power as the compromise candidate of rival Muslim Mouride clans. Senghor frequently attended the Mourides' annual 'Great Magal' festival to give speeches such as 'The Role of the Mourides in Building African Socialism'.[113] In 1963, at the annual 'Great Magal' festival, Senghor was obliged to praise the Khalifa as a 'socialist': 'Once more, what is socialism if not, essentially, the socio-economic system which gives primacy and priority to work? And who has done this better than Amadu Bamba and his successors, including you, El Hadj?'[114] To a large extent the power and influence of this famous African nationalist leader Senghor was a consequence of this obscure Sufi Muslim brotherhood.

Land Rights

Given the importance of African agricultural production to the world economy at that time, the attention of the British authorities naturally focused on land ownership as the main mechanism for preserving their exploitation system in Africa once colonialism ended. But preserving these archaic land tenure arrangements meant aggravating ethnic tensions. For example, in the mid-1950s, it was obvious to the American Africanist James Smoot Coleman that Britain's land tenure policy would exacerbate tribalism in Nigeria,

> The policy of preserving traditional institutions appeared also in the economic sphere in connection with the system of land tenure . . . Except in urban centres, this meant that existing ethnic groups were virtually frozen in the areas they occupied when the British arrived. In the balance, such a policy tended to perpetuate localism and foster tribalism.[115]

Since they did not respond to such criticism, it seems that, for the British, tribal tensions in newly independent Africa were a price worth paying so long as they could continue to operate their non-political exploitation of the continent after colonialism. Tragically,

Britain's land tenure policy was to be almost wholly adopted by independent Nigeria.

On their own, each clause of independent Nigeria's 1963 Republican Congress seemed perfectly innocuous. But in combination they proved greater than the sum of the parts. For example, the constitution's Section 27 guaranteed the freedom of every Nigerian to move freely throughout Nigeria and to reside in any part of the country. Yet a crucial exemption to this law was buried away in 'Subsection 3'. That stated that 'nothing in Section 27 shall invalidate any reasonably justified law that imposes restrictions on the acquisition or the use of land or other property in Nigeria'.[116]

This provision had the effect of legitimizing the 1962 Land Tenure Law introduced by the northern states, which placed the southerners on the same footing as foreigners in respect to landholding in any part of the north. Ojo records that the northern rulers backed this discriminatory legislation on the grounds that they feared 'the possible expropriation of many peasant landholders by sophisticated southern property speculators'. By appealing to anti-speculator sentiments, the emirs sought to secure popularity at the expense of southern market traders.

As a pro-market counterweight to legislation reinforcing the status of the emirs in the northern territories, the colonial authorities had demanded hut taxes be paid in cash. This helped to integrate the more marginal societies into market relations in the run-up to independence and enabled the southern Ibos to extend their trading businesses in the North. For the Tiv, who lived in the backward Plateau zone which was officially part of the Northern Region but was occupied by pagans and Christians, the tax requirement forced them to start selling beniseed as a cash crop (previously it had just been used as a relish). This caused the demand for land to increase.

> *When beniseed became a cash crop, its acreage increased many-fold. Manifestly, there has been an increased demand on the land . . . In addition, new transport facilities as well as safety for travellers and long-distance traders, have enabled Tiv to sell foodstuffs in non-Tiv markets. Every day truckload after truckload of food is exported from Tivland; as a result more land is put into production.*[117]

Inevitably some successful Tiv began to move beyond trading just to pay taxes to trading to secure a profit. This development began to subvert the traditional Tiv social structure. The Bohannons spelt out the tensions that these economic developments had caused among the Tiv: 'Tiv elders deplore this situation and know what is happening, but they do not know where to place the blame . . . [They] curse money, the Europeans who brought it, and the Ibo traders it brings.'[118] Yet if the beniseed crop had brought the Tiv elders a decent income as well, then nothing more would have been said. The overall inadequacy of the market has been obscured by the Bohannons here.

Isolated Ibo traders were an easy target. Thousands of them were to be slaughtered in northern Nigeria countryside in September 1966. Contrary to popular understanding, most of the killing of Ibos was not done by Muslims but by the north's Christian and pagan minorities like the Tiv, whose way of life had become increasingly precarious as the market made inroads into their lives while delivering less and less as a result. By the mid-1960s, the West was beginning to reduce its reliance on African agriculture. In fact, the EEC and USA were starting to look upon Africa as a suitable site to offload their agricultural surpluses. From then on, Africa was only considered by the world economy as a mineral source. One result of this change in Western priorities was the Nigerian Civil War of 1967–70. Unlike the rural pogrom of Ibos the previous year, this war was the first full-scale ethnic bloodbath between African urban élites – and millions died as a result.

Urban Ethnicity

As we saw above, the concept 'marginal man' had been developed to explain why ethnicity tended to survive in urban society. The urban immigrant sought sanctuary in his primordial traditions to relieve himself from the dislocations of modern life.[119] Economist Abner Cohen preferred a more material explanation. From his studies in the Yoruban city of Ibadan, Cohen observed that its Hausa immigrants maintained economic ties with the Hausa cattlemen of northern Nigeria to enable them to control the city's cattle trade. This economic fact put a premium on retaining an ethnic link with their northern brethren. At the same time, however, Cohen recognized that this ethnic system arose out of overall economic weakness: 'To rationalise the [cattle] trade and to put it on a modern basis will require a complete social and economic revolution covering almost every stage in the chain of the trade.'[120] Cohen pessimistically concluded, 'this at present is not feasible'. What makes this response especially gloomy is that it came at the height of the biggest expansion of capitalist production the world has ever seen.

Cohen's wider analysis is pertinent towards a material understanding of modern urban ethnicity, but the immediate economic link to Hausa ethnicity is too unusual for general application. In general, there are no such direct material connections to explain the survival of urban ethnicity. In part, the popularity of the 'marginal man' analysis derives from its non-economic, psychological explanation for the survival of ethnicity in the urban environment. The real explanation for the persistence of urban ethnicity lies elsewhere – out of Africa.

As we have seen in the case of Senegal, the urban élite was kept out of the African countryside by the colonial authorities and thus made dependent on the chiefs and religious leaders for getting the vote out at elections. According to William Graf, in the case of Nigeria:

> The aspiring political leaders were forced to concede the traditional rulers' pivotal role in securing mass support for their ethnically grounded parties. Traditional constituencies thus became the initial and most reliable source of the 'new' elite's mass support. Before and after independence, therefore, the political leaders courted the traditional leaders with all the inducements which the 'new' system could provide: seats in the upper house, political appointments (in particular ministries without portfolio) with their corresponding salaries and benefits, and much more.
>
> At the same time, the traditional rulers, increasingly deprived by the 'modernising' political system of their status, were compelled to look elsewhere for an institutional basis of security and prestige, without which their ability to provide for their 'constituency' and hence their traditional popular support would be jeopardised. Inevitably, they turned to the political parties who for reasons of

legitimation were interested in gaining the emirs', the chiefs' and obas' support.[121]

But ethnicity was not restricted solely to rural society in Africa. It seeped into urban Africa itself. In Nigeria, for example, the British aimed to protect the urban masses from the nationalist fever as well. As James Coleman remarks, 'In its early stages nationalism in Nigeria was a wholly urban phenomenon, but it was not a phenomenon of *all* urban centres'.[122] People who travelled to established cities in Nigeria from other areas found themselves excluded as tribal 'strangers':

> *As traditional city authorities controlled land rights and the political system, 'strangers' were compelled to settle on the outskirts of the city in specifically demarcated zones and were excluded from political life . . . The tribal homogeneity of indigenous people was to a large extent preserved . . . [Though] the tribal stranger sectors have been the centers of nationalist activity.*[123]

Coleman then remarks that in this discrimination the traditional city leaders were 'of course' supported by the British authorities. In a footnote to this passage, Coleman argues that while discrimination in the Yoruba-dominated cities of Western Nigeria was necessarily limited – after all, the population of Lagos had been a mixture of ethnic groups from all over West Africa since the days when Nigeria was known as the 'Slave Coast' – in the Hausa–dominated Northern cities it was organized to achieve a 'logical' political objective:

> *In the Northern Region both the ruling emirs and the British authorities had good political reasons for maintaining the separation between the traditional sector and the stranger sector. It was a logical corollary of indirect rule, but it also served to shield the peoples of the indigenous sector from the unsettling political ideas and from active contact with the more nationalist-minded southerners living in the* sabon garis *[strangers' ghetto].*[124]

Once the colonial powers left, therefore, for African nationalist politicians even to reach many of the urban masses, they were forced to approach the traditional authorities first. As the significance of the African countryside and therefore its population steadily diminished for the world economy through the 1960s, the existence of these urban ethnic vehicles took on an increased importance.

We have already seen how ethnicity was sponsored by the authorities to mollify militancy among Zambian copper miners in the 1930s. But, in an essay written in 1952, James Coleman has convincingly demonstrated how, through 'Tribal Associations' organized by proto-nationalists but sponsored by the authorities, ethnicity got a hold over the nationalist movement itself. Tribal associations were almost contemporary with the decolonization process.

Organized by newly arrived rural immigrants, Coleman locates the formation of the first urban Nigerian tribal association in 1928 – the Ibibio Welfare Union. By the end of the Second World War, tribal associations had been formed by 'virtually all the tribes in Nigeria except those in the Muslim areas of the far North'.[125] He observed how official policy gravitated towards them: 'Official policy has been one either of toleration or of active encouragement of the associations, but always insistent that efforts for reform must be channelled through the Native Authority.'[126]

Eventually, the British succeeded in turning the tribal associations into 'a powerful influence for the democratization of native authority councils'.[127] This growth of urban tribal associations made Coleman more optimistic than most about the prospects of modernization in Africa. Against official fears about 'detribalised natives', Coleman counselled that: 'The urbanised Nigerian is not as "detribalised" as early observers described him. Through the tribal associations he has been able to retain those elements of the traditional culture which are still meaningful to him.'[128]

Nevertheless, we have noted how chiefs and other upholders of 'traditional culture' were swept up by the nationalist tide and elsewhere Coleman accepts this is so.[129] Moreover, Coleman admits that many of the tribal associations of Nigeria served as embryonic vehicles for nationalist movements – notably Nnamdi Azikiwe's National Council of Nigeria and the Cameroons (NCNC) which began life as the Ibo Federal Union based in the capital Lagos. Furthermore, writing in 1952, Coleman conceded 'a new group of intellectuals' had arisen in Nigeria 'with a genuine national or regional outlook who are either indifferent or hostile to such associations because of the evils of parochialism and tribalism'.[130] But once this intellectual layer became fearful of the mobilized mass movement and disillusioned with the nationalist project, the ethnic side of the tribal associations that they had formerly tried to suppress asserted itself over the nationalist side. Favouring the ethnic side meant pursuing the interests of the particular ethnic group rather than concentrating on eradicating the colonial influence for the benefit of all.

Constitutionalism: The Recasting of Ethnicity as a Right

Given the failure of the nationalist project, the manipulation of foreign aid by the Western regimes, and their sponsorship of ethnic institutions in urban Africa as well as rural Africa, the nationalists were ready to submit to the introduction of ethnicity when it was advanced by the colonial powers. Nevertheless the ethnicity accepted by the nationalists took the innovative form of extreme equality, or ethnic 'rights', ethnic 'balance' or 'proportionality'. Each ethnic group in the country was to be allocated resources and positions in the new state according to their proportion of the overall population – as determined by official census.

The potential for creating immediate antagonism through the adoption of this principle of equality was immense. In theory, it meant the reordering of all the traditional tribal arrangements left by the colonial administration. Hence in Uganda, the Acholi, Kakwa and other northern tribes had been cultivated as military personnel for years by the British and consequently dominated the officer corps of the new Ugandan army. In Nigeria, it was the Christian minorities of the Northern Region who mainly ran the army.[131] Under the provisions of ethnic balance, however, soldiers from other 'tribes' could legitimately demand officer status.

Simply in terms of pre-empting ethnic violence, the ethnic rights policy proved to be a great success. Some commentators, wearing ethnic spectacles, see the influence of ethnicity in everything that happens in Africa, yet, except for a handful of well-known cases (Nigeria, the Sudan, Rwanda and Burundi, Zanzibar) the instances of ethnic rivalry were few and far between up to the 1990s. The main reason for this is that the West had little interest in stirring up ethnic strife among the African élites. On the contrary, they hoped to separate the élites from, and strengthen them against, the still insurgent masses. Generally speaking, the colonial authorities only resorted to provoking tribal conflict when they felt they were about to lose control. Under decolonization, the colonial authorities gradually grasped back the initiative after the nationalist upsurge peaked in 1948. Where ethnic rivalries did break out, it was usually for specific reasons. Western rivalry over Nigerian oil wealth resulted in the ethnic bloodbath there. Similarly the long-running civil war between the northerners and southerners in the Sudan was a product of Western efforts to limit the influence of the radical Nasserite regime in Egypt on Sudan and the rest of Africa.

Overall, however, it was the adoption of the concept of ethnic rights by nationalism that proved to be the decisive achievement by the colonialists. It handed over to the foreign offices of the Western powers – in particular the Red-obsessed USA – a highly sophisticated tool to adjust the policies of 'Independent' Africa from a distance, rather than directly and therefore 'imperialistically'. The West were not about to destroy the élite with whom they had established this key relationship by pressing the button marked 'tribal war'. As a secondary factor, the wealth pouring into the continent as a result of the marketing of African primary produce meant that disputes among the élite were limited to sharing out the profits rather than negotiating cutbacks, always a more traumatic procedure.

This success of the ethnic balance policy had a big impact among African politicians. Though it was a legacy of colonial rule imposed on the nationalists during the constitutional negotiations, ethnic proportionality eventually acquired such distinction that African nationalist sympathizers came to accept the principle of ethnic balance as their own. According to Saadia Touval,

> The pluralistic character of most African states has led to the development of mechanisms of adjustment enabling the accommodation of the interests and needs of diverse ethnic groups. Most have developed norms and procedures enabling the maintenance of an ethnic balance within the political and administrative institutions.[132]

This seemingly democratic form of ethnicity enabled African politicians to, at one at the same time, claim that they had risen above primitive tribalism, the cruder expressions of which they disparaged unmercifully, while manoeuvring to improve their ethnic constituencies.

As an illustration of how this contradiction was dealt with by African nationalists, it is useful to refer to the experience of the Luo tribal association in Kampala, the Ugandan capital, where Aidan Southall mentions the opprobrium that overt expressions of tribalism attracted the higher that local politicians advanced. Consequently, the Luo Union 'addressed themselves very consciously to this issue, endeavouring to define their association in non-ethnic terms by making qualification for membership not to be a Luo by birth but to have the welfare of the Luo people at heart'.[133] Through this adoption of equal ethnicity by nationalists, African ethnicity and African nationalism converged into each other, thereby cutting ethnicity's links to rural Africa and linking it to the fortunes of the urban African élite.

Donald Rothchild has uncovered numerous examples of how independent African governments and political parties engaged in this 'ethnic arithmetic' during the independence period.[134] In the past, the London journal *The Economist* has enthused over the benefits gained by Kanu, the ruling party of Kenya's President Daniel arap Moi, through fixing tribal deals:

> *Kanu says it preserves the country's stability, and certainly ensures its own, by fixing deals between members of the tribal elites, among whom urban jobs, influence, and the chance of profit, are subtly shared out. This is hardly democratic, but marvellously limits government spending. Instead of wooing millions of voters with public-sector projects and wage hikes, the government merely has to reward a few hundred tribal and regional bosses with state contracts, opportunities and favours.*[135]

Nairobi claimed this system helped keep tribalism in check, but *The Economist* more soberly accepted that 'inter-tribal deals do not eliminate tribal tensions, indeed they institutionalise them'.[136] Although President of Senegal Abdou Diouf had been the favoured candidate of the powerful Mouride clan, in 1984 he was obliged to set up a commission to eliminate the factional wrangling that was tearing his ruling Parti Democratique Senegalaise apart: 'The personalisation of politics at the grass roots or maintenance of local or national power proves that, in the party, there exists only clans founded on groupings of people swept along by the demons of electoralism, division, and clientelism.'[137]

What is missing from all these accounts is any notion of colonial responsibility for the promotion of ethnicity. African nationalism inculcated ethnicity solely through the debilitating effects of the decolonization process. This process was primarily visible through the negotiation of a series of constitutions with the interested African parties – usually conducted at Lancaster House in London. Given the absence of any written British constitution to imitate, these constitutions served a somewhat different function from the unwritten British constitution.[138] Despite the existence of Welsh, Scottish, Ulster and English elements making the 'United Kingdom', the British constitution has historically been strongly centralist. Yet pluralism was very much in vogue with the authors of the African Independence constitutions. This was particularly clear in their emphasis on ethnic rights. The only possible conclusion is that the constitutions were designed to make the newly independent states more vulnerable to outside interference.

In regard to these ethnic arrangements that the British managed to impose upon independent Africa, their insertion into all the constitutions had the effect of elevating colonial divisive tribalistic policies into legal rights. Thus, according to Fred Burke, in the Ugandan colony 'the 1949 [Local Government] Ordinance in effect provided a legal basis for the institutionalisation of parochial tribally oriented local governments'.[139] This legal gloss made it easier for the hesitant nationalist leaderships to accept tribalism. Until then, the notion of ethnic *rights* was a purely intellectual concern (more or less confined to the few scholars preoccupied with recording ethnic histories, ethnic languages, etc.). By presenting ethnic demands as local rights that formed a natural stepping-stone to the full national right to self-determination, the British made the prospect of national division more easy to swallow for the nationalist élite.[140]

To reiterate, the reason why ethnic 'rights' could not be a stepping-stone to national rights was because African ethnicity was fostered by the imperial powers to thwart the African liberation struggle, which had adopted a nationalist form. In those cases where ethnicity did exhibit proto-nationalist features – such as the Congo, Kenya, etc. – it was portrayed in Europe as atavistic primitivism. In most cases, then, while ethnic 'rights' were freely handed down by colonial administrations, national rights had to be extracted from them with great difficulty. Today the concept of 'rights' is being redefined to mean protection *by* the government. But rights only have substance if they mean protection *from* the government. The demand for the right to national self-determination threatened colonial rule. Ethnic rights were advanced by the colonial administration to divide the anti-colonial movement along tribal lines, and to legitimate foreign interference in independent Africa once colonialism had ended. Since colonialism was abolished, their historic success has been their consistent ability to get even the most radical African nationalist movements to adopt ethnic 'balance' as a guiding principle.

According to Africanist James Coleman, the Burkean conception of nationalism was intellectually decisive in this respect. Edmund Burke, one of the founders of British conservatism and a contemporary critic of the French Revolution, opposed a hierarchial conception of nationalism to the revolutionary centralist Jacobin conception. Burke insisted on loyalty to family as a priority, then town and then region. Only then, could loyalty to nation be admitted:

> *Whereas most Englishmen – and some Nigerians – would be instinctively attracted to a Burkean concept of nationalism, Nigerian nationalists seeking the rapid transformation of Nigeria into a modern and united state would incline more to a Jacobin nationalism, which extinguishes all obstructive intermediate groups.*[141]

If we accept for the sake of argument that the majority of Nigerian nationalists were 'Jacobins' in the mid-1950s, it is evident that the Burkean nationalists eventually succeeded in consolidating their more limited agenda. The reason for this was that African leaders were sensing that the mass nationalist movement was becoming more of a threat than an opportunity.

The Ashante Question in Ghana: The Peaceful Road

The case of the Ashante in Ghana is an excellent example of how colonialism successfully dealt with radical nationalism. To tame the Convention People's Party led by Kwame Nkrumah, London sponsored a political movement based on the powerful Ashante tribe in order to extract important constitutional concessions from Nkrumah. This enabled them to convert the CPP to 'equal' ethnicity and thus drop the Ashante once Ghanaian independence was achieved. The Ashante subsequently played only a minor role in Ghanaian politics throughout the whole independence period. Meanwhile, the CPP became a spent force, riven by factions, and its disgruntled supporters deserted it in droves. To his credit, even when Nkrumah was most isolated, he only became more bitter against imperialism. So he was deposed and sent into exile.

We have already explored in Chapter 3 how the British authorities reacted to the 1948–51 events in Ghana and thereby adapted their policy of indirect rule. This crisis was forced on the British to a large extent because the chiefs, including the Ashante, joined the CPP 'young men' in the late 1940s to get a better price for their in-demand cocoa. By the mid-1950s, however, the British had managed to set these two groups at each others' throats. When Nkrumah won the June 1954 general elections, he seemed to be in an unassailable position to achieve independence on his terms. But Governor Sir Charles Arden-Clarke – who we last encountered as a district officer bringing civilization and taxes to the people of the Nigerian Plateau – was 'working behind the scenes' and: 'managed, by reference to British parliamentary procedure, and using the good offices of Sir Emmanuel Quist, the Speaker, to get the Assembly to accept the Speaker's ruling that the NPP should be recognised as the official opposition.'[142]

The NPP was the Northern People's Party. It had 'emerged at the last moment' to win 12 out of 21 seats in the Northern Territories (the CPP won the others), yet the British wanted it made the official opposition. Three months later, the spokesman for the Ashantahene (King) set up the National Liberation Movement (NLM) to uphold Ashante cocoa interests. The Colonial Office then suggested federalism along Nigerian lines as a possible structure for independent Ghana, an idea that the NLM quickly took up.

The British government, however, backed Nkrumah and refused to consider federalism. They realized that the days of indirect rule and directly confronting nationalists with tribal solutions were counter-productive. Instead, they were holding out for transforming the CPP into an ethnically based organization. Hence, whilst maintaining a formal position of opposition to federation in his dealings with Nkrumah, Arden-Clarke commented on the new constitution to his wife just one month before independence:

> *The result of our efforts, which are not yet completed, will I think produce a weird and wonderful constitution which both sides will reluctantly agree to work and that is as much as anyone can expect at the present time. It has to deal with the political realities of the moment which are themselves pretty weird and wonderful. The shortest part of the constitution will deal with the fundamentals of parliamentary democracy and by far the longest part will be devoted to such details as how to change the boundaries of a region and how to create new ones, or how to arrange for the devolution of authority to Regional Assemblies which are not yet set up.[143]*

Arden-Clarke concluded his letter with the hope that 'they will not find it too easy to change'. Regionalism or federalism – what did it matter so long as the CPP was forced to be more tuned into ethnicity? Under this pressure, the CPP was changing. In June 1949, Nkrumah's CPP programme sought '3. To secure and maintain the complete unity of the Chiefs and people of the Colony, Ashanti, Northern Territories and Trans-Volta'.[144] Under British prodding, however, the CPP began dabbling with ethnicity in order to outmanoeuvre the Ashante 'threat'. Co-operation with the chiefs was now on their agenda.

To conciliate the Ashante, Nkrumah offered them a regional council, while encouraging the Brong minority in Western Ashanti to separate. In Kumasi, the capital of the Ashante, CPP activists mobilized its Fanti, Ga, Ewe, and northern Muslim inhabitants against the NLM. In a study of the Northern territories, we can see how the CPP compromised with the northernmost rural élite in Ghana.

P. A. Ladouceur recounts how the CPP undermined the northern-based NPP by approaching sympathetic chiefs for their support, holding out the carrot of aid funds for those that complied, and threatening trouble for those who did not. In the former case, the CPP was 'not without success in its approaches to the chiefs, notably in Gonja, Navrongo and Tumu'.[145] In the case of the latter, the CPP appealed to dissident elements 'including malcontent lesser chiefs and claimants to chieftaincies, and subject ethnic groups eager to throw off the yoke of chiefs imposed from outside'.[146] By exerting pressure on the chiefs, they obliged their political representatives to join the CPP. Ladouceur concludes:

> Both parties [the CPP and the NPP] relied on a system of 'patron politics' by which a comparatively small number of political patrons dominated particular areas through their influence over the local traditional elements. In the end it was the astute manipulation of this small group of patrons, through their traditional supporters, which resulted in the rapid reversal of the political situation in the North, paving the way for the undisputed rule of the Convention People's Party.[147]

As a result, by 1958, 'most CPP leaders in the North were from "princely" backgrounds'.[148] To all appearances, it seemed as if Nkrumah had won a tremendous victory over the forces of reaction in Ghana. It is true that the Ashante in particular have remained a marginal force in Ghanaian politics ever since. In reality, by incorporating ethnicity into his party, Nkrumah had been forced to accept the rural élite as a definite feature of the new Ghana. In time, the influence of the rural élites declined in importance in Ghana as agriculture shifted from being the source of income to a burden. The crucial development, therefore, was not the CPP's incorporation of the rural élite, but its acceptance of ethnicity, the convergence of African nationalism with ethnicity. It was this accommodation to non-Ashante ethnicity by the radical CPP which permitted the British to dispense with the Ashante and they were subsequently pushed to the political margins throughout the independence period. Though the British never imposed formal federalism upon Ghana, as they did in neighbouring Nigeria, the CPP was driven to adopt informal regionalism instead.

The Case of the San: A Setback for the West's Campaign for Ethnic 'Rights'

In southern Africa, the assimilation of the Bushmen or 'San' of the Kalahari desert of Bechuanaland (present-day Botswana) into African society was only represented as their 'extinction' as independence was drawing near. The British wanted Bechuanaland to become

Independent Botswana so as to block South Africa's northward expansion. Even so, it was useful to talk up a minority issue in order to be able to keep the Gaborene regime under pressure. In 1966, the London-based Anti-Slavery Society accused the majority Tswana people of Botswana of 'exterminating or enslaving' the San:

> *Driven, whether they like it or not, into the inhospitable area of the Kalahari desert, being exterminated or enslaved by the Bantu in the areas in which they live, the larger proportion of these people live in Bechuanaland where we at this time have a direct responsibility because shortly Bechuanaland is to receive independence . . . our first priority should be to do all in our power to produce safeguards in the Bechuanaland constitution protecting the rights of the Bushmen.*[149]

The colonial authorities subsequently ensured that there was a special department to monitor Bushmen affairs in the new Botswana state structure. The Gaborene regime, however, steadily resisted international campaigns to grant special constitutional 'rights' to the Bushmen, on the grounds that this would replicate the apartheid policies of their racist South African neighbours.

Independent Nigeria: On the Road to Constitutional Peace

It would be a mistake to imagine that ethnic conflict was always seen as desirable by the colonial authorities. For example, the Nigerian Governor Sir John Macpherson had privately expressed concern at the rise in tension between the Ibo and the Yoruba in June 1948:

> *I am very concerned about the growth of ill feeling between the Yorubas and the Ibos and I am inclined to think that the [Egbe Omo Oduduwa] Society is mainly concerned with resistance to Zik and the Ibos rather than with a constructive programme.*[150]

The European powers usually only resorted to stirring up tribal strife when they felt they were losing their grip. Through decolonization, ethnicity became a policy option and the colonialists concentrated upon transforming the nationalist parties into bodies which would take ethnicity into account rather than try to eradicate it. Regulation rather than wrecking was the object of decolonization.

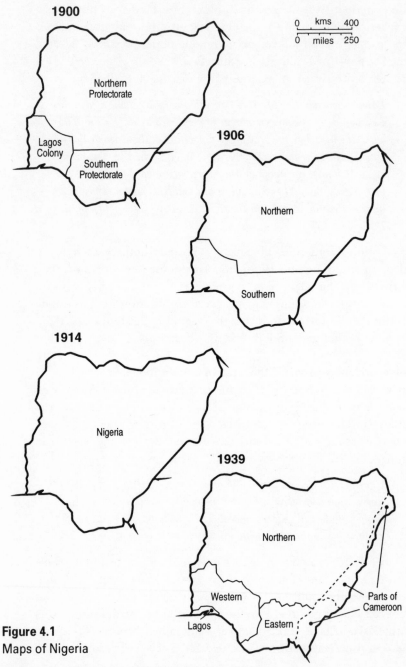

Figure 4.1
Maps of Nigeria

Source: I. L. Griffiths, *An Atlas of African Affairs*, p. 80.

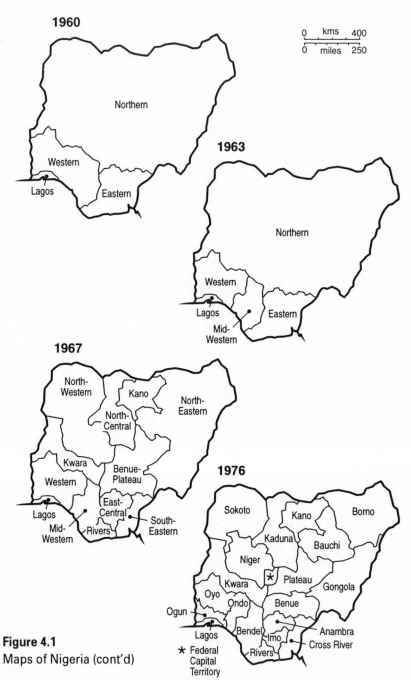

Figure 4.1
Maps of Nigeria (cont'd)

Source: I. L. Griffiths, *An Atlas of African Affairs*, p. 81.

These days hardly anyone is surprised by the outbreak of the Nigerian civil war in 1967. For those who hold the colonial perspective, only Pax Britannica could ever keep the peace in Africa. They see tribal animosity as being so ingrained in Africans that it is only a matter of time before, assuming there is no outside intervention, they all try to butcher each other to death. For the radicals, too, the civil war was inevitable in Nigeria so soon as its ethnic politicians began to manipulate the census population figures to give themselves bigger constituencies. But neither of these analyses can explain why the rest of independent Africa was not engulfed in a similar cauldron.

In reality, independent Nigeria was on the road to prosperity and development. The war only came about for reasons that had nothing to do with Nigeria. The point is that, when the war did break out, it took an ethnic form because of the conditions imposed on Nigeria during its decolonization. So how can we say that Nigeria was on the 'road to constitutional peace' like Ghana?

We have already seen how the flawed Nigerian 'national' constitution contained a colonial legacy of laws that promoted the interests of each Nigerian élite within its own area, while discriminating against them in other regions. It was not these laws themselves that were so important so much as the effect they had on helping to create an atmosphere of suspicion. During the Nigerian constitutional negotiations, for example, the British would emphasize the sharp capitalistic practices of the southerners to northern delegates, and then remind southerners of the reactionary feudal/slave-trafficking vices of the northerners. Regarding Nigeria, colonial administrator Andrew Cohen predicted that,

> rapid advance beyond the new constitution is not likely to be demanded by a majority of opinion for some time to come . . . Although there is a vocal political party in Lagos and the south which demands early self-government, the balance of power at present lies heavily with the more backward rural areas, particularly in Northern Nigeria; here there is strong opposition to rapid change.[151]

Nigerian nationalism did manage to challenge the Richards Constitution. However, Colonial Secretary Oliver Lyttelton later informed Churchill's Tory cabinet that the situation was still more favourable in Nigeria than Ghana because:

the collapse of the cumbrous Constitution established under the auspices of the Labour Government had provided an opportunity of according a larger measure of autonomy to the 14 million Moslem inhabitants of the Northern provinces who were more favourably disposed to this country than the Southern Nigerians.[152]

Under his Lyttelton Constitution introduced in 1954, regional divisions were considerably increased in Nigeria – all in the guise of furthering ethnic 'rights'. In the local elections that year Nnamdi Azikiwe's nationalist National Council of Nigeria and the Cameroons (NCNC) were squeezed into the Eastern Region, whilst the Yoruban-based Action Group won the West and the emir-led Northern People's Congress won the North. Consequently, 'No single nationalist party with a significant cross section of urban workers and peasants of many ethnic backgrounds would ever emerge in Nigeria.'[153]

During the 1951–4 period the NCNC had stood out for unitary independence for Nigeria. At its third convention in Kano in August 1951, the NCNC adopted the following policy:

That in view of recent divisionist tendencies in the country and to accelerate attainment of our goal for a united Nigeria, a unitary form of government with the acceptance of the principle of constituencies will be better for Nigeria and the Cameroons.[154]

This policy was kept until Azikiwe accepted the premiership of Nigeria's eastern region after the 1954 constitutional elections. Azikiwe thereafter reverted to his pre-1951 position: the abolition of Britain's three regional divisions but only so they could be replaced by the even greater number of organic ethnic divisions:

I am opposed to the division of a great country like Nigeria with an area of 372,674 square miles and a population of about 25 million into three regions, because it is an artificial system and must inevitably tend towards Balkanisation and the existence of chronic minority problems, I suggest instead the division of the country along the main ethnic and/or linguistic groups in order to enable each group to exercise local and cultural autonomy within its territorial jurisdiction.[155]

This was essentially the same position as that of Obafemi Awolowo's Yoruba-dominated Action Group.[156] The NCNC and the Action

Table 4.1   Nigeria's Constitutions

1862–1922:	The Lagos Constitution – covered Lagos colony only
1914–22:	The Lugard Constitution – unified Northern and Southern Nigerian protectorates
1922–45:	The Clifford Constitution – jurisdiction limited to southern Nigeria
1945–51:	The Richards Constitution – divided Nigeria into three regions of North, West and East
1951–54:	The Macpherson Constitution – granted legislative powers to the three regions
1954–60:	The Lyttelton Constitution – further diminished central powers: federalism
1960–63:	Independence Constitution
1963–79:	Republican Constitution

Source: Abiola Ojo, 'Law and Government in Nigeria'.

Group were hostile rivals to each other and regularly staged confrontations in Lagos. Faced by ethnically based 'nationalist' politics like this, no wonder Cohen and Lyttelton were so complacent about Nigeria compared to Ghana.

From their point of view, it was nationalism – not tribalism – that was the chief cause of conflict in Africa. Indeed, in a 1963 essay, the American scholar James Coleman argued that tribalism helped sustain Africa's freedom: 'The tribal and sectional pluralism of African states could make dictatorship less possible by providing countervailing power centres which cannot be coerced or regimented into a single authoritarian system'. He was satisfied that the division of Nigeria into three had solved the issue:

> In Nigeria, however, it could be argued that the tensions between the three regions, each one the political core of a major cultural group, and each unable either to dominate or to separate from the others, has created a structured, multiparty system that is largely responsible for the fact that, at the federal level, Nigeria is unquestionably the most free and open polity in independent Africa.[157]

Writing at the same time as Coleman, anthropologist Clifford Geertz was less sure. He noted how 'each [Nigerian regional] party attempts, with some success, to capitalise on minority resentments within their opponents' strongholds.'[158] Geertz believed that, to effectively counter ethnic disruption, ethnic pluralism had to penetrate every Nigerian institution. Geertz advised newly independent states not to deny or belittle groups advocating primordial [ethnic] sentiments but to 'domesticate' them:

> They must reconcile them with the unfolding civil order by divesting them of their legitimizing force with respect to governmental authority, by neutralising the apparatus of the state in relation to them, and by channelling discontent arising out of their dislocation into properly political rather than parapolitical forms of expression.[159]

This is reminiscent of Malinowski's sympathy for indirect rule in order to acclimatize (or acculturalize) Africans to modern society. In the mid-1960s, however, revolutionary phraseology was fashionable and Geertz was imaginative in calling his strategy to convert nationalism to ethnicity 'the integrative revolution'. Donald Rothchild has spelt out how such integration tended to stifle the new African regimes as effective operators on the world's markets:

> In brief, the political coalition acknowledges ethnic diversity and seeks, by including all key groups in the decision-making process, to reduce anxiety and hostility. It co-opts to induce collaboration and exchange. Such a strategy facilitates negotiated settlement, but not without a cost in terms of decisive leadership in developmental or foreign policy matters.[160]

Unfortunately for Rothchild, Coleman and Geertz, one unforeseen consequence of the transformation of urban nationalism with the infusion of rural tribalism was the complete rejuvenation of ethnicity. Despite the abolition of the anti-colonial movements, modern tribalism based on the urban élites was a more dynamic force in African society than tribalism had been when it was merely a rural phenomenon sponsored by the colonialists to thwart the mass nationalist movement.

At the same time, however, it is important to recall, so as to properly periodize ethnicity during the independence era, its relatively restrained character compared to contemporary ethnicity. In their overwhelmingly hostile book on African dictators, Robert Jackson and Carl Rosberg make the important qualification that the experience of ethnicity was limited to the circles inhabited by the political élite and rarely went beyond them:

> *Insofar as African rulers deal with such questions, they do so in terms of the stratagems and resources of personal rule – that is, offering or withholding patronage mostly, coercing occasionally. However, ordinarily it is the elite representatives and fiduciaries of ethnic groups, more than the general members, who gain privileges or suffer punishments under systems of personal rule.*[161]

Jackson and Rosberg are unable to explain this phenomenon, except to ascribe it to the personal whim of the dictator, but the real reason was continuing Western support for the African rulers. In the 1980s, this support was to crumble and modern ethnicity was to come into its own. The full force of modern urban ethnicity was first experienced, not in the Congo or the Mau Mau, but during the Nigerian civil war where Western intervention combined with the urban African élite to produce a devastating conflict.

The Nigerian Civil War

The Nigerian Civil War, 1967–70, would have been little more than a petty squabble if the West had not decided to exploit Nigerian oil reserves in the wake of the June 1967 Arab–Israeli War, which exposed Western dependence on Middle Eastern oil.

At independence in 1960, to thwart his Yoruban opponents, the Eastern region premier Zik joined the Northern emir-led coalition government as Governor-General. In 1963 he became Nigeria's first president. But his government was overthrown by junior army officers in January 1966. They were mainly Ibos who stood by the radical NCNC 1951–4 'Unitary State' programme for Nigeria. Major Nzeogwu, who led the coup in Kaduna and executed the Sardauna of Sokoto, pronounced the reason for the coup in a radio broadcast, which represented an indictment of Zik's opportunism:

> *Our enemies are the political profiteers, the swindlers, the men in high and low places that seek bribes and demand 10 per cent; those that*

*seek to keep the country divided permanently so that they can remain
in office as ministers or VIPs at least; the tribalists, the nepotists,
those that make the country look big for nothing before international
circles; those that have corrupted our society and put the Nigerian
political calendar back by their words and deeds . . . We promise that
you will no more be ashamed to say that you are Nigerian.*[162]

Further military action against the 'tribalists' was blocked by senior
army officers who had the coup leaders arrested. Nevertheless, they
introduced a 'Unitary Decree' in May 1966 to abolish the federal
Nigeria left behind by the British. Anti-Ibo rioting immediately
broke out in the northern region – mainly led by the Christian
minorities who had been campaigning for their own states there.
The unitary regime was then overthrown by northern army officers
at the end of July, and after an immense pogrom directed against
Ibos was relaunched in the North. An estimated 30,000 died and
1.5 million fled south to Eastern Nigeria. Even so, the Civil War
did not break out until eight months later, when the Ibos declared
the eastern region to be independent in May 1967 and called
it 'Biafra'.

It was only after they had succeeded in eliminating the Unitary
army leadership that the northern army, led by Colonel Yakubu
Gowon, changed over from backing northern secession to posing
as the defenders of a Federal Nigeria. Their coup had been code-
named *Araba* (separateness) and they flew the flag of 'The Republic
of Northern Nigeria' over their Ikeja barracks in Lagos. Evacuations
of northern civil servants and civilians had begun. Colonel Gowon's
first radio broadcast on 1 August had initially been to announce
secession, but was hastily redrafted at the last minute to back the
status quo ante. It was pressure from the West that forced the
northerners into backing federalism, which would leave the post-
independence system constructed by the British intact.

It still took months of systematic harassment to turn the
demoralized Ibos from 'Unitary State' supporters into Biafran
secessionists. The former military governor of Eastern Nigeria and
Biafran leader, Chukwuemeka Odumegwu-Ojukwu, or Emeka
Ojukwu for short, expressed the extent of that demoralization when

he addressed an abortive OAU (Organization of African Unity) peace conference in Addis Ababa in August 1968:

> Year after year, we made concessions and compromises to ward off the secessionist threats of the Northern Nigerians and save the unity of the Federation. The pogrom of 1966 ended all that, because it killed the will to maintain this precarious and inhuman association called Nigeria.[163]

The Biafran secession collapsed in January 1970, with tens of thousands of its supporters dying of starvation.

Political Ethnicity Summed Up

During the independence period [1949–89], the strategy of ethnic balancing by urban political élite had been implemented in order to counter divisive tribalism. For many years it proved relatively successful – primarily because it suited Western interests to restrain any ethnic tendencies. Western Africanist experts actively helped the African regimes to develop mechanisms to mollify these ethnic susceptibilities. However, once it no longer suited Western interests to prop up the African state – as became increasingly apparent throughout the 1980s – the negative effects of the ethnic balancing strategy came to the fore.

Published in 1975, David Smock and Kwamena Bentsi-Enchill's *The Search for National Integration in Africa* contained contributions by such Africanist notables as Ali Mazrui, Donal Cruise O'Brien and Aidan Southall among others. The entire contents of this volume was dedicated to enhancing the African state's 'manipulation' of ethnicity, for example through managing language and education programmes, in order to improve national integration. But only a decade later it had become *de rigeur* in the West to label such ethnic balancing practices by African politicians only in negative terms.

By the end of 1980s, however, growing Western disillusionment with Keynesian statist solutions to economic recession encouraged both the left and right to view the African state as inherently problematic. For example, see the collections of essays edited by Zaki Ergas, *The African State in Transition* (1987) and Donald Rothchild and Naomi Chazan, *The Precarious Balance: State and Society in Africa* (1988). Thanks to the African state's ethnic balancing policies, some now viewed it as irrevocably infected with tribalism and therefore incurably 'irrational'. According to radical left-winger Craig Charney,

> *In the African context, the 'neutral state' does not mean an objective, impersonal state; it means tribal balance in patronage . . . The excessive consumption, low rates of investment and economic 'irrationality' which mark African bureaucracies must be viewed in the light of this political logic.*[164]

This view that tribalism was a plague upon the African state was reinforced by the events that erupted in Africa after the fall of the Berlin Wall in November 1989.

After the initial panic over the supposed 'primordial' ethnicity of the African masses began to subside in the early 1990s, however, NGO intellectuals discretely began to advance a new version of African history. This contended that African nationalist regimes possessed a notorious disregard for ethnic sensitivities. According to leading NGO intellectual Alan Fowler, for instance:

> *In order to overcome ethnic differences exploited by colonial powers, many African governments systematically negated traditional social organisations. The official view was that traditional associations reinforced an unwanted ethnic awareness and, through their values and practices, acted as barriers to rapid growth and modernisation.*[165]

The growing influence of these Western paradigms that relied upon the assumption that ethnicity was both omnipotent and universal, either as a plague or as a source of true humanity, helped spread despair among African nationalists. According to Dr Eghosa Osaghae of Nigeria, tribalism could not be ignored because it was quite capable of destroying the African state. He therefore confesses that it was wrong even to try to eradicate tribalism in the first place, 'The whole point about managing (or mismanaging) ethnic conflicts is the acknowledgement that they cannot be wished away or eradicated'.[166] Dr Osaghae's solution to preserving the African state from the tribal threat was to drastically reduce its economic powers. This is tantamount to emasculating the state. Without its economic powers, Africa's state institutions became merely military bodies and started to lose their credibility among the African masses too. Just as non-politics were being urged upon African politicians, so their state was to be a non-state too. Osaghae's deeply pessimistic conclusion is that, 'Ultimately it is only when resources, wealth and privilege can be created outside of the state realm that ethnic management can be most meaningfully pursued'.[167] Unfortunately there is no evidence that ethnic tensions will be resolved once the state's assets are fully privatized. Nevertheless with the sole instrument disabled that enabled Africans to exert some influence on the world, the African state, the West and its NGOs could now move in to solve Africans' problems for them.

The principal problem with the ethnic balancing strategy pursued by the nationalists was the fact that it meant that they effectively endorsed the principle of ethnicity – and therefore organizing along ethnic lines. So long as the African state structures – and its all-important subsidy mechanisms – remained intact, this recognition of ethnicity could be handled, and it even helped to bring a certain stability to the regimes. However, as soon as the state structures began to unravel under Western pressure, the state bureaucracy found it more difficult to regulate ethnicity inside its own structures. With the African nationalist alternative discredited, through their NGOs the West could impose its own definition of ethnicity on African society.

Petty disputes always existed among the ethnic élites feeding off the independent African state. These bickerings steadily grew worse, however, as the issue turned from sharing out the pie equally, to sharing out the misery equally. In the African context, the fragmentation of society meant that, when the NGOs moved in and began to spread their message of moral ethnicity, state personnel gradually quit their jobs so as to secure more lucrative posts as NGO volunteers.

The first African nationalists struggled to build a society that was anything but local and ethnic. The overwhelming conclusion drawn from the failure of the nationalist project is that they experimented too much. Davidson and others now say that they should never have tried to challenge precolonial Africa's political and cultural systems. But, given their experiences, a more constructive and positive conclusion could be that they did not try hard enough. It is feasible to argue that far from centralization and democracy causing ethnic conflict, their comprehensive implementation would have been the only way to avoid it.

Notes

1. Basil Davidson, *The Black Man's Burden*, pp. 75–6. S. N. Sangmpam takes this homage to precolonial Africa one step further with his argument that the 'dynamism' of its lineage ideology managed to neutralize the impact of capitalism in Africa (*Pseudocapitalism and the Overpoliticised State*, p. 16).

2. Basil Davidson, *The African Slave Trade*, pp. 241–2.

3. P. Darby, *Three Faces of Imperialism*, p. 16.

4. Cited in John Ellis, *The Social History of the Machine Gun*, p. 82.

5. It should be noted that Davidson's 'superior' tribal states were subdued by much less resources – little more than a couple of machine-guns – than had to be deployed to emasculate the 'Western influenced' African nationalist movements a few decades on.

6. Frederick Lugard, *The Dual Mandate in British Tropical Africa*, p. 199.

7. In 1839 Lord Durham produced a report recommending local self-determination for the internal provinces and states of the white colonies (later dominions) of Canada, Australia, New Zealand and the Cape Colony after a small disturbance in Canada two years before. After the 1857 mutiny, the principle was also applied in the Indian Raj.

8. Andrew Roberts (ed.), *The Cambridge History of Africa*, p. 34. The concept of 'educated native' has marked similarities to the Spanish/Portuguese 'mulatto' and the American 'half breed'. In addition, in 1928 Robert Park, the president of the American Sociological Society, formulated the pseudo-scientific concept of the 'Marginal Man' who 'lives in two worlds': 'The Christian convert in Asia or in Africa exhibits many if not most of the characteristics of the marginal man, the same spiritual instability, intensified self-consciousness, restlessness, and malaise. It is in the mind of the marginal man that the moral turmoil which new cultural contacts occasion manifests itself in the most obvious forms' (cited in Grant Dyer, *Scientific Conceptions of the 'Other'*, p. 44).

9. Roberts, *The Cambridge History of Africa*, pp. 38–9.

10. Lugard, *The Dual Mandate*, p. 217.

11. Ibid., p. 218.

12. Ibid.

13. Ibid., p. 201. The title 'Emir' was introduced by the British.

14. Cited in P. K. Tibenderana's 'The Role of the British Administration in the Appointment of the Emirs of Northern Nigeria, 1903/1931', p. 232.

15. Lugard, *The Dual Mandate*, p. 288.

16. Ibid., p. 294.

17. Ibid., p. 295.

18. This is the point that Frantz Fanon makes in *The Wretched of the Earth*, p. 87.

19. Lugard, *The Dual Mandate*, p. 313.

20. Cited in Tibenderana, 'The Role of the British Administration', p. 257.

21. David Rooney, *Sir Charles Arden-Clarke*, p. 30.

22. Ibid., p. 12.

23. Geoffrey Bing, *Reap the Whirlwind*, p. 87. Or rehabilitated. In the mid-1920s, the Prince of Wales toured the Gold Coast and was introduced in Kumasi to the Ashantehene, Prempeh, who, after many years spent in exile, 'had seen the light and been allowed to return on a comfortable pension, a good Christian now and an active participant

in Church and municipal work'
(V. Kiernan, *The Lords of Human Kind*,
p. 210).

24. Lugard, *The Dual Mandate*, p. 199.

25. Paul Kennedy, *African Capitalism*,
p. 51.

26. Cited in Kennedy, *African Capitalism*,
p. 392.

27. Cited in John Iliffe, *A Modern
History of Tanganyika*, pp. 321–2.

28. Ibid., p. 323.

29. Ibid., p. 324.

30. Ibid., p. 325.

31. Jan Jorgensen, *Uganda*, p. 82.

32. Cited in Crawford Young, 'The
Colonial State and its Legacy', p. 50.

33. Robert O. Collins, *Shadows in the
Grass*, p. 474.

34. Ibid., pp. 170–1.

35. Ibid., p. 173.

36. The Nuer were convinced that their
magic had stopped the bombing. As the
Nuer lacked any chiefs, the British
invented some for them. For a brief
account of the RAF's air war against the
Nuer, see Charles Townsend, *Britain's
Civil Wars*, p. 197.

37. Adam Kuper, *The Invention of
Primitive Society*, pp. 197–201. In his later
books on the Nuer, Evans-Pritchard
amended his conclusions to show that
Nuer kinship and territorial patterns co-
existed, though not exactly.

38. 20 July 1910. Cited in William
Cohen, 'The French Colonial Service in
French West Africa', p. 497.

39. Ibid.

40. *Ame de Chef* (Paris, 1920), p. 208
cited in William Cohen, 'The French
Colonial Service', p. 499. These chiefs
had no popular legitimacy. For example,

by December 1957 in French Guinea,
'the African masses were increasingly
alienated from their chiefs. Suppression
of the canton chieftaincy in accordance
with the *loi-cadre* of 23 June 1956
aroused no regrets among the
population' (Claude Rivere, *Guinea*,
p. 44).

41. *Ame de Chef*, p. 48, in Cohen, 'The
French Colonial Service', p. 511.

42. *Ame de Chef*, p. 50, in Cohen, 'The
French Colonial Service', p. 511.

43. Ibid., p. 512. The Belgians and the
Portuguese both went to the opposite
extreme from the French, and did their
best to prevent the emergence of any
educated African élite (which also
reduced their options in tackling the
nationalist challenge).

44. J. Clyde Mitchell, *The Kalela Dance*,
p. 16.

45. John McCracken, 'Tribal Identity
and the Growth of Modern Politics,
1920–1940', pp. 647–8.

46. Crawford Young, *Politics in the
Congo*, p. 252. Professor Terence Ranger
discusses the significance of the outburst
in African witchcraft in the 1920s and
1930s as an embryonic anti-colonial
response in his 'Colonial and
Postcolonial Identities', pp. 278–9.

47. According to V. Kiernan, this
hostility of Christianity towards
traditional African religions produced
the well-known phenomenon of
Ethiopianism, which was not unlike
Taiping Christianity in China (which
Gordon had fought against before he
went to Khartoum) and even the
Madhist Islamic cult in the Sudan: 'Here
[in Africa] as in Taiping China,
Christianity fused with local cults to
produce new sects, often of a messianic
cast . . . "Ethiopianism", the impulse
towards separatist churches run by
Africans themselves instead of by white

men, was appearing from 1884. It was an African minister, John Chilembwe, who headed the small rebellion of 1915 in Nyasaland [present-day Malawi], a milestone of modern African history . . . Some years before this a Nyasalander called on his people to emulate "our fellow country Japan"'(V. Kiernan, *The Lords Of Human Kind*, p. 235).

48. Lugard, *The Dual Mandate*, p. 594. The Sudan Government's Foreign Office official handbook No. 98 (1920) stated; 'Christian churches and schools are allowed only in Khartum [*sic*] city . . . Outside Khartum no Christian missionary is authorised to preach in any part of the Northern Sudan'(p. 593). In a paper written in 1955, American Africanist James S Coleman blamed, among other factors, 'indiscriminate missionary education' and 'an intensive and at times intolerant Christian evangelization' for subverting 'the cohesiveness of traditional African society' (James Smoot Coleman, *Nationalism and Development in Africa*, p. 49).

49. Cited in Crawford Young, 'The Colonial State and its Political Legacy', p. 35. Also see ch. 9, 'The Debate about Indirect Rule in the Thirties', in Jeremy White, *Central Administration in Nigeria 1914–1948*, pp. 216–29.

50. Cited in Robert O. Collins (ed.), *Problems in the History of Colonial Africa 1860–1960*, pp. 154–5.

51. This theme seems to be staging something of a reappearance today. Reviewing an exhibition commemorating missionary David Livingstone, art critic Brian Sewell condemned the over-population of Africa brought about by medicine – and the destruction of the rainforest – and remarked how 'Christianity reduced the domestic institutions of the African to dereliction, destroying the mutual

support of extended families united by polygamy, monogamy a miserable substitute . . . [Livingstone] was a decent enough man to recognise the probability of damage to black African societies, warning that if contact with the European did not elevate the discovered native, deterioration must be the inevitable consequence' ('Through the past darkly', *Evening Standard*, London, 11 April 1996, p. 28).

52. Lord Hailey, 'Some Problems Dealt with in *An African Survey*', p. 202.

53. Robert Desmond Pearce, *The Turning Point in Africa – British Colonial Policy 1938–48*, p. 48.

54. The problem of the 'educated native', the 'rootless cosmopolitan' or 'marginal man' continued to beset the colonial authorities until the end. The concept 'marginal man' was invented by American sociologist Robert Ezra Park. See Grant Dyer, *Scientific Conceptions of the 'Other'*, pp. 41–6.

55. John M. Lee, *Colonial Development and Good Government*, p. 44.

56. Ibid., p. 45.

57. R. F. Holland, *European Decolonisation 1918–1981*, p. 128.

58. Yusuf Bangura, *Britain and Commonwealth Africa*, p. 42.

59. Cited in J. Kent, 'The British Empire and the Origins of the Cold War, 1944–49', p. 179.

60. Holland, *European Decolonisation*, p. 227.

61. Pearce, *The Turning Point*, p. 96.

62. Gareth Austin, 'The Emergence of Capitalist Relations in South Asante Cocoa-Farming 1916–33', pp. 260–2.

63. Phillip Darby, *Three Faces of Imperialism*, p. 129. Darby continues: 'The international commodity

agreements of the thirties provided a precedent for Third World attempts in the sixties and seventies to maximise economic returns and derive political leverage through the establishment of mineral and food cartels. Interest in orderly marketing led to the development of marketing boards during and after the war, which later became a general and permanent feature of the development strategy of the independent states.'

From the 1960s, a high world commodity price for cocoa was acting to conceal the fact that the 'independent' Ghanaian cocoa producer really only represented an insignificant input for one of the world's 'Big Four' cocoa processors: Cadbury/Schweppes, Gill and Duffus (British) and Nestlé/Rowntree (Swiss) who today control up to 80 per cent of the world's total cocoa sales between them (B. Dinham and C. Hines, *Agribusiness in Africa*, p. 34). The 'reserve' system that channelled Ghana's cocoa wealth into British coffers was not ended until the 1967 sterling devaluation.

When the world price of cocoa collapsed in the 1970s and 1980s, Ghana's cocoa producers faced destitution. The IMF/World Bank campaign against state intervention in Africa is a campaign against a European creation. Interestingly, the radical campaign against the IMF/World Bank structural adjustment policies demands a return to 'orderly marketing'. Neither solution has anything new to offer.

64. Rhoda Howard, *Colonialism and Underdevelopment in Ghana*, pp. 195, 197.

65. See Josephine Milburn, *British Business and Ghanaian Independence*, p. 35.

66. 'Balance of Payments: Production of Dollar-Earning Colonial Commodities', in Public Records Office, Kew, London, Cabinet memoranda and minutes (hereafter PRO/CAB) 129/Vol. 20/CP(47)242/23 August 1947.

67. Milburn, *British Business and Ghanaian Independence*, p. 48.

68. Basil Davidson, *Black Star – a View of the Life and Times of Kwame Nkrumah*, p. 109.

69. Milburn, *British Business and Ghanaian Independence*, p. 20.

70. Pearce, *The Turning Point*, p. 78.

71. Cited in Pearce, *The Turning Point*, pp. 33–4.

72. Ibid., p. 35.

73. Ibid., p. 122.

74. Rita Hinden (ed.), *Fabian Colonial Essays*, p. 13.

75. Ibid., p. 90.

76. Ibid., p. 97.

77. Cited in Pearce, *The Turning Point*, p. 103.

78. Cited in Pearce, *The Turning Point*, p. 159.

79. Cited in Pearce, *The Turning Point*, p. 152.

80. Ibid., p. 166.

81. Cited in Pearce, *The Turning Point*, p. 153.

82. Ibid., p. 170.

83. David Ernest Apter, *The Gold Coast in Transition*, p. 173.

84. Cited in George Edgar Metcalfe, *Great Britain and Ghana*, p. 689.

85. Cited in Metcalfe, *Great Britain and Ghana*, p. 690.

86. PRO/CAB 129/Vol. 36III/CP(49)199/8 October 1949.

87. Cited in Metcalfe, *Great Britain and Ghana*, p. 693.

88. Geoffrey Bing, *Reap the Whirlwind*, pp. 93–4. This tendency of chiefs to side with the nationalists became a common feature of all African independence struggles.

89. Richard Crook 'Decolonisation: The Colonial State and Chieftaincy in the Gold Coast', p. 10.

90. Cited in Pearce, *The Turning Point*, p. 168.

91. PRO/CAB 128/Vol. 16/58(49)/13 October 1949.

92. Public Records Office, Kew, London, Colonial Office papers (hereafter PRO/CO) 936/198, p. 4.

93. Ibid.

94. The colonial authorities did not hesitate to launch panics about primeval tribalism, despite their longstanding promotion of 'authentic' African culture as against the threat of the 'educated native' and then 'marginal man'. Crawford Young has recorded how the authorities stigmatized as 'tribalistic' national liberation movements they sought to control; 'The colonizer, anxious to manage decolonization in such a way as to ensure the emergence of moderate leaders well-disposed to preservation of metropolitan economic interests and warm post-independence political ties, found in ethnicity an irresistibly deadly weapon against aggressive and radical politicians and movements (stigmatization of the UPC in Cameroon as a Bamileke movement, Lumumbism in Zaire as a Kusu plot, Mau Mau as a Kikuyu aimed at ethnic domination, for example)'. Crawford Young, 'Ethnicity and the Colonial and Post-Colonial State in Africa', p. 84.

95. Stephen Weissman, *American Foreign Policy in the Congo 1960–1964*, pp. 67–8.

96. Jules Gerard-Libois, *Katanga Secession*, p. 17.

97. Ibid., p. 296.

98. Herbert F. Weiss, *Political Protest in the Congo*, p. 123.

99. Ibid., p. 115.

100. Weissman, *American Foreign Policy in the Congo*, p. 77.

101. Young, *Politics in the Congo*, p. 574. Interestingly, Young claims that the colonial authorities were responsible even for this embryonic ethnicity: 'The refusal of the colonial administration to tolerate African political movements until after the first elections had diverted the ablest leadership and organisational energies into tribal associations' (p. 575).

102. Weiss, *Political Protest in the Congo*, p. 258.

103. Ibid., p. 299.

104. M. G. Smith, 'Pluralism, Race and Ethnicity in Selected African Countries', p. 224.

105. Ntieyong U. Akpan, *Epitaph to Indirect Rule*, p. 26.

106. Kwame Nkrumah, *Africa Must Unite*, p. 191.

107. Jean-Paul Sartre, 'Preface', p. 19.

108. Frantz Fanon, *The Wretched of the Earth*, p. 87.

109. Walter Rodney, *How Europe Underdeveloped Africa*, p. 250. Pretoria initiated its infamous Bantustan (tribal homeland) policy in the 1960s.

110. Young, *Politics in the Congo*, p. 235.

111. Donal Cruise O'Brien, *The Mourides of Senegal*, pp. 3, 234.

112. Ibid., p. 282.

113. Ibid., p. 277.

114. Ibid., p. 219.

115. James Coleman, *Nigeria*, p. 325.

116. Quoted in Abiola Ojo, 'Law and Government in Nigeria', p. 59.

117. Paul and Linda Bohannon, *Tiv Economy*, p. 98.

118. Ibid., p. 248.

119. For one commentator, in berating marginal man, the West was really responding to a sense of its own marginalization during the decolonization process. Imperialism became the hate-word of the era, yet 'By denying imperialism the Western elite was denying itself' (Frank Furedi, *The New Ideology of Imperialism*, p. 92).

120. Abner Cohen, *Custom and Politics in Urban Africa*, p. 190.

121. William Graf, 'Nigerian Grassroots Politics', p. 110.

122. Coleman, *Nigeria*, p. 79.

123. Ibid., pp. 78–9.

124. Ibid., p. 437, fn. 22. The Eastern Delta region was the least urbanized part of Nigeria and, from the 1950s, its relatively new cities served as experiments for Andrew Cohen's elected local council scheme.

125. James Coleman, 'The Role of Tribal Associations in Nigeria', p. 17.

126. Ibid., p. 18.

127. Ibid.

128. Ibid.

129. See ibid., p. 136.

130. Ibid., p. 19.

131. 'British colonial [army] recruiters concentrated on the northern groups, but not the Hausa so much as the so-called Middle Belt groups. Ethnic communities such as the Tiv, Ika-Ibo, Angas or Birom fit the colonial model for rank-and-file soldiery. These were small communities which felt overwhelmed by large indigenous groups and they welcomed foreigners as protectors. They were less developed politically and so posed little threat, and were deprived in terms of literary and commercial experience so that the military became an attractive option. It was out of these groups that Major Gowon came' (Cynthia Enloe, *Ethnic Soldiers*, pp. 156–7). Gowon led the July 1966 coup that ousted the brief nationalist regime in Nigeria.

132. Saadia Touval, 'Partitioned Groups and Inter-State Relations', p. 224.

133. Aidan Southall, 'The Concept of Elites and their Formation in Uganda', p. 358.

134. For numerous examples of the 'Proportionality Principle', see Donald Rothchild, 'State–Ethnic Relations in Middle Africa'; Donald Rothchild, 'Hegemony and State Softness'; and Donald Rothchild and Michael Foley, 'African States and the Politics of Inclusive Coalitions'. Indeed, Rothchild's enthusiasm for identifying the ethnic origins of African cabinets and party leaderships sometimes get the better of him. Thanks to colonialism's efforts to preserve ethnicity, any African can be inserted into an ethnic category no matter how irrelevant that is. For that matter, so could many members of Western European and American cabinets and political parties, but only the most lame analysts still base their assessments of Western politics on ethnic origin. Personally speaking, my own 'Campbell clan' status has thankfully been completely irrelevant for me.

135. Nicholas Harman, 'East Africa: Turning the corner'.

136. For his part, Kenyan president Daniel arap Moi has taken on board Lonsdale's ethical ethnicity with alacrity. In reference to Rwanda, he noted that tribalism was bound to wreck the African continent. Then he spoke out in favour of moral ethnicity: 'Most of the

problems facing Africans arose from their refusal to abide by their age-old system of moral principles. Africans had to abide by their cultural moral values.' BBC Monitoring Service, 'Kenyan Broadcast Corporation, Nairobi 18/10/96', radio report.

137. Diouf, quoted in Robert Fatton 'Clientelism and Patronage in Senegal', p. 75. In his most recent account of the Mouride movement, Donal Cruise O'Brien describes how it has fragmented along with the regime it sustained for so long throughout the independence period (see Donal Cruise O'Brien, 'A Lost Generation?', pp. 60–1).

138. According to Crawford Young, this failure to transfer British standards of justice to the African colonies was deliberate: 'By the time of the British imperial occupation of African territory, the dangers to colonial hegemony in indiscriminate transfer of British legal practices was well recognised. Thus, there was no question of application of the jury system in criminal law, which had so undermined the effectiveness of the law as a vehicle for colonial control in Ireland and in the North American colonies' ('The Colonial State and its Political Legacy', p. 35).

139. Fred Burke, Local Government and Politics in Uganda, p. 39.

140. The Irish nationalist leader Michael Collins also sought a 'stepping-stone' to independence and accepted Partition.

141. Coleman, Nigeria, p. 323. Coleman relied heavily for his definition of nationalism upon Carlton Hayes's analysis in The Historical Evolution of Modern Nationalism.

142. David Rooney, Kwame Nkrumah, p. 80. Rooney adds: 'This incident, trivial in itself, raised the more significant issue of tribalism or ethnicity.'

143. D. Rooney, Sir Charles Arden-Clarke, p. 208, my emphasis.

144. Rooney, Kwame Nkrumah, p. 44. At this time, the chiefs were working with the CPP nationalists.

145. P. A. Ladouceur, Chiefs and Politicians – the Politics of Regionalism in Northern Ghana, p. 178.

146. Ibid.

147. Ibid.

148. Ibid., p. 177. Cynthia Enloe goes so far as to accuse Nkrumah of tribalism, claiming that he set up a personal guard in 1959 composed entirely Nzima, his own ethnic group (Ethnic Soldiers, p. 154).

149. Anti-Slavery Society 'Annual Report for the Year Ending 31 March 1966', cited in David Stephen, The San of the Kalahari, p. 10. In May 1996, the House of Lords forced the government to send the British High Commissioner to investigate allegations that the Gaborene government had evicted the San from their Kalahari refuge 'in cattle trucks' ('Bushmen find few friends', Daily Telegraph, 17 May 1996, p. 18).

150. Cited in F. Furedi, Colonial Wars and the Politics of Third World Nationalism, p. 261.

151. PRO/CO 936/198, p. 4.

152. PRO/CAB 128/Vol. 26I/(53)34/27 May 1953.

153. Manning Marable, African and Caribbean Politics from Kwame Nkrumah to Maurice Bishop, p. 62.

154. Cited in Coleman, Nigeria, p. 324.

155. Speech of 3 April 1950, in Nnamdi Azikiwe, Zik, p. 108.

156. See James Coleman, 'The Ibo and Yoruba Strands in Nigerian Nationalism'.

157. Reprinted in Coleman, *Nationalism and Development in Africa*, p. 98.

158. Clifford Geertz, 'The Integrative Revolution – Primordial Sentiments and Civil Politics in the New States', p. 151.

159. Ibid., p. 128.

160. Donald Rothchild, 'State–Ethnic Relations in Middle Africa', pp. 83–4.

161. R. Jackson and C. Rosberg, *Personal Rule in Black Africa*, p. 47.

162. Cited in Z. Cervenka, *The Nigerian Civil War 1967–70*, p. 256.

163. Ojukw E, *Biafra*, vol. 1, p. 325.

164. Craig Charney, 'Political Power and Social Class in the Neo-Colonial African State', p. 60.

165. Alan Fowler, *Institutional Development and NGOs in Africa*, p. 10.

166. Eghosa Osaghae, *Ethnicity and its Management in Africa*, p. 1.

167. Ibid., p. 42.

CHAPTER 5

Tribalizing Talk

We have established a thematic framework for modern ethnicity and also indicated its specificity as compared to previous forms of political ethnicity. We now turn to consider the theoretical assumptions that underpin the literature on theories of ethnicity.

Social constructionism is the theoretical basis for moral ethnicity. It is based on the notion that individuals can construct their own ethnic identity through interpersonal relationships with each other – people talking tribalism to each other. As a victim-orientated philosophy, it poses a moral alternative that supersedes all the other theories of ethnicity: the colonial record of imposing an invented tribalism on Africans from the outside; the primordialist determinism of ancient blood relations; the instrumentalist account of communities mobilizing ethnicity to compete with each other for access to resources. Yet for all its high moral tone, its origins lie in the most diehard conservative theories that glorify in the supremacy of flexibility, particularism and localism.

The Colonial Invention of Tribalism
The 'political ethnicity' we reviewed in the previous chapter has recently been 'deconstructed' by social constructionists. The allegation is that this legacy of colonially invented tribalism is responsible for much of ethnic strife that afflicts Sub-Saharan Africa today.

For old-school imperial apologists, demonstrating the widespread existence of pre-modern tribes in Africa formed an important part of their justification for imperialism, that is, 'We at least helped to modernize Africa'. However, as respect for modernism declined in the West and respect for primitivism grew, pro-colonial historians came around to admitting that colonial administrations were indeed responsible for promoting tribalistic policies. This admission might contradict traditional imperial justifications for the Europeans' mission in Africa; yet it helped gloss over the record of imperialism in Africa through presenting it as being pro-ethnic, while also providing a subtle demonstration of the power of colonialism to make things happen in Africa. As the colonial record has been gradually unearthed by historians, this latter aspect favouring colonialism's tribal policies has more and more come to the fore.

It is interesting to note, however, that though pro-colonialists are prepared to acknowledge that the European authorities undertook the creation of African tribes, they are reluctant to admit this to be a deliberate conspiracy. The colonial promotion of indigenism was driven on by a concern to meet the rising challenge of African nationalism. According to conservative historian Philip Gulliver, 'this emphasis on tribe was strengthened in the later opposition of colonial officials to growing nationalism'.[1] After listing a number of 'invented' aboriginal groupings in Uganda and Tanganyika, Gulliver makes the significant remark that they were created 'as much by unconsidered reaction as by positive policy'.[2]

From this perspective, politicizing a selection of African cultural practices and manufacturing them into 'tribes' is far from a conspiracy orchestrated by the West. It might more closely resemble a panic response by colonial authorities reacting to the prospect of rising instability. In this latter aspect, the promotion of ethnicity by imperialism seems to originate more from its sense of weakness when confronted by the threat of opposition rather than from any overwhelming confidence in its abilities: its tribal policies were attempts to react to a society going out of control.[3]

For pro-colonial historians like Philip Gulliver, there was one supreme justification for the plans of the colonial administrations to foster tribalism in Africa: stability. Though writing at the end of the 1960s, he notes how the tribe is in reality a flexible concept, open to being politically manipulated both for ill and for good purposes:

> *Both the concept and the operative groups denoted by the term 'tribe' are flexible, sometimes very highly so. The cultural forms and symbols can be, and are, manipulated to conform to and give support to*

differing groups (ie tribes) for differing purposes and interests. Thus the groups on the ground are capable of variable cultural definition according to circumstances. There are no absolute groups of people, defined and delineated once and for all, and to be labelled tribes. This is a general characteristic of particularism within wider society.[4]

Gulliver here gives a modern interpretation of the long conservative tradition of emphasizing the predominance of the local, or the particular, in politics. This tradition reaches back at least to the days of Edmund Burke and Joseph de Maistre, both vigorous opponents of the French Revolution, if not to medievalism before them.

We have already noted how some of the most conservative sections of the Western establishment express an affinity towards certain African tribes like the Zulus or the Bushmen. In April 1996, an editorial in *The Times* enthusiastically greeted the inauguration of Mrs Lynne Symonds, a schoolteacher from Norfolk, as tribal chief of the Mamprusi of northern Ghana:

Mrs Symonds is not a charity worker or a Unesco official; she is a teacher from an ordinary English village. Personal friendships bind and inspire more than any aid programme. To those who nourish such human links belong tribal honour and glory.[5]

In Uganda, the coronation of Ronald Mutebi as the new Kabaka (King) of Buganda in July 1993 was greeted by a chorus of Western approval (Britain's Labour government had deposed the last Kabaka in 1966). Some observers interpreted the event as an act of political manipulation by Ugandan president Yoweri Museveni and predicted further upheavals for Uganda since it seemed to restore the domination of the Baganda there. Others claimed, however, that the ritual 'represents the realities of black African allegiance': 'I speak of the re-emergence of the *tribe* as the only political entity that in the long run is going to work effectively in post-colonial Africa'.[6]

The point about the Kabaka of the Baganda is that it is widely seen as a pro-British institution. Its revival in the 1990s thereby seems to suggest that the explicitly imperial party that still exists in Britain was right all along. The Kabaka had been completely transformed as an institution by the British from 1890 onwards.[7] According to African historian Ali Mazrui, 'The capacity of the

Baganda to be deeply anglicized and at the same time profoundly traditionalist remains one of the fascinating aspects of those people'.[8] Since the Kabaka-ship had almost become a venerable British institution (Mazrui describes it as an 'Anglo-African institution'[9]) it is no surprise that the ceremony provoked nostalgia among the old colonial brigade for the days of the empire. But is it legitimate to talk about the colonial invention of tribalism? Were the European powers ever that powerful in moulding African society?

Primordialism: A Contested Ethnicity

Oxford historian and leading proponent of social constructionist theories of ethnicity, Terence Ranger has cleverly reposed the colonial 'invention' of tribes as less than the exercise of omnipotent colonial authority and more as the outcome of a contest between the colonial authorities and their African subjects. Instead of the image of powerful Europeans inventing African culture, Ranger demonstrates how the European powers transformed originally nebulous African customs into a rigid structure to suit their own purposes of cultivating a hierarchical African élite of chiefs and kings, etc. In his essay on the Manyika of eastern Zimbabwe, Ranger demonstrates how, though European missionaries and colonial authorities may have been responsible for slotting Africans into ethnic categories in the first place, Africans were able to respond flexibly to this development and even turn it to their advantage: 'Whites and especially missionaries played a key role in the definitions of the Manyika identity but in such a way that the idea was open for all sorts of uses by Africans.'[10]

It was in his celebrated essay 'The Invention of Tradition in Colonial Africa'(1983), that Ranger propounded his view that the strength of pre-colonial identity was derived from its flexibility:

> *Almost all recent studies of nineteenth century pre-colonial Africa have emphasised that far from being a single 'tribal' identity, most Africans moved in and out of multiple identities, defining themselves at one moment as subject to this chief, at another moment as a member of that cult, at another moment as part of this clan, and at yet another moment as an initiate in that professional guild.*[11]

Through exhibiting such flexibility, Africans could apparently avoid the colonial discourse and pursue their own, more organic versions. Again, in his book on the Zimbabwean liberation struggle, Ranger mentions how white Rhodesian attempts to cultivate a bogus layer of loyal chiefs could not compete with the more flexible Shona spirit-mediums and so they only recruited 'a sequence of very aged men'.[12] Many of these collaborators were subsequently shot by the guerrillas. On the other hand, the Shona mediums brought peasants and guerrillas together in what Ranger calls a 'community of resistance' against the white occupiers.[13] This rural religion 'prevented the past from being expropriated in its turn by the "belated" traditionalism of Rhodesia Front "tribal politics"'.[14]

Ranger has correctly grasped that tribalism is a mediated form, in those times a resultant product of Africans struggling to free themselves from the colonial yoke. He has successfully rubbished the notion of colonial omnipotence through the invention of tribes, but it has all been at significant cost. Rather than concede that the strength of African nationalism alone would have been sufficient to extract concessions from its colonial foe, Ranger's perspective emphasizes the flexibility of African ethnicity as the real source of African nationalism's power. But how much substance can we attribute to his notion of a flexible African ethnicity that is capable of transcending the colonial experience and, indeed, holding more responsibility than nationalism for ultimately defeating it?

It is as well to remember that the notion of racial or ethnic flexibility has a long and conservative pedigree. Ranger has twisted the conservative notion of weak and suggestible human personalities into a critique of imperialism, though with its reactionary origins remaining intact. Any theory that bases itself on the fundamental pliability of the human personality, as does the theory of the social construction of ethnicity, contains within itself the reactionary kernel that assumes that individual human beings cannot be expected to make rational decisions. Indeed the odious medieval belief in Fate habitually presented life as comprising a series of erratic yet implacable incidents, which the individual could not hope to avoid but had to adapt to as best one could. For example, in Carl Orff's splendid cantata *Carmina Burana*, based on thirteenth-century monkish writings, Christian piety is mixed with paganism in a lament against the fickleness of Fate: 'O Fortune, changeable as the Moon! . . . Monstrous Fate, you turning wheel . . . I weep from Fortune's blows.'

Austrian physician F. A. Mesmer (1734–1815) first revealed the suggestibility of individuals under hypnotism. *Fin de siècle* French sociologist Gustave LeBon proposed that mobs could also be mesmerized or manipulated by a charismatic personality once they had been whipped into a state of mass hysteria. LeBon's seminal work – *Psychologie des Foules* (Paris, 1895) – was originally written to explain away the success of revolutionaries during the Paris Commune of 1870, but it was then adopted by various establishment figures to argue for the deliberate inculcation of racism and militarism among the European masses.[15]

Colonialist notions that assume the flexibility of ethnicity go back much further than Gulliver, who wrote in the late 1960s. The first study of an African ethnic group written from the standpoint that ethnicity is also flexible was published in 1942. Siegfried Nadel – a Viennese professor who served as an anthropologist for the Anglo-Sudanese administration – produced a study of the Nupe of Northern Nigeria, *A Black Byzantium*. In it, he subjectively defined the African tribe as 'a group the members of which claim unity on the grounds of *their* conception of a specific common culture', and he drew a clear distinction between the openness of bottom-up cultural communities and the rigidity of top-down political units, 'The political unit, unlike culture and community, is exclusive . . . Cultural groups and communities have fluid boundaries; the association (in our case the political unit) is or is not rigid; but its boundaries . . . are by definition rigid.'[16] Nadel obtained this distinction between political associations and cultural communities from American sociologist R. MacIver. By Nadel's time the idea that ethnicity is fluid and Africans could chose their own ethnic identity had become very much an isolated standpoint. Only the most diehard conservatives would respond to its appeal to the supremacy of personal malleability and particularism.

As we have noted already, 50 years before Nadel, the German-American anthropologist Franz Boas had posited the existence of many 'cultures', all equally valid, against the singular notion of Culture, meaning the state of civilization that any society can aspire to. Boas also allowed for the impact of migration on societies, making the important concession that cultures can vary under external influence and therefore admitting their fluidity. Boas influenced a whole generation of American anthropologists and sociologists but, by the time of the Second World War, his epigones like Ruth Benedict had distorted his themes by hardening them. Benedict maintained that a society's culture was so decisive that it could mould individuals from birth into traits that they kept for life. Benedict's determinist model of 'cultural pluralism' verged on substituting cultural explanations of human diversity for racist biological ones.

Boas the individual was seen as radical because of his explicit anti-racism, and he was therefore shunned. But many colonial administrators found they could identify with Boasian themes – particularly when they were reinterpreted by his epigones. According to Elazar Barkan, British anthropologists who advised the colonial administration, like Bronislaw Malinowski and Alfred Radcliffe-Brown, might affect a disdain towards Boasians like Ruth Benedict and Margaret Mead, yet they all, 'under different names, but with similar effect . . . resurrected Rousseau's noble savage, and presented the primitives as a source of envy to Western society'.[17]

According to Peter Novick, cultural pluralism became particularly popular during the inter-war years because 'a certain detached scepticism towards the norms of one's own society became common' among leading anthropologists after the barbarities of the First World War.[18] During the Second World War and through the 1950s, however, Boas went into steep decline – the zenith of American hegemony – as anthropology turned to stress 'the unity rather than the variety of cultures' and the concept of development came into its own.[19] Thanks to the post-war boom in the West, during which capitalism experienced its most sustained period of growth ever, Siegfried Nadel's insights remained marginal for the next 40 years.

Nadel's – and social constructionism's – moment finally came at a moment when anomy and alienation, risk and chaos, globalization and niche marketing, became the buzz words of the 1990s' generation. Ethnic flexibility was rescued from the traditional right and adopted by radical academics in despair at the failure of their socialist and African nationalist projects. Far from the popularity of social constructionism arising out of a close inspection of African social trends, it solely derives from the intellectual confusion precipitated by the disintegration of Western society.

This explains why constructionist theories – though around for many decades – have spent so long on the margins of Africanist thought. Only once respect for the old Western traditions had been lost could the old African tribal kings and kingdoms, that duplicated the British monarchy and parliament, and encapsulated 'African tribalism', be replaced by the environmentally sustainable African ethnic minority seeking solace in contemplating their past culture, tolerating other identities, and generally feeling satisfied with living in a multicultural milieu (unless and until they are cruelly manipulated by unscrupulous politicians). Unconsciously social constructionists are transposing categories generated through the fragmenting crisis of Western society on to the Third World.

In 1969, the year of the Woodstock pop festival and during mass protests against the Vietnam War, colonialism was never so unpopular. As the first rumbles of the new era of stagnation were heard, and while Gulliver was hastily rehashing imperial history, radical Scandinavian anthropologist Fredrik Barth wrote: 'We give primary emphasis to the fact that ethnic groups are categories of ascription and identification by the actors themselves, and thus we have the characteristic of organising interaction between people.'[20] The following year, Aidan Southall also declared war on traditionalist conceptions of tribalism: 'To hammer home the importance of interlocking, overlapping, multiple collective identities is one of the most important messages of social and cultural anthropology.'[21]

Crawford Young's *The Politics of Cultural Pluralism* and Nelson Kasfir's *The Shrinking Political Arena* – both published in 1976 and both written from the 'new' perspective – helped launch it as a mainstream intellectual current among Africanist scholars in the West. During the 1980s – and especially since the end of the cold war – the social constructionist school of African ethnicity became the dominant paradigm among the Western intelligentsia.[22]

The eminent Africanist Crawford Young has probably set out the most systematic appraisal of social constructionism as it applies to African ethnicity in his *The Politics of Cultural Pluralism*. For Young, ethnic identity is 'a subjective self-concept' and is peculiarly suited to encapsulating the experience of the *urban* African:[23]

Urban residence places persons in juxtaposition and social interaction with culturally differentiated individuals, perceived as groups from far more diverse provenience than would be characteristic in the countryside. For both self and other it is inconvenient to interpret social reality through too complex a mapping system. A reductionist process occurs, whereby roughly similar groups in language or even in general area of origin are grouped together in ordinary discourse. Reductionism is most pronounced in the perception of others.[24]

Young limits society's role to 'others' in his self-conception of ethnicity: 'Subjective identity itself is affected by the labels applied by others. Through a feedback process, it is gradually internalised by the group itself.'[25] He also makes the useful point that the original epithets 'Negro' and 'Indian' were eventually adopted by the targets of abuse themselves. Young concludes with the proviso though that, although identity is subjective and fluid, it is 'not infinitely elastic' since physical attributes like skin colour remain more or less indelible.[26] Nevertheless, the interaction of individual imaginations is always allocated more weight in the production of ethnicity by constructionists like Young than, say, wider concerns like socio-economic developments or the impact of international relations upon African society.

Until the end of the 1980s, Ranger's insight that ethnic identity could be a product of a contest or struggle between the colonial authorities and the African masses was dominant. In the aftermath of the collapse of the Soviet bloc, however, references to struggles or masses were frowned upon and subsequently labelled 'primordialist' or 'essentialist'. Ranger's stress on the elasticity of ethnicity has secured his reputation as the emphasis swung against primordialism. Basil Davidson, however, has been increasingly sidelined, despite the welcome that his *Black Man's Burden* (1992) initially received for its assault upon the African nationalist state.[27]

The problem with the African state according to Davidson was that it was not under sufficient mass pressure. Rejecting Western 'nation statist' influences, Davidson called for a return to the model of precolonial tribalism which he alleges was more responsive to the masses. But Davidson even hesitates to adopt the notion of ethnic flexibility:

If one were to make a comparative listing of political structures in precolonial Africa the result would confirm that precolonial political structures undoubtedly displayed great diversity, but an even greater unity of underlying concept. So much nonsense has been written over the last hundred years about the arbitrary and unpredictable nature of precolonial African political communities and their modes of existence that their systematic regularities, and the reasons for these realities, have been hugely obscured.[28]

Later Davidson describes the deleterious impact of the West upon Africa and, in a phrase that is reminiscent of the 'rootless Marginal Man' theorists of the 1950s, praises an account of Master-Sergeant Samuel Doe, the Liberian dictator who seized power in 1980, which labels him as a 'cultural hybrid' who is 'lost between two worlds'. For Davidson, this expression best sums up African dictators such as Doe and Mobuto: 'This saying has at least the merit of suggesting the mental state in which their seizure of power forces them to live.'[29]

Here Davidson completely counterposes himself to the social constructionist agenda of ethnicity which, far from criticizing marginal man as 'lost', suggests that it is only through becoming cultural hybrids themselves that Africans can begin to make sense of their environment and come to terms with it. Basil Davidson has been superseded because his primordialist elevation of precolonial tribalism as well as his rejection of ethnic hybridity confines him to the sidelines of mainstream Africanist ethnicity debate.

Anthony Smith has tried to restate the case for primordial ethnicity in the 1990s. But he distinguishes himself from discredited mass primordialism by describing himself as 'ethno-symbolist'. Indeed Smith defensively notes that 'there is no necessary connection between ethnicity and conflict' and stresses the functions performed by ethnicity for social integration.[30] Smith emphasizes instead the cultural contribution of myths, memories and symbols which he maintains are 'as old as the historical record itself':[31] 'There has been a resurgence of ethnicity in the modern world, as the intelligentsias have rediscovered ethnic roots as an antidote to the impersonality of bureaucratic rationalism.'[32]

This reprise of the 'marginal man' theories of the 1950s cannot explain why ethnicity made such a huge impression only after the cold war ended in 1989.

Instrumentalism: Pork-barrel Ethnicity

In the 1990s, the intellectual emphasis of ethnicity theory has steadily swung away from cohabiting with mass ethnicity, or primordialism, and towards focusing upon the individual or rather interpersonal construction of ethnic identity by communities. In 1983, using his South-east Asian experiences, Benedict Anderson's *Imagined Communities* brilliantly captured this new version of social constructionism by arguing that local Third World communities imagined their own identity.[33] Hence for Jean-François Bayart, the editor of *Politique Africaine*, Davidson's vision of a large number of well-established ethnic communities in pre-colonial Africa is a myth:

> *The very notion of ethnic group, at least in the form in which it is usually imagined, that of a given entity, going back over centuries and corresponding to a limited geographical area does not square with fact . . . If this extreme diachronic flexibility of ethnicity were recognised historically, one would see that pre-colonial black Africa was not, strictly speaking, made up of a mosaic of ethnic groups.*[34]

Referring to the Kirdi, Mofu, Foule, Peul and Bamileke of the Cameroons, Bayart proposes that 'they do not seem to have existed for much longer than the [independent] state itself'.[35] He suggests instead that the imagination is prioritized, since for him 'there may even be such a thing as an ethnic awareness without an ethnic group'.[36] For Wyatt MacGaffey, the difference between an African ethnic group and an African tribe also depends on whose imagination was at work:

> *In Kongo [a province in Zaire], an area where one would expect to find tribes if such things existed, we find instead a constant flux of identities . . . Although both 'tribes' and 'ethnic groups' are imagined communities, the difference between them may be that while an ethnic group imagines itself, a tribe has been imagined by others.*[37]

Here we can see how those scholars influenced by Anderson's imagined communities differ from the Ranger/Davidson school of struggles over ethnic identity. The grubby masses no longer have any role to play at all. Anderson's theory of ethnic identity was a hybrid construct, the outcome of a negotiation between different imaginations, a dialogue to be negotiated between élites rather than a contest between classes.

The development that effectively removed the masses from the arena at the same time permitted the emergence of a new, instrumentalist school of social constructionism that saw ethnicity entirely in terms of community pressure groups manipulating their ethnic heritage to secure access to resources. The origins of instrumentalism probably lie in the Manchester school of ethnicity (Mitchell, Epstein and Gluckman) of the 1950s. The Manchester scholars sought to resolve the problem of persisting ethnicities in an urbanized Africa of the early 1950s, but Anderson laid down the intellectual background for its mainstream adoption in the 1990s. As can be seen from the contributions to the 1993 Rhodes conference, instrumentalism became the dominant school in the field of African ethnicity in the wake of the confusion caused by the collapse of the Soviet bloc.[38]

Instrumentalists abhor primordialism because it allegedly paves the way for ethnic fanaticism, for fundamentalism, for – in academic parlance – essentialism. In addition, primordialists never really get around to explaining why ethnic sentiments should stay submerged for prolonged periods and only surface in society occasionally. The notion of Identity (with a capital 'I') is inherently dependent upon the past, upon background, on your 'roots'. Both primordialist and instrumentalist wings cannot avoid this aspect of identity in their definitions of ethnicity, but the primordialists stress it more than the instrumentalists. Primordial ethnic identity is therefore overtly conservative, and this is what instrumentalists find repugnant about it.

For their part, instrumentalists lay stress on the flexibility of ethnic identity (though supposed primordialists like Ranger also emphasize it). But we have seen how the notion of malleable identities also possesses reactionary antecedents. Even so, the instrumentalists' notion of ethnic fluidity seems more radical than ethnic Identity's rigid conservativism because it ties ethnicity to conceptions like globalism, risk and the uncertain – all of which became trendy in the 1990s.

According to Louise de la Gorgendiere, 'Instrumentalism, as a situational, competitive form of collective and individual self-interest, is too crude for understanding the complexities of peoples' lives'.[39] But the popularity of instrumentalism cannot be put down to its theoretical inconsistencies. Its influence is more due to the collapse of institutions and movements that people traditionally looked to for both protection and advancement – such as the Labour and Communist parties, the trade unions in the West and the nationalist movement in Africa. In the Western society today, the idea that you survive by swopping between identities, rather than joining a movement, has acquired the status of orthodoxy. This notion began in lesbian and gay studies and then spread into gender and racial issues – and from there into Third World and African studies.

We have seen how Ranger located African ethnicity's superiority over nationalism in its ability to provide alternative identities into which Africans could manoeuvre. For the constructionists, then, ethnic multiplication – or fragmentation – does not pose a problem but is rather a cause for celebration. As far back as 1969, Fredrik Barth noted that the persistence of ethnic identity depended upon the supply of alternative identities to the individual: 'What matters is how the others, with whom one interacts and to whom one is compared, manage to perform, and what alternative identities and sets of standards are available to the individual.'[40]

Instrumentalism is the philosophy of ethnicity as a survival 'scam'. Instrumentalism and the chaos of the global market contradict themselves by definition, but instrumentalists do not advocate a direct confrontation with the market. Rather, they propose that ethnic groups survive by manipulating their flexibility in order to discover a niche for themselves in the market. Instead of being manipulated by outsiders, therefore, the ethnic group is encouraged to manipulate itself into positions of advantage. These pork-barrel tactics are the hallmark of instrumentalism. Dissatisfaction with the immorality of instrumentalism has proceeded apace.

The 'primordialist' critique of instrumentalism is that it is superficial because it never explains exactly where the appeal of ethnicity derives from in the first place. Hutchinson and Smith criticize instrumentalism for 'taking the ethnic nature of organisations for granted' and failing to account for the 'mass passions evoked by ethnic ties and cultural symbols'.[41] Some instrumentalists have even managed to detach the link between ethnicity and the past. Abner Cohen thinks that London stockbrokers are an ethnic group.[42] Anthropologist Eugeen Roosens also claims that ethnicity is not a primitive phenomenon but a modern one because ethnic minorities seek to maximize (or minimize) the display of their identity so as to obtain greater access to high-technology goods. Furthermore, the desire to obtain these goods will in time erode away ethnic identities:

> *In many cases, a kind of transcultural consensus is reached about the value of a number of products of the modern world . . . It may take some time, but in the long run high-quality goods win consensus about their worth in widely different cultures. Consequently there is a steady movement in the various cultures towards uniformity.*[43]

To primordialists, therefore, instrumentalism is not so much a theory as a description of society approximately one degree less valuable than the musings of a tabloid editorial. For those who believe that ethnicity is the universal human condition, the instrumentalist heresy is that there is every reason to expect ethnicity will become redundant when circumstances so dictate. Hutchinson and Smith, for instance, have 'anti-essentialists' deconstructing ethnicity into an 'optional identity often overshadowed by other (gender, class, regional) identities.[44]

We can now draw some conclusions about the debate between primordialists and instrumentalists. Both hold assumptions influenced by social constructionism, but where primordialists perceive ethnicity as a mythical entity emerging out of the past to engulf society, instrumentalists accuse them of essentialism and even complicity in racism. For their part, instrumentalists are certain that ethnicity is an entirely modern phenomenon, a ploy constructed simply to attract scarce resources, a scam. Any indigenous authenticity, and all ethnic morality, is, by definition, denied by them. Primordialists ask where the ethnicity of the instrumentalists comes from. Yet the protagonists of the instrumentalist standpoint began to prevail over their primordial rivals as soon as the celebrations at the collapse of the Soviet bloc and the African nation-state in the 1980s turned into groans as western institutions, too, began to crumble in the 1990s. Instrumentalist theories of ethnicity were only briefly flavour of the month, however. The immorality of instrumental ethnicity was frowned upon as tending to exacerbate social instability.

Recognition that the primordial and the instrumentalist perspectives are inadequate has recently led to efforts to transcend them both. In 1991, Henrika Kuklick rewrote the historiography of British anthropology to demonstrate that primitive societies were morally superior to colonialism, claiming that the 'social ideal' of Evans-Pritchard and Malinowski and company 'were to be found in simple societies'.[45] Despair at the intricacies of human existence has led other protagonists in a more mystical direction. For Richard Fardon, it is impossible to answer such basic questions about ethnicity as: is it real? has it been invented? do ethnic groups have histories? – because ethnicity is far too complex to understand. Fardon therefore retreats from reason into the irrational world of tarot cards:

> *The project of Tarot precipitates complex resemblances in the world by virtue of the ways in which human efforts have been called forth and governed. The problems of conceptualizing the inception (or even invention) of ethnicity are rather similar to those involved in the historicity of the Tarot.*[46]

As we have seen, others like Cambridge don John Lonsdale, have sought to base ethnicity upon equally mystical Christian notions of morality. The debate between primordialists and instrumentalists over what ethnicity means has been fierce, but their inadequacies are now being transcended by moral or mystical conceptions of ethnicity.[47]

Social Constructionism and Moral Ethnicity

The appropriateness of social construction theory to contemporary moral ethnicity can be located in its celebration of passive individuals who can only enter into local relations with other people.

By themselves, the ethnicity theses of social constructionism contain a number of contradictory propositions. If we assume that constructionism is correct to assert that all social phenomenon are merely contingent constructions, what happens when ethnicity itself is demystified? Instead of assigning a privileged place to indigenism, let's debunk (or 'deconstruct' in the parlance) it too. If ethnicity is really so fluid, how can cultural diversity be maintained over time?

Patently, if cultures are compatible, and can flow into each other, then diversity must eventually be abolished.[48] Again, if there are limits to fluidity to maintain ethnic diversity, what are they? And are they generally applicable? Meanwhile, what is it about localism that makes it relevant to the modern condition, especially in these globalizing times? If ethnicity is globally relevant, and the limits that preserve it are generally applicable, how can constructionism also maintain that universals are essentialist? Or is ethnicity itself culturally essentialist, as Ruth Benedict would presumably argue? If so, how does this differ fundamentally from racial theories of African tribalism? Caught as it is between universalism and particularity, the concept of fluid ethnicity is left emasculated.[49]

Both social constructionism's ethnic universality and its alleged localism are empty abstractions. This leaves its much vaunted fluidity looking rather wooden. It is to resolve these internal contradictions that social constructionism has to rely upon mixing identities only at the level of individual discourse. An effort to rescue the concept can be seen in the recent rise in popularity of the equally irrational concept of 'the diaspora'. This seems to represent a backdoor attempt by them to smuggle ethnicity back on to the agenda even after it has been disposed of by their own notions of 'hybridity' and the flexibility of identities.

Apart from Boas and LeBon, the crucial strand in the formation of social constructionism theory was provided by Edmund Husserl (1858–1936), who together with Boas was also a product of the nineteenth-century German school of conservative philosophy. It is only through Husserl's stance on interpersonal subjectivity that social constructionism has been able to overcome its obvious contradictions.

Husserl postponed the issue of whether objective reality exists or not: we cannot know whether our ideas are real representations of an objective world – so he left that question on one side ('bracketed off'). For Husserl, while the term 'subjective' refers to a single consciousness, 'objectivity' is reduced to mean those perceptions that had been verified by their common possession in a community, rather than admit any idea of external reality. Instead of the modern expression 'the social construction of reality', Husserl preferred 'an objective consensus between subjects' or the 'intersubjective constitution of the world'. According to James Heartfield, with this theme 'Husserl influenced sociologists like Max Scheler, Alfred Schutz and Raymond Aron, and philosophers like Martin Heidegger and, through him, Jean-Paul Sartre'.[50] Through Sartre, Thomas Kuhn and then Michel Foucault social constructionism took on a radical dimension. For example, see Jacques Derrida's *Speech and Phenomena and Other Essays on Husserl's Theory of Signs* (1967).

Social constructionism recognizes the contingent character of capitalism, but maintains self-imposed limits on its sometimes useful insights. Social constructionism does not mean that society constructs. On the contrary, for social constructionists 'social' only ever means the interaction of individuals – never society as a whole. 'Construction' is the extrapolation of these individual interactions to form a – albeit contingent – community. Thus social construction-ism is the philosophy of the inadequate, primitivized individual *par excellence*. As such, social constructionism provides a much needed intellectual sustenance to the mish-mash of Western primitivism that NGO volunteers pick up before they leave for Africa.

Herein lies social constructionism's real flaw. Its presumption that interpersonal relations are able to impose themselves directly on capitalist society is erroneous. In fact, they only impinge indirectly – once they have been mediated through the 'invisible hand' of the market. Society cannot simply be extrapolated from an immense accumulation of interpersonal ties.[51] On the contrary, the forms that interpersonal relations take are determined by more social forces.

Ethnicity was never just an immutable African tradition. But neither is it in a permanent state of flux, as the constructionists would have it. Indeed, the theme of a 'global maelstrom' advocated by adherents of ethnic thinking has been much exaggerated. The market is more responsible for any flexibility that ethnicity may possess than any choices made by interpersonal relationships. Ironically, it is the volatile market that also organizes social relations in a capitalist society, if only to a limited extent. Indeed, the market both organizes and disturbs, integrates and atomizes capitalist society. To stress one aspect at the expense of the other leads to an unbalanced approach. The constructionists tend to emphasize uncertainty in the world today at the expense of the orderly because, with the designation of the market as *natural*, its responsibility for *social* organization under capitalism has been shrouded. And the more the market is naturalized, the more its socializing inclinations are hidden.

Formerly, apologists for capitalism assumed production relations to be eternal, with the opportunity for social transformation restricted to intervention in the marketplace. Nowadays, however, the market is assumed to be natural as well. When the transactions of the market are greeted with the same sort of fatalistic resignation as the weather, the implication is that the scope for social experimentation is drastically reduced – mainly to the narrow sphere of immediate personal relationships. To compensate, social constructionists try to garnish this forlorn remnant of social activity by sponsoring the adoption of ethnic identities as a liberating impulse.

Whence, then, the appeal of social constructionism that individuals can really determine their identity in society? First, the failure of traditional projects for nationalist or socialist emancipation was essential. But the decisive factor was the elevation of the suffering African victim into a moral status symbol by a diminished West. This establishment ratification of the philosophy's primitivist assumptions confirmed moral ethnicity as potentially adoptable by everyone. Fluid ethnicity already contained the notion of the pliant individual. Technology like the internet and the satellite telephone is welcome so long as it also helps foster the notion of the diminished individual and the marginal community. Now ethnicity can be applied globally to everyone and everyone can become ethnic – so long as they are prepared to adopt the moral demeanour of the victim. This bizarre conception that people talking tribal identities to each other can actually determine the direction of society could only get a grip in a time when the belittling of the individual is positively celebrated as a moral virtue.

Since it is so full of contradictions, it scarcely can come as a surprise to learn that social constructionists frown upon any analysis that probes beneath the surface. A world made up of multiplying identities seemingly expresses creativity and makes for the best possible world. From this perspective, anything that impedes the elasticity of the interchanges of these minorities, which seeks to impose definition upon the undefinable, is not only wrong – it is dangerous. To attempt to define ethnicity any more deeply smacks of 'totalitarianism',

'Western conceit', 'male arrogance' or, in academia, 'essentialism'. By placing indigenism into rigid categories or boundaries, essentialism provides the intellectual rationale for ethnic cleansing.

By going on the offensive against primordial ethnicity, social constructionism has caused itself one or two intellectual problems. It has redefined ethnicity so it can now mean almost anything globally. But what does it actually mean specifically in the case of Africa? For Edwin Wilmsen, 'the package of meanings wrapped in the word "ethnicity" has grown exponentially'.[52] Jan Pieterse also seems overwhelmed by the variety of interpretations of ethnicity: 'Ethnic politics are highly contextual and local because they are affected by so many variables – socioeconomic change, changing center–local relations, political transformation, historical mortgages'.[53] Unfortunately anyone attempting to provide an answer to the meaning of ethnicity risks being denounced as an essentialist even for asking the question.

Logical consistency – or even meaning – is not critical, however, for the success of the social constructionist project. It is far bigger than any academic requirement for theoretical rigour. Ultimately, even the instrumentalists prefer to accommodate to ethnicity rather than see it abolished. Social constructionists celebrate primivitism and the diversity of minorities, not out of any altruistic generosity to other cultures, but first to excuse the West from having to explain why it has failed to modernize Africa, and second, to excuse the West from having to explain why it has lost faith in the ability of its own system to deliver decent living standards.

The present vogue is for the morally inclined theories of ethnicity that can sanitize Africans. But which morality? Approval for ethical theories of ehnicity has only intensified the pressure to establish an original source for indigenism that can be beyond reproach. In general, the trend has been to depict ethnic communities as morally appropriate because they stand close to nature. In other words, indigenism is naturalized. The ethnic is biological. Despite their profound aversion for anything that smacks of essentialism, with ethical ethnicity social constructionists have fashioned a doctrine that sanctions the same sort of quasi-biological determinism that they have spent their careers attempting to refute.

Though they are virulently opposed to any essentialist analysis of the concept of ethnicity, the central assumption that informs all social constructionist analyses is that ethnicity is an eternal characteristic of humanity. From this perspective, it is impossible to see what demarcates contemporary African society from its preceding forms since the assumption is that they are all being driven by ethnicity. Ultimately, if ethnicity represents the essence of humanity, then the modern world must be no different from society at the dawn of history. Despite their anti-primordial intentions, we therefore find that social constructionist theories of ethnicity are also imbued with the same mysterious influences as primordial theories. For both instrumentalism and moralism, primitive forms of human organization are exerting their conservative impact upon every subsequent form of human organisation. As a result, the dominant paradigm today in modern ethnic theory is that those limits that constrained ancient primitive societies are just as valid for Africa's local communities today, as indeed they are for the modern world.

Notes

1. Philip Gulliver (ed.), *Tradition and Transition in East Africa*, p. 15. In the cases of the Congo and Kenya, Crawford Young and Frank Furedi both confirm that the colonial authorities managed to thwart the development of a conventional nationalist movement through this official sponsorship of a tribal agenda. See C. Young, *Politics in the Congo*, p. 575; and F. Furedi, *The Mau Mau War in Perspective*, p. 5.

2. Gulliver (ed.), *Tradition and Transition in East Africa*, p. 15.

3. Thanks to Suke Wolton for this point.

4. Philip Gulliver (ed.), *Tradition and Transition in East Africa*, p. 34.

5. *The Times*, 8 April 1996, editorial.

6. Tom Stacey, 'Crowned to a chorus of approval', *Independent*, 3 August 1993, his emphasis.

7. See Thomas Pakenham, *The Scramble for Africa*, p. 416 passim.

8. Ali Mazrui, *Soldiers and Kinsmen in Uganda*, p. 180.

9. Ibid., p. 173.

10. Terence Ranger, 'Missionaries, Migrants and the Manyika', p. 142.

11. Terence Ranger, 'The Invention of Tradition in Colonial Africa', p. 248.

12. Terence Ranger, *Peasant Consciousness and Guerrilla War in Zimbabwe*, p. 251.

13. Ibid., p. 206.

14. Ibid., p. 14.

15. See Robert Nye, *The Origins of Crowd Psychology*.

16. Siegfried F. Nadel, *A Black Byzantium*, pp. 17–18. Interestingly, Nadel's book was warmly welcomed by indirect rule advocate Lord Lugard, who wrote the foreword to it.

17. Elazar Barkan, *The Retreat of Scientific Racism*, p. 119.

18. Peter Novick, *That Noble Dream*, p. 144.

19. Ibid., p. 549.

20. Fredrik Barth (ed.), *Ethnic Groups and Boundaries*, p. 10. Barth has been cited as an original authority on the flexibility of ethnicity ever since, but the first 'modern' social constructionist was actually Paul Mercier, who mentions Nadel's influence in his 'Remarques sur la Signification du "Tribalisme" en Afrique Noir', pp. 64–7. According to Michael Schatzberg, 'As early as 1961 Paul Mercier observed that all regions of the continent could furnish examples demonstrating that one is not simply a member of a single, immutable ethnic group . . . Mercier wrote that an ethnic group could be defined in whatever way its members chose' (Michael Schatzberg, *Politics and Class in Zaire*, p. 26).

21. Aidan Southall, 'The Illusion of Tribe', p. 36.

22. See for example, from the 1980s onwards, Benedict Anderson, *Imagined Communities*; Michael Banton, *Racial and Ethnic Competition*; Paul Brass, *Ethnic Groups and the State*; Dov Ronen (ed.), *Democracy and Pluralism in Africa*; Henrika Kuklick, *The Savage Within*; Bruce Berman and John Lonsdale, *Unhappy Valley*; Jean-François Bayart, *The State in Africa*; Thomas Hylland Eriksen, *Ethnicity and Nationalism*; Edwin Wilmsen and Patrick McAllister (eds), *The Politics of Difference*.

23. Crawford Young, *The Politics of Cultural Pluralism*, p. 41.

24. Ibid., p. 42.

25. Ibid., p. 43.

26. Ibid.

27. See Davidson's *The Black Man's Burden*.

28. Ibid., p. 63.

29. Ibid., p. 246.

30. John Hutchinson and Anthony Smith, *Ethnicity*, p. 3.

31. Ibid.

32. Ibid., p. 10.

33. Benedict Anderson, *Imagined Communities*.

34. Jean-François Bayart, *The State in Africa*, pp. 46, 50.

35. Ibid., p. 47.

36. Ibid.

37. Wyatt MacGaffey, 'Kongo Identity, 1483–1993', pp. 1035–7.

38. Wilmsen and McAllister (eds), *The Politics of Difference*.

39. Louise de la Gorgendiere, 'Ethnicity', p. 13.

40. Barth (ed.), *Ethnic Groups and Boundaries*, p. 25. The discrepancy in periodization between the inception of the academic debate on ethnicity and the popular explosion of interest in the issue at the end of the 1980s was not due to any functional requirement that sufficient time must elapse before conceptual innovations seep into the public arena. Much academic discourse never reaches the popular domain anyway. It can be better accounted for by two other factors. First, it is far easier to relinquish an intellectual outlook than drop, albeit decrepit, ideologies which, none the less, serve to prop up society; and second, unlike academia, the establishment did not willingly endure the relativisms of the constructionist standpoint and has only adopted it once their traditional convictions had been found demonstrably deficient in the aftermath of the Soviet crisis.

Furthermore, the meaning of instrumentalism has also altered because of disenchantment with political movements. Whereas instrumentalists used to portray social classes and movements inventing ethnic identities to achieve ambitious goals, like the preservation – or the overthrow – of colonialism, their perspective has considerably narrowed over the years to the current condition, where instrumentalism usually means depicting small clusters of people forging indigenist roots as a survival strategy to access scarce resources or to alleviate discrimination.

41. Hutchinson and Smith, *Ethnicity*, p. 34.

42. Abner Cohen, *Two-dimensional Man*, p. 15.

43. Eugeen Roosens, *Creating Ethnicity*, pp. 157–8.

44. Hutchinson and Smith, *Ethnicity*, p. 12.

45. See 'The Glorification of Innocence', in Henrika Kuklick, *The Savage Within*, pp. 264–71.

46. Richard Fardon, 'Crossed Destinies', p. 128.

47. There was no conception of a 'moral' ethnicity at the April 1993 Rhodes conference on ethnicity and identity in South Africa. However, in a more recent social constructionist text – Richard Werbner and Terence Ranger (eds), *Postcolonial Identities in Africa* – moral ethnicity has a much higher profile, especially in Patrick Chabal's essay (in which Lonsdale in cited approvingly).

48. As Eugeen Roosens has successfully argued, see his *Creating Ethnicity*, pp. 157–8.

49. At the philosophical level, criticism of social constructionism can be taken much further. While it readily admits that globalism is an abstraction (albeit mysterious – hence 'chaos theory') and the nation-state is also abstract (but in an incompetent and even dangerous way – 'risk society'), it insists that its privileged localism somehow remains pragmatically practical. Little does it realize that this 'concrete' parochiality will remain abstract too so long as it is abstracted from the universal. As will, vice versa, any universal theory that is disconnected from local reality. Marxist philosopher Istvan Meszaros's remarks on modernity and post-modernism are pertinent here: 'In this respect it does not really matter whether "universality" or "particularity" dominates in the theories in question. In the end it comes to the same thing. For the dominance of "universalism" in "modernity" can only amount to *abstract* universality. And, by the same token, the cult of "difference" and "particularism" in "postmodernity" remains constrained by the inherent limitations of *abstract* particularity.' (Istvan Meszaros, *The Power of Ideology*, p. 45). In other words, it is only by tracing the mediating links between the universal and the particular that can make them both socially relevant.

50. James Heartfield, 'Marxism and Social Construction', pp. 8–9. It would be churlish to associate social constructionism with the notorious subjectivism of Bishop Berkeley (1685–1753), who argued that nothing exists objectively except as collections of ideas produced by the mind.

51. Thanks to James Heartfield for this point. Hence, coming from the opposite direction, Thomas Eriksen is mistaken when he imagines that sufficient inter-ethnic marriages could eventually abolish ethnicity in the case of Mauritius: 'If the trend of interethnic marriages continues, an ultimate effect may be the end of ethnicity as we know it today' (Eriksen, *Ethnicity and Nationalism*, p. 159).

52. Wilmsen and McAllister (eds), *The Politics of Difference*, p. 4.

53. Ibid., p. 42.

CHAPTER 6

Primitivizing Marx?

It is vital to consider Marx's views on primitive society because his extensive notes on the subject permit us to challenge today's dominant paradigm that the conditions that governed primitive communist societies in the past can still be applied to backward societies today. 'Just as each century has its own Nature, so it produces its own primitives'[1] to which we may perhaps add, 'and its own Marx'. Apparently Karl Marx also once said 'What is certain is that, as for me, I am no Marxist'.[2] From the beginning Marx was caricatured. To an extent this is an inevitable consequence for anybody who wishes to express themselves publicly. But today we can conclude that the caricature of Marx is so much more dominant than the legacy of the man himself that it has become worthless to use the label Marxist. At best, Marxism does not mean anything much anymore. At worst, Marxism is in danger of being subsumed under the general primitivist sentiments of our times. Primitive communism, rather than world communism, is the new ideal society. Stalinism first turned Marx into an icon and, as the most renowned icon of communism, Marx might just be set to return as a primitive idol.

Throughout the cold war years, the Marxist tradition was lambasted for its failure to understand both ethnicity and nationalism.[3] As we saw in Saul Dubow's comment in the introduction to this book, Marxism has also been derided for its assessment of ethnicity as 'false consciousness'.[4] But today it is increasingly assumed that, as a Communist, Marx would have sympathized with the victims of ethnic persecution and generally supported the notion that a new society would amount to a revival of the freedom, equality and tolerance of primitive communities.

For a number of reasons, therefore, it would be productive to review what Marx and Frederick Engels actually wrote about 'primitive communism': to establish what primitive communism was and to thwart the idolization of Marx; to clear up the confusions that social constructionism has created over the impact of interpersonal relations in ethnic communities; to dispose of the erroneous notion that humanism is compatible with primitivism; but chiefly to demonstrate that the primitive world has gone for ever and there is no relation between it and local communities in Africa today.

Karl Marx wrote about primitive communism with Engels in *The German Ideology* (1845–6); in the *Grundrisse* (1857–67) and *Capital* at the same time; and his ethnological notes on Morgan and others (1879–82). Engels's work on the subject is contained in *Anti-Duhring* (1877–8) and *The Origins of the Family, Private Property and the State* (1884). Both Marx and Engels were strongly influenced by the American anthropologist Lewis Morgan's work *Ancient Society, or Researches in the Lines of Human Progress from Savagery through Barbarism to Civilisation* (1877). The main illustrations that Marx, Engels and Morgan used were the Native Indian tribes of the Americas, the old Greek and Latin tribes, the German and Irish tribes, and the castes of the Indian subcontinent. They wrote very little about Africa at all. Nevertheless it is useful to make explicit at this point the main assumption they operated under since it stands in such stark contrast to those of mainstream cultural relativism. Once we have done this it will be obvious why what Marx and Engels wrote also applied to primitive communities everywhere.

This assumption is that different levels of production determine different forms of society, but within those forms people are the same irrespective of any other difference, cultural or temporal.[5] Thus this assumption implies that Greek society of the fourth century BC can be compared to that of the Iroquois based around the New York area in fifteenth century AD.[6] Morgan's title – from savagery through barbarism to civilization – lists the different divisions of 'ancient society'. The division between savagery and barbarism is somewhat arbitrary: Morgan used the standard of whether the use of pottery had developed. The divide between barbarism and civilization is judged to be the abolition of gentile social forms – that is, society organized around blood or kin relationships – by the rise of the state (demarcated by territory).

Originally, primitive man was thought to be an isolated individual, a Robinson Crusoe figure or Rousseau's 'noble savage'. In a footnote to *The Communist Manifesto* written by Engels in 1888, the true communal origin of man is set down:

> *In 1847, the prehistory of society, the social organisation existing previous to recorded history, was all but unknown. Since then, Hathausen discovered common ownership of land in Russia, Maurer proved it to be the social foundation from which all Teutonic races started in history, and by and by village communities were found to be, or have been the primitive form of society everywhere from India to Ireland. The inner organisation of this primitive communistic society was laid bare, in its typical form, by Morgan's crowning discovery . . .*[7]

These, then, are our assumptions. In respect to primitive communities, and therefore primitive communism, the principal questions we want to answer is: did Marx and Engels considers individuals free and equal in them? were they democratic? and were they tolerant of their different neighbours?[8]

Were individuals free and equal under primitive communism? According to Lawrence Krader, Marx opposed the romanticized Rousseau version of the free primitive individual with his own notion of 'non-despotic bonds' imposed on the individual by the community:

> *In the negative sense, Marx posited the unfreedom in the primitive condition, in contradistinction to Rousseau, as the non-despotic bonds of the group. Rousseau's notion of the chains of civilisation as opposed to the primitive state of freedom was reconceived by Marx as chains of primitive bondage which were satisfying and comforting. Despotic, dissatisfying, discomforting are the bonds of civilisation.*[9]

For Marx, the individual in a primitive communist community was little more than an item of communal property, albeit one that is carefully looked after:

The reproduction of presupposed social relations – more or less naturally arisen or historic as well, but become traditional – of the individual to his commune, together with a specific objective existence predetermined for the individual, of his relations both to the conditions of labour and to his co-workers, fellow tribesmen, etc – are the foundation of development, which is therefore from the outset restricted . . . The individuals may appear great. But there can be no conception here of a free and full development either of the individual or of the society, since such development stands in contradiction to the original relation.[10]

Marx's views on primitive communism are comprehensively summed up in his famous remark on the impact of British colonialism on the 'idyllic' village communities of India:

Sickening as it must be to human feeling to witness those myriads of industrious patriarchal and inoffensive social organisations disorganised and dissolved into their units, thrown into a sea of woes, and their individual members losing at the same time their ancient form of civilisation and their hereditary means of subsistence, we must not forget that those idyllic village communities, inoffensive though they may appear, had always been the solid foundation of Oriental despotism, that they restrained the human mind within the smallest possible compass, making it the unresisting tool of superstition, enslaving it beneath traditional rules, depriving it of all grandeur and historical energies.[11]

Marx and Engels were fully aware of the negative side of civilization, that is capitalism's, achievements. Civilization was a thousand times more progressive than those Indian villages, but it was a thousand times more brutal as well:

Civilisation achieved things of which gentile [that is, primitive] society was not even remotely capable. But it achieved them by setting in motion the lowest instincts and passions in man and developing them at the expense of all his other abilities. From its first day to this, sheer greed was the driving spirit of civilisation . . . If at the same time the progressive development of science and a repeated flowering of supreme art dropped into its lap, it was because without them modern wealth could not have completely realised its achievement.[12]

Marx, making the same point as Engels, indicated that the source of primitivism's morality was based on the assumption of a diminished humanity, where production is geared to existing human need; as compared to modernity, where humanity has apparently been chained to the unlimited expansion of production: 'Thus from the old view, in which the human being appears as the aim of production, regardless of his limited national, religious, political character, seems to be very lofty when contrasted to the modern world, where production appears to be the aim of mankind and wealth as the aim of production.' The development of society's productive forces required the sacrifice of all presuppositions, all preconditions, where man strives not to remain something that he has already become, but where all limited, one-sided aims are sacrificed to secure the full development of human mastery over the forces of nature. 'This is why the childish world of antiquity appears on one side as loftier. On the other side it really is loftier in all matters where closed shapes, forms and given limits are sought for. It is satisfaction from a limited standpoint; while the modern gives no satisfaction; or, where it appears satisfied with itself, it is vulgar.'[13]

In his book on the German objective idealist Hegel, Hungarian Marxist Georg Lukacs refers to this contradiction between the morality of tribal society as compared to the progressiveness of modern society while reviewing Hegel's remarks on the Greek tragedy, *Antigone*:

> *What is striking about Hegel's view of the* Antigone *is the way in which the poles of this contradiction are maintained in a tense unity: on the one hand, there is the recognition that tribal society stands higher morally and humanly than the class societies that succeed it, and that the collapse of tribal society was brought about by the release of base and evil human impulses. On the other hand, there is the equally powerful conviction that this collapse was inevitable and that it signified a definite historical advance.*[14]

Primitive society's high moral standards were bought at the price of ensuring that its individuals were kept at the level of the lowest common denominator, that is, they remained childish and naïve about the wider world. In such a society, the notion of democracy is meaningless. People were ruled by their customs and they 'voted' accordingly. Even to talk about 'individuality' or 'personality' is to show a cavalier disregard for their meanings.

In market society, people generally relate to each other as commodities, rather than personally. Money, the supreme commodity, is social power and hence can determine the fate of even the most intimate of relationships. In primitive communist society, however, money has little or no value and the personal seems to reign supreme. In reality, however, personal and interpersonal relationships in primitive communism are only a faint semblance of the modern phenomenon. No personal ties could ever transgress the restrictive customs of communal life. Expulsion from the community was a frightful penalty – it meant almost certain death. Even the powers of the chiefs were so limited by custom, that is, not by democracy.

Primitive communism meant a 'levelling down' to basics, but for Marx this 'crude communism' was unnatural, an

> *abstract negation of the entire world of culture and civilisation, and the return to the unnatural simplicity of the poor, unrefined man who has no needs and who has not even reached the stage of private property, let alone gone beyond it.*[15]

The primitive was not much of a personality. Marx consistently maintained that the primitive individual was a diminished individual, an embryonic human. In his opinion, ancient society was founded either 'on the immature development of man individually, who has not yet severed the umbilical cord that unites him with his fellowmen in a primitive tribal community, or upon direct relations of subjection'.[16] According to Krader, Marx was so convinced that relations in primitive society were collective, not personal, that he contradicted Morgan on this point.[17] Krader continues: 'It is an inconsistency to think that because the number of people in a primitive society is small, for which reason the members may relate to the chief personally, the governmental or judiciary or other relations are personal.'[18] The collective relations of the primitive community bear within them both private and impersonal elements. It is true that these became more and more differentiated as the amount of tribal property increased and the office of chief became more clearly delineated. This only took place over generations, however.

The typical communal personality was the complete nonentity. Once this point has been grasped we can begin to appreciate the peculiar meaning of democracy in a primitive communist society. A definite chief was selected in advance – maybe many years in advance – and then elected into power by the community as a whole at the appropriate moment. The selection was more a matter of following the norms of traditional society than as the result of any democratic process.

Marx discusses this issue of the election of communal leaders, or chiefs, in his notes on Sir Henry Sumner Maine's *Lectures on the Early History of Institutions* (1875). For Marx, the tribal chief was only in theory elected, whereas in practice the office was transmittable. Following a principle known as 'Tanism', chiefs were formally elected but the elect was invariably the nearest mature male relative of the dying chief.[19] This is an early form of hereditary succession, whose origins are derived in the endless repetition of this procedure, and – given an increase in the material possessions of the primitive community – the elections are eventually dispensed with and an aristocracy installed.[20] Such electoral procedures are also followed for the post of witch-doctor or traditional healer, where an important requirement of the profession is access to rituals, rites and indigenous wisdom passed on by predecessors, who for this reason retain a great measure of power over the community through their ability to train and select their heirs. Needless to say, even their magical powers were limited by the collective constraints imposed by communal life.

Great efforts have been put into refuting the Hobbesian notion that primitive communities were constantly in a state of war with each other, and to posit instead the image of an array of peaceful communes tolerating each other's identities and cultural differences. Given that primitive communities were neither at peace nor at war all the time, the truth must lie somewhere in between. To properly deal with this question we will have to spend some time with the 'gloomy science', economics.

Marx ridiculed those bourgeois economists who treated cavemen as the first capitalists. For him, exchange only existed at the edges of primitive society and had marginal impact within it:

> It is simply wrong to place exchange at the centre of communal society as the original, constituent element. It originally appears, rather, in the connection of different communities with one another, not in the relations between different members of a single community.[21]

This exclusion of exchange to the margins of primitive communities had an important influence on shaping them. Whereas labour to produce items for exchange with another community is indirect, that is, its products are not for immediate use. They are to be exchanged for something else. On the other hand, labour within the primitive community can be said to be directly social, that is, its products can be immediately useful for society. In fact, we can be speaking about the same item – say, meat. One community that had caught too much meat to eat themselves might exchange it, say for an excess of fish caught by some other community. Whereas relations with other communities are mediated through a material relationship, relations within the community can therefore remain direct and collectively social. While internal community relations are immediately or directly social, relations with other communities are mediated through the market-place, such as it is.

Even without the impetus provided by war or conquest, the gradual division of labour developing within the community enables these external exchange relations to penetrate the internal economy of the community and eventually come to dominate it, leading to its transformation. Engels's works trace in detail the transformation of the primitive communist community under the impact of the specialization of labour, the subsequent growth of wealth, and the development of classes and the state. We need only note here that Marx believed that the notion of private wealth germinated among primitive communities and nomadic tribes. For example, he took note of Morgan's idea that 'the possession of domesticated animals – which are capable of infinite multiplication – gave the first idea of wealth to the human mind'.[22] The origin of money, for Marx, was also primeval:

> Nomadic races are the first to develop the money-form, because all their worldly goods consist of movable objects and are therefore directly alienable; and because their mode of life, by continually bringing them into contact with foreign communities, solicits the exchange of products.[23]

Given the limitations and restrictions on allowing market relations to penetrate communal life, conflicts within the community could be easily regulated by the tribal authorities. It was otherwise between communities, however, where conflicts were not restricted by traditional custom.[24] It is not so much, therefore, that they were no conflicts within or between primitive communities. It is rather than the collective barriers within the community placed limits on conflict that did not exist between communities, where conflict could therefore go much further (the vendetta, the feud, blood-debts, slaving, etc.). For Engels, the rosy image of tolerant primitive communities is only feasible when applied within the tribe. Otherwise, the contrary assumption holds good: 'Outside the tribe was outside the law. Wherever there was not an explicit treaty of peace, tribe was at war with tribe, and wars were waged with a cruelty which distinguishes man from other animals . . .'[25]

The moral code of the primitive communist community was for their own members only. Generally, they treated everyone else like beasts. Engels dramatically makes the point that, in respect to the primitive communist community, the development of slavery was 'a great step forward'.[26] First he makes the point that, as Man sprang from beasts, he had no alternative but to use bestial means in order to extricate himself from barbarism. But these 'bestial means' were directed outside of the community, at least initially. The necessary growth in the productive forces required an increased division of labour, and thus the 'simplest and most natural form' of this was to enslave prisoners of war. Engels dryly points out that slavery could be considered an advance even by the slaves themselves: 'The prisoners of war, from whom the mass of slaves were recruited, now at least saved their lives, instead of being killed as they had been before, or even roasted, as at a still earlier period.'[27]

Engels reproaches those who turn up their noses at ancient Greek society for being based upon slavery. Without such slavery there would be no Acropolis, no Greek science, no Socrates, Plato and Aristotle, and no plays, including *Antigone*. In Marx's famous phrase, 'Force is the midwife of every old society pregnant with a new one. It is itself an economic power.'[28]

The suspicion here is that if primitive society was tolerant and respected the culture and identity of others, it was only because it was itself barren and content to remain a marginal, diminished collectivity of humanity. Toleration can be a lovely euphemism for stagnation. What seems clear is that, in so far as primitive communities were peaceful, they were inert. But it is also the case that, in so far as they were violent, it was an entirely external phenomenon which made little or no impact on the internal structure of the commune.

We can now return to the 'flaw' in the social constructionist argument which we discovered in the previous chapter in order to examine its source. We can now see how, in reviewing Marx and Engel's relatively balanced remarks on primitive communism, the example of primitive communism exerts a powerful appeal for those seeking the moral regeneration of their own societies. It can easily be understood how, then, they might seek in the structures of those same communities a means by which the impact of a chaotic globalized market can be alleviated.

This motive has persuaded the social constructionists to overlook the realities of primitive communism, and especially the fact that their 'directly social' character entailed the obliteration of individual personalities and interpersonal relations (which was no real loss to the communities in question since such phenomena would not become a general experience until the development of modern society). Furthermore, they were also persuaded to distort the real impact of market relations on ethnic communities today. All of them more or less assume that Marx and Engels, and Morgan's, descriptions of primitive communities still apply today. Indeed, given the general contempt that money-making and capitalism in general is held in today, the fashion is to present the globalized world as tending towards a post-market one, that is, where a global community of ethnicities will have recovered the moral certainties of primitive communism.[29]

We have already asserted in the previous chapter that the market is more responsible for any flexibility that ethnicity displays than any choices made by the interpersonal relationships advanced by the social constructionists. In the same way, capitalism in the 1990s is responsible for the shape that modern primitivism takes, which is why Marx, Engels and Morgan's accounts of primitive society – written in the last century – no longer apply.[30] As Marx said, each century produces its own primitives.

The Real and the Formal Subsumption of Labour under Capital

Marx distinguished between two different stages of capitalist development: the formal and the real subsumption of labour under capital.[31] In the *formal* subsumption of labour under capital, capital extracts profit from labour working with pre-capitalist techniques. It is called formal, because it is only formally different from those pre-capitalist modes of production. In the *real* subsumption of labour under capital, on the other hand, capitalism extracts profits by revolutionizing the labour process. It is called real, because it is the specifically capitalist mode of production. Despite the motivation of the individual capitalist to generate profits for himself, and despite the immense barbarities committed in its name to keep this contradictory process in gear, the fact is that this system modernized the whole world.

Chronologically, the real subsumption arose out of the formal relationship. The real subsumption became the dominant form of capitalism throughout the world in this century. Logically, then, we must begin with this latter process now established and examine how it is changing. The stagnation of the capitalist economy, the broad support for environmentalism, the antipathy towards unlimited science and technology, the prioritization of people over profits, the flight towards the primitive – these all indicate that the specifically capitalist mode of production is breaking down in the 1990s.

For Marx, the real subsumption of labour under capital 'begins only when capital sums of a certain magnitude have directly taken over control of production'.[32] Once in the driving seat it can begin operating on the basis of its own specifically capitalist laws, bending everything to itself, even transforming technology so that the regulation of nature can be considered a feasibility for the first time in human history. Yet it is precisely these progressive features of capitalism that have come under most suspicion today. The unlimited pursuit of science and technology in the cause of greater profits, in other words, capitalism's sole progressive aspect, has become the target of primitivist hostility. Every feature of capitalism that emphasizes the possibility of extracting relative surplus value is continually criticized, while those aspects of capitalism that depend upon the direct exploitation of people are celebrated as 'sustainable'. Major aid projects like dams and electricity installations are cancelled, while the village pump has made a comeback. The back-breaking hoe and the plough that are still the most widely used tools in African agriculture are praised to the skies, while the tractor and the combine-harvester are condemned for polluting the environment.

This celebration of absolute surplus value recalls the formal subsumption of labour under capital, with which it is irrevocably associated. The formal subsumption of labour under capital was the method of exploitation that dominated in the past, but a simple return to the past is not involved here. In the past, though conditions were primitive everywhere, people were inspired by the possibility of the spread of technology and other aspects of modernity to Africa. Nowadays, the machinery might be available but it is regarded as a problem that makes things worse. In the section dealing with merchant's capital in the third volume of *Capital*, Marx describes one typical instance of the formal subsumption of labour in capital – the independent furniture makers of London's East End:

> *The whole production is divided into very numerous separate branches of business independent of one another. One establishment makes only chairs, another only tables, a third only bureaux, etc. But these establishments themselves are run more or less like handicrafts by a single minor master and a few journeymen. Nevertheless, production is too large to work directly for private persons. The buyers are the owners of furniture stores. On Saturdays the master visits them and sells his product, the transaction being closed with as much haggling as in a pawnshop over a loan.*
>
> *The masters depend on this weekly sale, if for no other reason than to be able to buy raw materials or to pay out wages. Under*

these circumstances, they are really only middlemen between the merchant and their own labourers. The merchant is the actual capitalist who pockets the lion's share of the surplus-value . . . the merchant turns the small masters into his middlemen, or buys directly from the independent producer, leaving him nominally independent and his mode of production unchanged.[33]

The atomization of production, the breakdown of manufacturing industry into sub-units, sub-contracting and, eventually, home-working are becoming increasing common in the West, but in Africa there never really was any large-scale production outside of the mines. In respect to the 'independent' furniture masters of London who were really workers, Marx makes clear that,

Without revolutionising the mode of production, [this system] only worsens the condition of the direct producers, turns them into mere wage-workers and proletarians under conditions worse than those under the immediate control of capital, and appropriates their surplus-labour on the basis of the old mode of production.[34]

This way of merchandising the produce of the 'independent African farmer' is the typical of the technique adopted by the major Western food processors like the cocoa operations of Cadburys and Nestlé in Ghana and Côte d'Ivoire. According to Dinham and Hines, Brooke Bond Liebig (Kenya) has 'confined' itself to marketing tea for this reason as African farmers increasingly took over its plantations after independence:

Smallholder production of some crops can substantially benefit companies, for which the main source of profitability is in processing, marketing and distribution, because smallholders can deliver good quality crops at reasonable cost, and attract government and aid funding which would not be available to a foreign firm.[35]

The NGO community has taken this African smallholder framework on board, while covering it in a 'sustainable development' gloss. After studying 95 farming projects in eastern and southern Africa, the London-based International Institute for Environment and Development concluded that, by using inexpensive, small-scale appropriate technology adapted for local conditions, and encouraging them to work in groups, 'the small farmers in these countries could certainly double or treble their food production without genetic engineering or heavy investment in pesticides or fertilizers'.[36]

Yet, in the *Grundrisse*, Marx specifically mentions small-scale agriculture as an example of the 'most odious exploitation', because

> *what takes place is exploitation by capital without the mode of production of capital . . . The most odious exploitation still takes place in them, without the relation of capital and labour here carrying within itself any basis whatever for the development of new forms of production, and the germ of newer historic forms. Capital still appears materially subsumed under the individual workers or family of workers – whether in a handicraft business or in small-scale agriculture.*[37]

The formal subsumption of labour under capital should not, therefore, be mistaken for a return to pre-capitalist forms of production. It only occurs when any barriers to the extraction of surplus-value have been destroyed. For Marx, it relies on 'a purely financial relationship' between protagonists. Thus, the pre-capitalist mode of production which is based on directly social relations has not been revived. Moreover, the need to pursue the most barbaric form of profit extraction – that based on the exploitation of direct labour – means that the instruments of oppression need to be maintained close at hand.

It might seem surprising to associate NGO 'do-gooders' and the purveyors of 'Indigenous Knowledge Systems' with a more barbaric form of surplus value extraction, but that is the consequences of their 'small is beautiful' approach.[38] In so far as they employ technology, it is merely as consumer 'gadgets' to help reconcile people with their miserable existence rather than deploy the technology to boost production and thereby alleviate it. Nevertheless, as with any system of exploitation, instruments of repression need to be maintained close at hand. Under the former system of political ethnicity, the colonial authorities recast African primitive cultural traditions into hierarchical instruments of state repression. Under moral ethnicity, however, the élites cultivated by the NGOs police the diminished ethnic communities.

At this stage, it has become obvious that we will have to redefine primitivism. Up to this point, we have assumed that primitivism meant that people were more human the closer they came to nature. Our argument has been that this definition implies a degradation of humanity. Now it has been revealed that primitivism does not even mean bringing humanity closer to nature. Rather, primitivism means bringing people closer to capitalism, albeit a more basic form of capitalism.

Whereas primitive communism meant an inert existence, where nothing much ever happened, under primitive capitalism, the system's dynamism occasionally peeps out behind its diminished conception of ethnic life. Exploitation is systematic with the politically correct police awaiting to suppress those who rebel in an outburst of resentment, repression is draconian, with the ever-present danger of the Great Powers manipulating ethnic divisions (as in the Great Lakes region in the 1990s) and so causing death and destruction to millions.

Primitivizing Marx?

It is automatically assumed that Marxism takes the side of the victims and especially ethnic victims. From an ideology formerly devoted to forging a vanguard which would take society towards a brave new world, Marxism is being turned into a caring, sharing support system for the victims and the oppressed of the world. Marxism and Marxists are lined up with everyone else moaning about the sufferings inflicted upon either persecuted ethnic victims, or the sad casualties of ethnic violence. The strength of the victimizing agenda, the diminished individual, is so powerful that every political system – even Marxism – is seen through its spectacles. But it would be wrong to refer to Marx to justify the project to primitivize society, specifically to restore primitive communism as an ideal model of society. Our survey of Marx's notes on primitive society demonstrates, on the contrary, that the conditions that governed primitive communist societies in the past cannot be applied to backward societies in Africa today, which are fully integrated into capitalism.

Marx was interested in all forms of humanity, including the primitive. We have demonstrated that primitivism feeds on the suspicion that humanity is a problem. For Marx, however, humanity was the solution. Modern 'ethical' ethnicity is a profoundly conservative and reactionary force in Africa. It is perfectly possible to comprehend its meaning. Not only does it celebrate long-defunct cultures, it also implies that future social experimentation is risky and should be avoided.

If nature determines society, then it is impossible for humanity to transform it into something better. The current appeal to be ethnic represents an entreaty to accept the naturalization of society. The ethnic standpoint that to be human is to be closer to nature, helps to diminish the distinction between the social and the biologically determined. The acceptance of the naturalization of the market acts to detach human agency from anything but its most immediate functions. Finally, the fallacy that the norms of primitive society organically demarcate the boundaries for modern society elevates nature above humanity.

In the introduction we asked why, if modern ethnicity is so different from political ethnicity, it is an unjustified embellishment on behalf of social constructionism to characterize it as being in an endless kaleidoscope of motion. The explanation lies in the fact that the apparent fluidity of modern ethnicity is merely a complementary feature of its naturalization. As such, modern ethnicity is peculiarly suited to transforming the subject into the abject, personalities into cyphers.

Africa's own techno-shaman, the modern NGO volunteer, sits in his four-wheel drive vehicle with his satellite phone and his internet-compatible laptop computer, busy all day downloading ethnic identities to try to implant them in Africans – who would otherwise forget the whole business – as if they were alien abductees. The eradication of African ethnicity principally requires confronting Western primitivism.

Notes

1. Karl Marx, 'The Philosophical Manifesto of the Historical School of Law', p. 61.

2. For an interesting discussion on the origins and meaning of this remark, see the foreword in Hal Draper, *Karl Marx's Theory of Revolution*, pp. 5–11.

3. See, for example, Tom Nairn's seminal essay 'The Modern Janus', which begins in grandiloquent style: 'The theory of nationalism represents Marxism's greatest historical failure', p. 329.

4. For American political analyst Nelson Kasfir, radical analysts see ethnicity as 'false consciousness' because they see it as contradicting class interests: 'Since classes are based on objective economic relations, acting on the basis of ethnic loyalties can only be subjective. Second, ethnicity must be understood in terms of the elite (or bourgeois), not the masses. Finally, since ethnicity from this point of view is a tool used by the elite to consolidate its class position, it is clearly a question of rational self-interest and has little to do with fundamental values or psychic identity' (Nelson Kasfir, *The Shrinking Political Arena*, p. 68).

For instance, see these citations from the radical Messrs Mafeje, Sklar and Saul:

a) 'There is a real difference between the man who, on behalf of his tribe, strives to maintain its traditional integrity and autonomy, and the man who invokes tribal ideology in order to maintain a power position, not in the tribal area, but in the modern capital city, and whose ultimate aim is to undermine and exploit the supposed tribesmen. The fact that it works, as is often pointed out by tribal ideologists, is no proof that "tribes" and "tribalism" exist in any objective sense. If anything, it is a mark of false consciousness on the part of the supposed tribesmen, who subscribe to an ideology that is inconsistent with their material base and therefore unwittingly respond to the call for their own exploitation. On the part of the new African elite, it is a ploy or distortion to conceal their own exploitative role' (Archie Mafeje, 'The Ideology of Tribalism', p. 259);

b) 'Tribal movements may be created and instigated to action by the new men of power in furtherance of their own special interests which are, time and again, the constitutive interests of emerging social classes. Tribalism then becomes a mask for class privilege' (Richard Sklar, 'Political Science and National Integration – A Radical Approach', p. 6);

c) 'It is relatively easy to induce the lower strata of any given ethnic group to interpret the essence of their backwardness as being the result of a zero-sum game over the distribution of scarce resources played out between tribes rather than being primarily a result of class division, world-wide and local' (John Saul, 'The Unsteady State', p. 20).

Both Kasfir and these radicals are entitled to their opinions, but they should not be confused with a Marxist analysis of ethnicity. If ethnicity is 'false consciousness', as it is according to Mafeje, how should one regard African nationalism? Surely nationalism was much more effective in submerging the class interests of the masses behind the new African élite than tribalism? The superficial description of ethnicity as 'false consciousness' here merely raises a further question as to why the African élite felt they had to rely upon ethnicity as a mobilizing force when nationalism had proved more effective until then. And if tribalism is a mask for class privilege, then why did not Sklar go the whole hog and state that African nationalism was a class mask too? Saul seems to believe that class division reflects the true interests of the 'lower strata', but the Western socialist tradition concentrated on 'class' and 'working class' to the exclusion of everything else, yet they still sought to compromise with the capitalist establishment.

Contrary to Kasfir, classes are not 'based on objective economic relations'. And, equally, ethnicity cannot just be a 'subjective phenomenon' to be dismissed as an illusion, as 'false'. For Marx, the capitalist economy is a product of man's social relations that have been alienated and so seem to confront society as a natural object. In same way, other phenomena – such as classes and ethnicity – also acquire a material force if they grip society as much as the economy can. Their 'naturalness' is an appearance, albeit a real appearance, thanks to the peculiar material form that social relations take on in capitalist society.

There are no neat boxes in Marxism, with class as an objective or 'economic' category and ethnicity as a subjective one. From the Marxist perspective, any social phenomenon can be transformed into its opposite – given the right circumstances. For example, this book is a critique of modern 'moral' ethnicity, but it also includes circumstances where ethnicity acquires a progressive content as it gripped the masses when they initially confronted colonialism. [For more on the relationships between materialism and ideology, see Franz Jakubowski's *Ideology and Superstructure in Historical Materialism.*]

5. While these phases are commonly accepted in respect to prehistoric categorizations: the Stone Age, the Iron Age, the Bronze Age of Man, etc., the relativistic problem arises when the same principle is applied to more modern times. As we have seen, cultural relativists advance the claim that people are different irrespective of the fact that the whole world is now capitalist.

6. In *Capital*, Marx ridicules the contemporary idea that societies based upon communal property applied solely to Slavic and Russian communities. He points out that they could be found among the Romans, Teutons, Celts and Indians. See Karl Marx, *Capital*, vol. 1, (1954), p. 82.

7. Karl Marx and Frederich Engels, *The Communist Manifesto*, p. 13, fn. 2.

8. We have selected the attributes of freedom, equality and tolerance, because we imagine these are the qualities ostensibly belonging to primitive communities that modern primitivists would most like to associate themselves with. We therefore overlook entirely the routine practices of cannibalism, incest, paedophilia, etc., that prehistorians and anthropologists have attested to as present among primitive communist communities (see F. Engels, *The Origin of the Family, Private Property and the State*, pp. 29–30).

9. Lawrence Krader, *The Ethnological Notebooks of Karl Marx*, p. 60.

10. Karl Marx, *Grundrisse*, p. 487.

11. Karl Marx, 'The British Rule in India', p. 306.

12. Frederick Engels, *The Origin of the Family*, pp. 168–9.

13. Marx, *Grundrisse*, pp. 487–8.

14. Georg Lukacs, *The Young Hegel*, p. 412.

15. Karl Marx, 'Economic and Philosophical Manuscripts' (1844), p. 346.

16. Karl Marx, *Capital*, vol. 1 (1954), pp. 83–4.

17. Krader, *The Ethnological Notebooks of Karl Marx*, p. 416, fn. 16.

18. Ibid., pp. 9–10.

19. Ibid., p. 373, fn. 82.

20. Ibid., p. 173.

21. Marx, *Grundrisse*, p. 103.

22. Cited in Roman Rosdolsky, *The Making of Marx's Capital*, p. 117.

23. Marx, *Capital*, vol. 1 (1954), p. 92.

24. Or, if they were, they were at a different level. For example, 'If a young warrior [of the Karamojong people of Uganda] wanted to gain the respect of his peers and be sought after as a husband it was traditional for him to have raided cattle and to have killed an enemy' (Sarah Errington, 'The Karamojong of Uganda').

25. Engels, *Origin of the Family*, p. 88. Lest he be accused of racism and Euro-centrism, on the same page Engels sang the praises of the Zulus and 'the Nubians' (Mahdists) against the British infantry in Africa. In what may be seen today as a backhanded compliment, Engels expresses his regard for 'the dignity, uprightness, strength of character and courage of these barbarians'.

26. Frederick Engels, *Anti-Duhring*, p. 232.

27. Ibid. In this text, Engels later makes the point that 'cannibalism . . . it is now universally established, was the primitive form of using defeated enemies' (p. 234).

28. Marx, *Capital*, vol. 1 (1954), p. 703.

29. In reality, what is being abolished are the *excesses* of the market – usually exhibited by the smaller, poorer capitalists – and these are being replaced by environmentally sensitive ethical business practices, which can only be afforded by the larger capitalists. For an argument in favour of business ethics, see Sheena Carmichael, *Business Ethics*.

30. It was an old Stalinist and Maoist prejudice that peasants and small farmers were only pre-capitalist social formations and therefore their struggle for capitalism was progressive. The opposite is the case now as primitivists assume a pre-capitalist status of ethnic society as evidence of its progressiveness.

31. See 'The Results of the Immediate Process of Production', Karl Marx, *Capital* vol. 1 (1976), pp. 1019–38.

32. Ibid., p. 1027.

33. Karl Marx, *Capital*, vol. 3, pp. 329–30.

34. Karl Marx, *Capital*, vol. 3, p. 329.

35. Barbara Dinham and Colin Hines, *Agribusiness in Africa*, p. 111.

36. *Independent*, 12 February 1996, p. 13.

37. Marx, *Grundrisse*, p. 853.

38. Eric Schumacher, author of *Small is Beautiful*, was the founder of Intermediate Technology.

Bibliography

ActionAid, *The Roots of Reconciliation* (London: ActionAid, December 1993).

'Africa: the Curse of Tribal War', *Newsweek* (21 June 1993).

Africa Direct, *Submission to the UN Tribunal on Rwanda* (London, 1996).

African Rights, *Rwanda: Death, Despair and Defiance* (London: African Rights Publications, 1994).

African Rights, 'Great Expectations: the Civil Roles of the Churches in Southern Sudan', African Rights discussion paper No. 6, London (April 1995).

African Rights, *Facing Genocide: the Nuba of Sudan* (London: African Rights Publications, July 1995).

African Rights, *Presumption of Innocence: the Case Against Innocent Mazimpaka* (London: African Rights Publications, May 1996).

Akpan, N., *Epitaph to Indirect Rule: a Discourse on Local Government in Africa* (London: Frank Cass, 1967).

Anacleti, O., 'African NGOs – Do They Have a Future?', in Centre for African Studies, *Critical Choices for the NGO Community: African Development in the 1990s*, Seminal Proceedings No. 30, University of Edinburgh (May 1990).

Anderson, B., *Imagined Communities: Reflections on the Origin and Spread of Nationalism* (London: Verso, 1983).

Anonymous, 'Dzulekofe Mafia to Create Greater Eweland Region in West Africa', *The African* (March 1996).

Apter, D., *The Gold Coast in Transition* (Princeton, NJ: Princeton University Press, 1955).

Armstrong, L., 'Pretty cool', *Vogue* (July 1996).

Asiwaju, A. (ed.), *Partitioned Africans: Ethnic Relations across Africa's International Boundaries 1884–1984* (London and Lagos: C. Hurst, 1985).

Austin, G., 'The Emergence of Capitalist Relations in South Asante Cocoa-Farming 1916–33', *Journal of African History*, vol. 28, no. 2 (1987).

Azikiwe, N., *Zik: a Selection from the Speeches of Nnamdi Azikiwe* (Cambridge: Cambridge University Press, 1961).

Bangura, Y., *Britain and Commonwealth Africa: the Politics of Economic Relations 1951–75* (Manchester: Manchester University Press, 1983).

Banton, M., *Racial and Ethnic Competition* (Cambridge: Cambridge University Press, 1983).

Barkan, E., *The Retreat of Scientific Racism* (Cambridge and New York: Cambridge University Press, 1992).

Barth, F. (ed.), *Ethnic Groups and Boundaries: the Social Organisation of Culture Difference* (Bergen and London: Universitet-Forlaget/Allen and Unwin, 1969).

Bayart, J.-F., *The State in Africa: the Politics of the Belly* (London and New York: Longmans, 1993 [French original – 1989]).

BBC Monitoring Service, 'Kenyan Broadcast Corporation, Nairobi 18/10/96', *BBC Monitoring Summary of World Broadcasts: Africa* (26 October 1996).

Beck, U., *Risk Society: Towards a New Modernity* (London and Beverly Hills: Sage Publications, 1992).

Bentsi-Enchill, Nii K., 'Steps at the grassroots', *West Africa* (3 August 1987).

Berman, B. and Lonsdale, J., *Unhappy Valley: Conflict in Kenya and Africa* (London: James Currey, 1992).

Bing, G., *Reap the Whirlwind: an Account of Kwame Nkrumah's Ghana from 1950 to 1966* (London: MacGibbon and Kee, 1968).

Blunt, P. and Warren, D. M. (eds), *Indigenous Organisations and Development* (London: Intermediate Technology Publications, 1996).

Bohannon, P. and Bohannon, L., *Tiv Economy* (London: Longman, 1968).

Bookchin, M., *Re-enchanting Humanity* (London: Cassell, 1995).

Brass, P., *Ethnic Groups and the State* (London and Sydney: Croom Helm, 1985).

Bratton, M. and Walle, N. van de, 'Toward Governance in Africa: Popular Demands and State Responses', in

G. Hyden and M. Bratton (eds), *Governance and Politics in Africa* (Boulder, CO: Lynne Rienner, 1992).

Brooke, E., 'Slaves of the Fetish', *Independent on Sunday* (16 June 1996).

Burke, F., *Local Government and Politics in Uganda* (Syracuse: Syracuse University Press, 1964), p. 39.

Carey, J., *The Intellectuals and the Masses* (London: Faber and Faber, 1992).

Carmichael, S., *Business Ethics: the New Bottom Line* (London: Demos, 1995).

Carter, G. and O'Meara, P. (eds), *African Independence – the First Twenty-five Years* (London: Hutchinson, 1985).

Centre for African Studies, *Critical Choices for the NGO Community: African Development in the 1990s*, Seminal Proceedings No. 30, University of Edinburgh (May 1990).

Cervenka, Z., *The Nigerian Civil War 1967–70* (Frankfurt am Main: Bernard and Graefe Verlag Für Wehrwesen, 1971).

Chabal, P., 'The African Crisis', in R. Werbner and T. Ranger (eds), *Postcolonial Identities in Africa* (London and New Jersey: Zed Books, 1996).

Chambers, R., *Rural Development: Putting the Last First* (London: Longmans, 1983).

Charney, C., 'Political Power and Social Class in the Neo-Colonial African State', *Review of African Political Economy*, no. 38 (April 1987).

'City Council Elections in 97?', *Mozambique Peace Process Bulletin*, no. 17 (November 1996).

Cohen, A., *Custom and Politics in Urban Africa: a Study of Hausa Migrants in Yoruba Towns* (London: Routledge and Kegan Paul, 1969).

Cohen, A., *Two-dimensional Man: an Essay in the Anthropology of Power and Symbolism in Complex Society* (London: Routledge and Kegan Paul, 1974).

Cohen, J., 'Ethnic Federalism in Ethiopia', *Northeast African Studies*, vol. 2, no. 2, New Series (1995).

Cohen, W., 'The French Colonial Service in French West Africa', in P. Gifford and L. W. M. Roger, *France and Britain in Africa: Imperial Rivalry and Colonial Rule* (New Haven, CT and London: Yale University Press, 1971).

Coleman, J. S., 'The Ibo and Yoruba Strands in Nigerian Nationalism', *Nigeria: Background to Nationalism* (Berkeley and London: University of California Press, 1958).

Coleman, J. S., *Nigeria: Background to Nationalism* (Berkeley and London: University of California Press, 1958).

Coleman, J. S., 'The Role of Tribal Associations in Nigeria', *Nationalism and Development in Africa: Selected Essays* (Berkeley and London: University of California Press, 1994).

Coleman, J. S., *Nationalism and Development in Africa: Selected Essays* (Berkeley and London: University of California Press, 1994).

Collins, R. O. (ed.), *Problems in the History of Colonial Africa 1860–1960* (New Jersey: Prentice Hall, 1970).

Collins, R. O., *Shadows in the Grass: Britain in the Southern Sudan 1918–1956* (New Haven, CT, and London: Yale University Press, 1983).

Cosway, N. and Anawkum, S., 'Traditional Leadership and Community Management in Northern Ghana', in P. Blunt and D. M. Warren (eds), *Indigenous Organisations and Development* (London: Intermediate Technology Publications, 1996).

Crook, R., 'Decolonisation: the Colonial State and Chieftaincy in the Gold Coast', *Seminar Papers on Decolonisation in the 20th Century* (London: Institute of Commonwealth Studies, 1984–5).

Cruise O'Brien, D., *The Mourides of Senegal: the Political and Economic Organisation of an Islamic Brotherhood* (Oxford: Clarendon Press, 1971).

Cruise O'Brien, D., 'A Lost Generation? Youth Identity and State Decay in West Africa', in R. Werbner and T. Ranger (eds), *Postcolonial Identities in Africa* (London and New Jersey: Zed Books, 1996).

Darby, P., *Three Faces of Imperialism: British and American Approaches to Asia and Africa 1870–1970* (New Haven, CT: Yale University Press, 1987).

Davidson, B., *Black Star – a View of the Life and Times of Kwame Nkrumah* (London: Allen Lane, 1973).

Davidson, B., *The African Slave Trade* (Boston: Atlantic Monthly Press, 1980).

Davidson, B., *The Black Man's Burden: Africa and the Curse of the Nation State* (London: James Currey, 1992).

Deighton, A. (ed.), *Britain and the First Cold War* (London: Macmillan, 1990).

Derrida, J., *Speech and Phenomena and Other Essays on Husserl's Theory of Signs* (Evanston, WY: Northwestern University Press, 1973 [Original 1967]).

Destexhe, A., *Rwanda and Genocide in the Twentieth Century* (London: Pluto Press, 1995).

Dinham, B. and Hines, C., *Agribusiness in Africa* (London: Earth Resources Research Publications, 1983).

Draper, H., *Karl Marx's Theory of Revolution: Volume Two, the Politics of Social Classes* (New York and London: Monthly Review Press, 1978).

Dubow, S., 'Ethnic Euphemisms and Racial Echoes', paper delivered at conference on ethnicity at Institute for Social and Economic Research, Rhodes University, Grahamstown, South Africa, 20–24 April 1993. Published as 'Special Issue: Ethnicity and Identity in Southern Africa', *Journal of South African Studies*, vol. 20 (1994), pp. 355–70.

Dyer, G., 'Scientific Conceptions of the 'Other': American Social Science and the Third World 1918-1960', unpublished thesis University of Mississippi, Oxford MS (May 1993).

Economist Intelligence Unit, *Country Profile 1993/94: Ethiopia, Eritrea, Somalia, Djibouti* (London: Economist Intelligence Unit, 1994).

Ellis, J., *The Social History of the Machine Gun* (London: Cresset Library, 1987).

Emerson, R., *From Empire to Nation: the Rise to Self-Assertion of Asian and African Peoples* (Cambridge, MA: Harvard University Press, 1960).

Engels, F., *Anti-Duhring* (Beijing: Foreign Languages Press, 1976).

Engels, F., *The Origin of the Family, Private Property and the State* (London: Junius Publications, 1994).

Enloe, C., *Ethnic Soldiers: State Security in Divided Societies* (Harmondsworth: Penguin, 1980).

Ergas, Z. (ed.), *The African State in Transition* (New York: St Martin's Press, 1987).

Eriksen, T., *Ethnicity and Nationalism: Anthropological Perspectives* (London and East Haven: Pluto Press, 1993).

Errington, S., 'The Karamojong of Uganda', *BBC Focus on Africa*, vol. 7, no. 2 (April–June 1996).

Fanon, F., *The Wretched of the Earth* (Harmondsworth: Penguin, 1967).

Fardon, R., '"Crossed Destinies": the Entangled Histories of West African Ethnic and National Identities', in L. Gorgendiere, K. King and S. Vaughan (eds), *Ethnicity in Africa: Roots, Meanings and Implications* (Edinburgh: Centre of African Studies, 1996).

Fatton, R., 'Clientelism and Patronage in Senegal', *African Studies Review*, vol. 29, no. 4 (December 1986).

Fowler, A., *Institutional Development and NGOs in Africa* (Oxford and Holland: Intrac and Novib, 1992).

Furedi, F., *The Mau Mau War in Perspective* (London: James Currey, 1989).

Furedi, F., *Mythical Past, Elusive Future: History and Society in an Anxious Age* (London: Pluto Press, 1992).

Furedi, F., *The New Ideology of Imperialism: Renewing the Moral Imperative* (London and Boulder, CO: Pluto Press, 1994).

Furedi, F., *Colonial Wars and the Politics of Third World Nationalism* (London and New York: Tauris, 1994).

Gary, I., 'Confrontation, Cooperation or Cooptation: NGOs and the Ghanaian State during Structural Adjustment', *Review of African Political Economy*, vol. 23, no. 68 (June 1996).

Geertz, C., 'The Integrative Revolution – Primordial Sentiments and Civil Politics in the New States', in C. Geertz, *Old Societies and New States: the Quest for Modernity in Asia and Africa* (London: Free Press of Glencoe, 1963).

Geertz, C., *Old Societies and New States: the Quest for Modernity in Asia and Africa* (London: Free Press of Glencoe, 1963).

Gehrels, B. and Rankin, A., 'Conservation: Pandas before People?', *Orbit*, no. 59 (4th quarter 1995).

Gerard-Libois, J., *Katanga Secession* (Madison, WI: University of Wisconsin Press, 1966).

Giddens, A., *Beyond Left and Right: the Future of Radical Politics* (Cambridge: Polity Press, 1994).

Gifford, P. and Roger, L. W. M., *France and Britain in Africa: Imperial Rivalry and Colonial Rule* (New Haven, CT, and London: Yale University Press, 1971).

Gillott, J. and Kumar, M., *Science and the Retreat from Reason* (London: Merlin, 1995).

Gorgendiere, L. de la, 'Ethnicity: a Conundrum' in L. de la Gorgendiere, K. King and S. Vaughan (eds), *Ethnicity in Africa: Roots, Meanings and Implications* (Edinburgh: Centre of African Studies, 1996).

Gorgendiere, L. de la, King, K. and Vaughan, S. (eds), *Ethnicity in Africa: Roots, Meanings and Implications* (Edinburgh: Centre of African Studies, 1996).

Gourevitch, P., 'After the Genocide', *New Yorker* (18 December 1995).

Graf, W., 'Nigerian Grassroots Politics: Local Government, Traditional Rule and Class Domination', *Journal of Commonwealth and Comparative Politics*, vol. 24, no. 2 (July 1986).

Griffiths, I., *An Atlas of African Affairs* (London: Methuen, 1984).

Gulliver, P. (ed.), *Tradition and Transition in East Africa: Studies of the Tribal Element in the Modern Era* (London: Routledge and Kegan Paul, 1969).

Guyer, J. (ed.), *Feeding African Cities: Studies in Regional Social History* (Manchester: Manchester University Press, 1987), pp. 46–7.

Hailey, Lord, 'Some Problems Dealt with in *An African Survey*', *International Affairs* (March–April 1939).

Hanlon, J., *Mozambique: Who Calls the Shots?* (London: James Currey, 1991).

Harman, N., 'East Africa: Turning the corner', *The Economist* (20 June 1987).

Hayes, C., *The Historical Evolution of Modern Nationalism* (New York: Macmillan, 1948).

Heartfield, J., 'Marxism and Social Construction', in S. Wolton (ed.), *Marxism, Mysticism and Modern Theory* (London: Macmillan, 1996).

Hinden, R. (ed.), *Fabian Colonial Essays* (London: Allen and Unwin, 1945).

Hobsbawn, E. and Ranger, T. (eds), *The Invention of Tradition* (Cambridge: Canto, 1992).

Holland, R., *European Decolonisation 1918–1981* (London: Macmillan, 1985).

Howard, R., *Colonialism and Underdevelopment in Ghana* (London: Croom Helm, 1978).

Hudson, P., *Travels in Mauritania* (London: Flamingo, 1991).

Hutchinson, J. and Smith, A., *Ethnicity* (Oxford and New York: Oxford University Press, 1996).

Hyden, G., 'Problems and Prospects of State Coherence', in D. Rothchild and V. Olorunsola, *State Versus Ethnic Claims: African Policy Dilemmas* (Boulder, CO: Westview Press, 1983).

Hyden, G. and Bratton, M. (eds), *Governance and Politics in Africa* (Boulder, CO: Lynne Rienner, 1992).

Iliffe, J., *A Modern History of Tanganyika* (Cambridge: Cambridge University Press, 1979).

Jackson, R. and Rosberg, C., *Personal Rule in Black Africa* (Berkeley and London: University of California Press, 1982).

Jakubowski, F., *Ideology and Superstructure in Historical Materialism* (London: Pluto Press, 1990).

Jenkins, S., *Accountable to None: the Tory Nationalization of Britain* (London: Hamish Hamilton, 1995).

Jorgensen, J., *Uganda – A Modern History* (London: Croom Helm, 1981).

Kajese, K., 'African NGO Decolonisation: a Critical Choice for the 1990s', in Centre for African Studies, *Critical Choices for the NGO Community: African Development in the 1990s*, Seminal Proceedings No. 30, University of Edinburgh (May 1990).

Kaplan, R., 'The Coming Anarchy', *Atlantic Monthly* (February 1994).

Kapuscinski, R., *The Emperor – Downfall of an Autocrat* (London: Quartet Books, 1983).

Kasfir, N., *The Shrinking Political Arena: Participation and Ethnicity in African Politics* (Berkeley and Los Angeles: University of California Press, 1976).

Keane, F., *Season of Blood: a Rwandan Journey* (London: Viking, 1995).

Kemp, R. and Kemp, J., *Kichepo Stick Fighting*, Channel Four TV (15 September 1996).

Kennedy, P., *African Capitalism: the Struggle for Ascendency* (Cambridge: Cambridge University Press, 1988).

Kent, J., 'The British Empire and the Origins of the Cold War, 1944–49', in A. Deighton (ed.), *Britain and the First Cold War* (London: Macmillan, 1990).

Kiernan, V., *The Lords Of Human Kind* (London: Cresset Library, 1968).

Kohn, H., *The Idea of Nationalism: a Study in its Origins and Backgrounds* (New York: Collier, 1944).

Kolarz, W., *Myths and Realities in Eastern Europe* (London: Lindsay Drummond, 1946).

Krader, L., *The Ethnological Notebooks of Karl Marx* (Assen, The Netherlands: Van Gorcum, 1972).

Krauthammer, C., 'The return of the primitive', *Time* (29 January 1996).

Kuklick, H., *The Savage Within: the Social History of British Anthropology 1885–1945* (Cambridge: Cambridge University Press, 1991).

Kuper, A., *The Invention of Primitive Society* (London and New York: Routledge, 1988).

Ladouceur, P., *Chiefs and Politicians – the Politics of Regionalism in Northern Ghana* (London: Longman, 1979).

Lawson, D., 'Bosnia is Europe's problem', *Spectator* (8 May 1993).

Lee, J. M., *Colonial Development and Good Government: a Study of the Ideas Expressed by British Official Classes in Planning Decolonisation 1939–1964* (Oxford: Clarendon Press, 1967).

Lefort, R., *Ethiopia: A Heretical Revolution?* (London: Zed Press, 1983).

Levinson, D. and Ember, M. (eds), *Encyclopedia of Cultural Anthropology*, vol. 2 (New York: Henry Hunt, 1996).

Lewis, W. A., *Politics in West Africa* (London: Allen and Unwin, 1965).

Leyden, N. van, 'Africa 95: a Critical Assessment of the Exhibition at the Royal Academy', *Cahiers d'Etudes Africaines*, 141–2, XXXVI–1–2 (1996).

Libewstein, G. von, Slikkerveer, L. J. and Warren, D. M., 'CIRAN: Networking for Indigenous Knowledge', in D. M. Warren, L. J. Slikkerveer and D. Brokensha (eds), *The Cultural Dimension of Development*

(London: Intermediate Technology Publications, 1995).

Lijphart, A., *Democracy in Plural Societies: a Comparative Exploration* (New Haven, CT and London: Yale University Press, 1977).

Lloyd, P. (ed.), *The New Elites of Tropical Africa* (Oxford: Oxford University Press, 1966).

Lonsdale, J., 'The Moral Economy of Mau Mau', in B. Berman and J. Lonsdale, *Unhappy Valley: Conflict in Kenya and Africa* (London: James Currey, 1992).

Lugard, F., *The Dual Mandate in British Tropical Africa* (London: Frank Cass, 1965). (Originally published, 1922.)

Lukacs, G., *The Young Hegel: Studies in the Relations Between Dialectics and Economics* (London: Merlin Press, 1975).

MacGaffey, J., *The Real Economy of Zaire: the Contribution of Smuggling and Other Unofficial Activities to National Wealth* (London: James Currey, 1991).

MacGaffey, W., 'Kongo Identity, 1483–1993', *South Atlantic Quarterly*, vol. 94, no. 4 (Fall 1995).

Macready, N., 'Female genital mutilation outlawed in United States', *British Medical Journal* (2 November 1996).

Mafeje, A., 'The Ideology of Tribalism', *Journal of Modern African Studies*, vol. 9, no. 2 (August 1971).

Malik, K., *The Meaning of Race: Race, History and Culture in Western Society* (London: Macmillan, 1996).

Mandela, N., 'South Africa's Future Foreign Policy', *Foreign Affairs*, vol. 72, no. 5 (November–December 1993).

Marable, M., *African and Caribbean Politics from Kwame Nkrumah to Maurice Bishop* (London: Verso, 1987).

Mare, G., *Ethnicity and Politics in South Africa* (London: Zed Press, 1993).

Marshall, A., 'Heart of Prejudice', *Independent* (20 November 1996).

Marshall, J., 'The Zippies', *Wired*, 2.05 (May 1994).

Marx, K., *Capital*, vol. 1 (Moscow: Foreign Languages Publishing House, 1954).

Marx, K., *Capital*, vol. 3 (Moscow: Foreign Languages Publishing House, 1959).

Marx, K., 'The Philosophical Manifesto of the Historical School of Law'(1842), cited in L. Krader, *The Ethnological Notebooks of Karl Marx* (Assen, The Netherlands: Van Gorcum, 1972).

Marx, K., 'The British Rule in India', in K. Marx, *Surveys From Exile* (Harmondsworth: Penguin, 1973).

Marx K, *Grundrisse* (Harmondsworth: Penguin, 1973).

Marx K, *Surveys From Exile* (Harmondsworth: Penguin, 1973).

Marx, K., 'Economic and Philosophical Manuscripts', in K. Marx, *Early Writings* (Harmondsworth: Penguin, 1975).

Marx, K., *Early Writings* (Harmondsworth: Penguin, 1975).

Marx, K., *Capital,* vol. 1 (Harmondsworth: Penguin, 1976).

Marx, K. and Engels, F., *The German Ideology* (London: Lawrence and Wishart, 1974).

Marx, K. and Engels, F., *The Communist Manifesto* (London: Junius Publications/Pluto Press, 1996).

Mazrui, A., *Soldiers and Kinsmen in Uganda: the Making of a Military Ethnocracy* (London: Sage Publications, 1975).

McCracken, J., 'Tribal Identity and the Growth of Modern Politics, 1920–1940', *Cambridge History of Africa, 1905-1940*, vol. 7 (Cambridge: Cambridge University Press, 1986).

McHugh, H., 'USAID and Ethnic Conflict: an Epiphany?', paper presented at conference on 'Development Assistance and Ethnic Conflict', Cornell University, USA (5–7 October 1995).

McNeely, J., 'IUCN and Indigenous Peoples: How to Promote Sustainable Development', in D. M. Warren, L. J. Slikkerveer and D. Brokensha (eds), *The Cultural Dimension of Development* (London: International Technology Publications, 1995).

Mercier, P., 'Remarques sur la Signification du "Tribalisme" en Afrique Noir', *Cahiers Internationaux de Sociologie*, no. 31 (1961).

Meszaros, I., *The Power of Ideology* (London and New York: Harvester Wheatsheaf, 1989).

Metcalfe, G., *Great Britain and Ghana: Documents of Ghana History 1807–1957* (London: Thomas Nelson, 1964).

Middleton, N., *Kalashnikovs and Zombie Cucumbers: Travels in Mozambique* (London: Phoenix Books, 1995).

Middleton, N., O'Keefe, P. and Moyo, S., *The Tears of a Crocodile: from Rio to Reality in the Developing World* (London and Boulder, CO: Pluto Press, 1993).

Milburn, J., *British Business and Ghanaian Independence* (London: C. Hurst, 1977).

Miles, W., 'Decolonisation as Disintegration: the Disestablishment of the State in Chad', *Journal of African and Asian Studies*, vol. 30, nos 1–2 (June 1995).

Mitchell, J. C., *The Kalela Dance*, Rhodes-Livingstone Papers no. 27 (Manchester: Manchester University Press, 1956).

Monbiot, G., *No Man's Land: an Investigative Journey Through Kenya and Tanzania* (London: Picador, 1994).

Morgan, L., *Ancient Society, or Researches in the Lines of Human Progress from Savagery through Barbarism to Civilisation* (Cambridge, MA: Belknap Press, 1964 [originally published 1877]).

Morris, D. and Marsh, P., *Tribes* (Exeter: Pyramid Books, 1988).

Morton, J., *The Poverty of Nations: the Aid Dilemma at the Heart of Africa* (London: Tauris, 1996).

Moynihan, D., *Pandaemonium: Ethnicity in International Relations* (Oxford: Oxford University Press, 1993).

Nadel, S. F., *A Black Byzantium: the Kingdom of Nupe in Nigeria* (Oxford: Oxford University Press, 1942).

Nairn, T., *The Break Up of Britain: Crisis and Neo-Nationalism* (London: Verso, 1981).

Nairn, T., 'The Modern Janus', in T. Nairn *The Break Up of Britain: Crisis and Neo-Nationalism* (London: Verso, 1981).

Nairn, T., 'The Incredible Shrinking State', *Demos* (9/1996).

National Lottery Charities Board, *International Grants Programme*, London (September 1996).

Ndegwa, S., *The Two Faces of Civil Society: NGOs and Politics in Africa* (West Hartford, CT: Kumarian Press, 1996).

Niamir, M., 'Indigenous Systems of Natural Resource Management among the Pastoralists of Arid and Semi-arid Africa', in D. M. Warren, L. J. Slikkerveer and D. Brokensha (eds), *The Cultural Dimension of Development*

(London: Intermediate Technology Publications, 1995).

Nkrumah, K., *Africa Must Unite* (London: Panaf Books, 1963).

Norval, A., 'Thinking Identities: Against a Theory of Ethnicity', in E. Wilmsen and P. McAllister (eds), *The Politics of Difference* (Chicago and London: University of Chicago Press, 1996).

Novick, P., *That Noble Dream: the 'Objectivity Question' and the American Historical Profession* (Cambridge and New York: Cambridge University Press, 1988).

Nugent, P., *Big Men, Small Boys and Politics in Ghana* (London and New York: Pinter, 1995).

Nye, R., *The Origins of Crowd Psychology: Gustave LeBon and the Crisis of Mass Democracy in the Third Republic* (London and Beverley Hills: Sage Publications, 1974).

Ojo, A., 'Law and Government in Nigeria', in D. Smock and K. Bentsi-Enchill, *The Search for National Integration in Africa* (New York: Free Press, 1975).

Ojukw, E., *Biafra*, vol. 1 (New York: Harper and Row Publishers, 1969).

Osaghae, E., *Ethnicity and its Management in Africa* (Lagos: Malthouse Press, 1994).

Pakenham, T., *The Scramble for Africa* (London: Abacus, 1991).

Pawson, J., *Minimum* (London: Phaidon, 1996).

Pearce, R. D., *The Turning Point in Africa – British Colonial Policy 1938–48* (London: Frank Cass, 1982).

Petterson, D., 'Ethiopia Abandoned?: an American Perspective', *International Affairs*, vol. 62, no. 4 (Autumn 1986).

Pirsig, R., *Zen and the Art of Motorcycle Maintenance: an Inquiry into Values* (London: Corgi Books, 1976 [originally 1974]).

Pina-Cabral, J. and Campbell, J. (eds), *Europe Observed* (London: Macmillan, 1992).

Post, L. van der, *The Lost World of the Kalahari* (Harmondsworth: Penguin, 1962 [originally 1958]).

Preston, R., *The Hot Zone* (London: Corgi Books, 1994).

Randall, H. and Polhemus, T., *The Customised Body* (London: Serpents' Tail, 1996).

Ranger, T., *Peasant Consciousness and Guerrilla War in Zimbabwe* (London: James Currey, 1985).

Ranger, T., 'Missionaries, Migrants and the Manyika: the Invention of Ethnicity in Zimbabwe', in L. Vail, *The Creation of Tribalism in Southern Africa* (Berkeley and Los Angeles: University of California Press, 1991).

Ranger, T., 'The Invention of Tradition in Colonial Africa', in E. Hobsbawn and T. Ranger (eds), *The Invention of Tradition* (Cambridge: Canto, 1992 [originally 1983]).

Ranger, T., 'The Tribalisation of Africa and the Retribalisation of Europe', *St Antony's Seminar Series: Tribe, State, Nation*, Oxford, (January 1994).

Ranger, T., 'Colonial and Post-Colonial Identities', in R. Werbner and T. Ranger (eds), *Postcolonial Identities in Africa* (London and New Jersey: Zed Books, 1996).

Renner, M., *Fighting for Survival* (Washington, DC: Worldwatch Institute, October 1996).

Revell, L., 'The Return of the Sacred', in S. Wolton (ed.), *Marxism, Mysticism and Modern Theory* (London: Macmillan, 1996).

Reyntjens, F., *Burundi: Breaking the Cycle of Violence*, international report 95/1 (London: Minority Rights Group, 1995).

Rhodes, C., *Primitivism and Modern Art* (London: Thames and Hudson, 1994).

Richards, P., *Fighting for the Rain Forest: War, Youth and Resources in Sierra Leone* (London: International African Institute, 1996).

Rieff, D., 'Rwanda: the Big Risk', *The New York Review of Books* (31 October 1996).

Rivere, C., *Guinea: the Mobilisation of a People* (Ithaca, NY, and London: Cornell University Press, 1977).

Roberts, A. (ed.), *The Cambridge History of Africa: 1905–1940*, vol. 7 (Cambridge: Cambridge University Press, 1986).

Rodney, W., *How Europe Underdeveloped Africa* (London: Bogle-L'Ouverture Publications, 1972).

Ronen, D. (ed.), *Democracy and Pluralism in Africa* (Boulder, CO: Lynne Rienner, 1986).

Rooney, D., *Sir Charles Arden-Clarke* (London: Rex Collins, 1982).

Rooney, D., *Kwame Nkrumah: the Political Kingdom in the Third World* (London: Tauris, 1988).

Roosens, E., *Creating Ethnicity: the Process of Ethnogenesis* (London and New Dehli: Sage Publications, 1989).

Rosdolsky, R., *The Making of Marx's Capital* (London: Pluto Press, 1977).

Rossiter, J. and Palmer, R., 'Northern NGOs in Southern Africa: Some Heretical Thoughts', in Centre for African Studies, *Critical Choices for the NGO Community: African Development in the 1990s*, Seminal Proceedings No. 30, University of Edinburgh (May 1990).

Rothchild, D., 'State-Ethnic Relations in Middle Africa', in G. Carter and P. O'Meara (eds), *African Independence – the First Twenty-five Years* (London: Hutchinson, 1985).

Rothchild, D., 'Hegemony and State Softness: Some Variations in Elite Responses', in Z. Ergas (ed.), *The African State in Transition* (New York: St Martin's Press, 1987).

Rothchild, D. and Chazan, N. (eds), *The Precarious Balance: State and Society in Africa* (Boulder, CO, and London: Westview Press, 1988).

Rothchild, D. and Foley, M., 'African States and the Politics of Inclusive Coalitions', in D. Rothchild and N. Chazan (eds), *The Precarious Balance: State and Society in Africa* (Boulder, CO: Westview Press, 1988).

Rothchild, D. and Olorunsola, V. (eds), *State Versus Ethnic Claims: African Policy Dilemmas* (Boulder, CO: Westview Press, 1983).

Sangmpam, S., *Pseudocapitalism and the Overpoliticised State: Reconciling Politics and Anthropology in Zaire* (Aldershot: Avebury, 1994).

Sartre, J.-P., 'Preface' to F. Fanon, *The Wretched of the Earth* (Harmondsworth: Penguin, 1967 [original 1961]).

Saul, J., 'The Unsteady State', *Review of African Political Economy*, vol. 5 (1976).

Schatzberg, M., *Politics and Class in Zaire* (London and New York: Africana Publishing, 1980).

Schatzberg, M. (ed.), *The Political Economy of Zimbabwe* (New York: Praeger, 1984).

Schumacher, E., *Small Is Beautiful: a Study Of Economics as if People Mattered* (London: Abacus, 1974).

Selincourt, K. de, 'Demon Farmers and Other Myths', *New Scientist* (27 April 1996).

Shillington, K., *Ghana and the Rawlings Factor* (London: Macmillan, 1992).

Sklar, R., 'Political Science and National Integration – a Radical Approach', *Journal of Modern African Studies*, vol. 5, no. 1 (May 1967).

Smillie, I. and Helmich, H., *Non-governmental Organisations and Governments: Stakeholders for Development* (Paris: Organization for Economic Co-operation and Development, 1993).

Smith, A., 'Ties that Bind', *LSE Magazine* (Spring 1993).

Smith, M. G., 'Pluralism, Race and Ethnicity in Selected African Countries', in J. Rex and D. Mason, *Theories of Race and Ethnic Relations* (Cambridge: Cambridge University Press, 1986).

Smock, D. and Bentsi-Enchill, K. (eds), *The Search for National Integration in Africa* (New York: Free Press, 1975).

Snyder, J., 'Nationalism and the Crisis of the Post-Soviet State', *Survival*, International Institute of Strategic Studies, vol. 35, no. 1 (Spring 1993).

Southall, A., 'The Concept of Elites and their Formation in Uganda', in P. Lloyd (ed.), *The New Elites in Tropical Africa* (Oxford: Oxford University Press, 1966).

Southall, A., 'The Illusion of Tribe', *Journal of Asian and African Studies*, vol. 5, nos 1–2 (January–April 1970).

Stephen, D., *The San of the Kalahari*, Report No. 56 (London: Minority Rights Group, November 1982).

Stephenson, N., *Snow Crash* (London: RoC, 1992).

Stocking, G., *Race, Culture and Evolution* (London and Chicago: University of Chicago Press, 1982).

Sub-Saharan Africa Survey, *The Economist* (7 September 1996).

Survival International, *Niger Delta Peoples*, leaflet (1995).

Survival Newsletter, no. 36 (1996).

Szeftel, M., 'Ethnicity and Democratization in South Africa', *Review of African Political Economy*, no. 60 (1994).

Thurow, L., *The Future of Capitalism: How Today's Economic Forces Shape Tomorrow's World* (London: Nicholas Brealey, 1996).

Tibenderana, P., 'The Role of the British Administration in the Appointment of the Emirs of Northern Nigeria, 1903/1931: the Case of Sokoto Province', *Journal of African History*, vol. 28, no. 2 (1987).

Tilly, C., 'A Bridge Halfway: Responding to Brubaker', *Contention*, vol. 4, no. 1 (Fall 1994).

Touval, S., 'Partitioned Groups and Inter-State Relations', in A. Asiwaju (ed.), *Partitioned Africans: Ethnic Relations across Africa's International Boundaries 1884-1984* (London and Lagos: C. Hurst, 1985).

Townsend, C., *Britain's Civil Wars: Counterinsurgency in the Twentieth Century* (London: Faber and Faber, 1986).

Uphoff, N., 'Preface', in P. Blunt and D. M. Warren, *Indigenous Organisations and Development* (London: Intermediate Technology Publications, 1996).

Vail, L., *The Creation of Tribalism in Southern Africa* (Berkeley and Los Angeles: University of California Press, 1991).

Vale, V. and Juno, A. (eds), *Modern Primitives: an Investigation of Contemporary Adornment and Ritual* (San Francisco: Re/Search Publications, 1989).

Walker, P., 'Indigenous Knowledge and Famine Relief in the Horn of Africa', in D. M. Warren, L. J. Slikkerveer and

D. Brokensha (eds), *The Cultural Dimension of Development* (London: Intermediate Technology Publications, 1995).

Warren, D., Slikkerveer, L. and Brokensha, D. (eds), *The Cultural Dimension of Development* (London: Intermediate Technology Publications, 1995).

Werbner, R. and Ranger, T. (eds), *Postcolonial Identities in Africa* (London and New Jersey: Zed Books, 1996).

Weiss, H., *Political Protest in the Congo* (Princeton, NJ: Princeton University Press, 1967).

Weiss, T. (ed.), *Humanitarian Emergencies and Military Help in Africa* (London: Macmillan, 1990).

Weiss, T. and Wiseman, H., 'Delivering Humanitarian Assistance in African Armed Conflicts: a Critical Commentary', in T. Weiss (ed.), *Humanitarian Emergencies and Military Help in Africa* (London: Macmillan 1990).

Weissman, S., *American Foreign Policy in the Congo 1960–1964* (Ithaca and London: Cornell University Press, 1974).

Weitzer, R., 'Continuities in the Politics of State Security in Zimbabwe', in M. Schatzberg (ed.), *The Political Economy of Zimbabwe* (New York: Praeger, 1984).

White, J., *Central Administration in Nigeria 1914–1948: the Problem of Polarity* (Dublin: Irish Academic Press, 1981).

Wilmsen, E. and McAllister, P. (eds), *The Politics of Difference: Ethnic Premises in a World of Power* (Chicago and London: University of Chicago Press, 1996).

Wolton, S. (ed.), *Marxism, Mysticism and Modern Theory* (London: Macmillan, 1996).

World Bank, *Sub-Saharan Africa: From Crisis to Sustainable Growth* (Washington, DC: The World Bank, November 1989).

Young, C., *Politics in the Congo: Decolonisation and Independence* (Princeton, NJ: Princeton University Press, 1965).

Young, C., *The Politics of Cultural Pluralism* (Madison, WI: University of Wisconsin Press, 1976).

Young, C., 'Ethnicity and the Colonial and Post-Colonial State in Africa', in P. Brass, *Ethnic Groups and the State* (London and Sydney: Croom Helm, 1985).

Young, C., 'The Colonial State and its Political Legacy', in D. Rothchild and N. Chazan (eds), *The Precarious Balance: State and Society in Africa* (Boulder, CO, and London: Westview Press, 1988).

Zola, E., *Rome* (Stroud: Alan Sutton, 1993).

Index